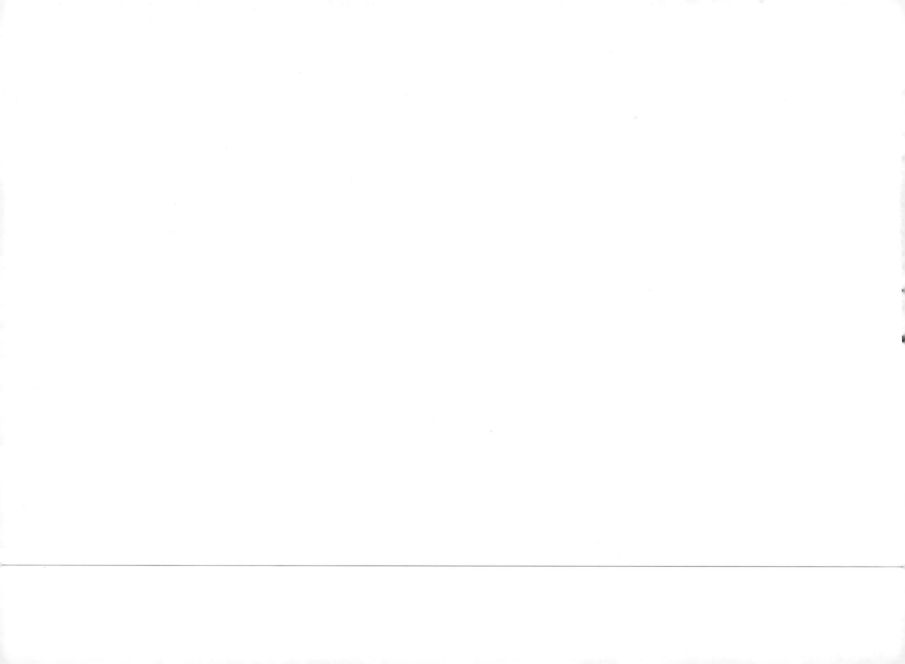

Across Colorado

RECIPES and RECOLLECTIONS

More Than a Cookbook by The Volunteers of the Colorado Historical Society

Published by
The Volunteers of the
   Colorado Historical
   Society
1300 Broadway
Denver, Colorado 80203

Distributed to the trade by
ROBERTS RINEHART
   PUBLISHERS
6309 Monarch Park Place
Niwot, Colorado 80503
TEL 303.652.2685
FAX 303.652.2689

3rd printing, 1999

ISBN 1-57098-203-1
$22.95

ON THE COVER:

A Sunday, after-church picnic at Olathe, on
the Western Slope, about 1911. From the
Garrison Photograph Collection, Colorado
Historical Society.

Pastel painting by Randi Eyre

Arlene Hansen	Project Director
Fern Wilson	Editor
Ann Douden	Book Designer
Cindy Adams	Photograph Coordinator
Ruth Koons	Artist
Margaret Erickson	Contributing Editor
Pauline Brown	Graphic Assistant
Lori Kranz	Proofreader

CONTENTS

Across Colorado

Across Colorado

FOREWORD

Thomas J. Noel, Ph.D., University of Colorado at Denver

Savor some morsels of Colorado's delicious past along with tomorrow's recipes from across Colorado.

Since 1879, volunteers at the Colorado Historical Society have been doing excellent work helping the Society collect, preserve, exhibit, and publish the best of Colorado's past. This book perpetuates that tradition of volunteers serving nutritious, tasty fare.

In 1963, the Volunteers published *Pioneer Potluck*, a cookbook of historic recipes. *Across Colorado* is an even bigger, better, and more ambitious effort focused on contemporary recipes. Whether you are looking for food for thought or tummy, you cannot go wrong with this intriguing book.

From all regions of the Highest State, *Across Colorado* offers you

- a cookbook,
- a collection of anecdotes, *and*
- superb photographs, many heretofore unpublished, from the Colorado Historical Society's fantastic collection of some 500,000 images.

Herein you will find excerpts from Augusta Tabor's diary and Charlie Brown's formula for his legendary Pit Barbecue in Maybell, in the state's northwestern corner. You will find choice recipes that reflect Colorado's diverse cultures. You will find a diary recording a courtship that flowered into marriage, left by the postmistress of Vega and coauthored by her husband-to-be.

These recipes include a starter for sourdough bread and Son of a Gun Stew. Some may sound exotic, but they are useful, tasty recipes, made from easily obtainable ingredients—except perhaps the roast pigeon casserole. All are modern formulas for twenty-first-century cooks.

The Colorado Historical Society Volunteers collected some 400 recipes from hundreds of people all around Colorado. They tested submissions from church groups, ethnic clubs, historical societies, museums, and individuals from Aguilar to Yuma. These are the top 150 plus, all tested repeatedly by cooks of various expertise. All earned rave reviews. You will rave too when you use them.

Along with *Across Colorado's* delicious meals, be sure to pass on some of its wonderful historical tidbits that add sugar and spice to this banquet of a book.

Colorado History Museum

with its fellow institutions in presenting outstanding, cooperative exhibitions.

From this building at 1300 Broadway stem all of the Society's programs, including its outstanding education program for schoolchildren, its quarterly history journal, *Colorado Heritage*, its monthly newsletter, *History Now*, frequent monographs, and other publications. The building also houses the Society's comprehensive collection of historical artifacts of the American West, some of which are on permanent display. Others are shown in special exhibits.

Located in Denver's cultural center, one block from the Denver Art Museum and across the street from the Denver Public Library, the Colorado History Museum is well located to contribute to the cultural base and history education of Colorado residents, to inform out-of-state visitors about the American West, and to collaborate

ON FOOD, RECOLLECTIONS, AND HISTORY   *Georgianna Contiguglia, President, Colorado Historical Society*

History is not

merely an

accumulation of

the stories of great

events, it is the

celebration of the

daily events of

our lives.

The stories associated with foods and foodways are delicious entrees to family, local, and regional history. I associate certain foods with members of my family. Take, for instance, Harvard beets. My Aunt Mary always made Harvard beets for special Sunday dinners. I didn't like beets, still don't, but I was much taken with the rich, red color and creamy, thick texture of the sauce. My Uncle Bill was a proud graduate of Harvard, and I always thought Aunt Mary made us Harvard beets to remind us of his accomplishments.

As a child I spent vacations with my older cousins on Cape Cod. I loved the time with them because my Aunt Elizabeth would always let me eat whatever I wanted at mealtime. One summer I gained eight pounds eating her moist, chocolate cake for breakfast each morning.

One of the most noted family recipes is that for "Contigooey Stewy," a dish made famous by my husband on Boy Scout outings, and cooked in aluminum foil over an open fire. I was introduced to the one-pot meal on a camping trip to Wyoming years ago. My husband's boyhood friends and I still recall with relish that rough-it meal.

My favorite food story is associated with the first birthday I celebrated after being married. I was living in New York, and my mother in Massachusetts baked and decorated a birthday cake for me. Then she inserted candles around the top, carefully placed the masterpiece in a see-through plastic box, and carted the loving gift to the post office. The postman said, "Lady, you can't mail that cake! It will get smashed to smithereens." Undaunted, my mother asked the postman how he planned to handle the delicate item. "Well, I'll be very careful, of course," he replied. "Well," my mother responded, "so will every other postal worker along the way." The cake arrived intact, delivered to my door, with only one candle slightly askew. It was the best birthday cake I ever tasted!

The Colorado Historical Society has been in the business of collecting, preserving, and educating the people of Colorado about the history of this state and region for over a century. We hope that as you use and savor these well-tested recipes and enjoy the snippets of history that accompany them, you will also think about the significance of foods and food traditions in your own family and community. It is often the quiet meals with family and special holiday feasts that give a piquant flavor to the history of our lives.

Across Colorado

Cookbook Committee

General Co-Chairmen	Arlene Hansen Cindy Adams	Photography Research	Cindy Adams Lucy Kissell
		(with special assistance from Eric Paddock and the Historical Society's staff)	
Honorary Chairman	Jane DeMerritt		
Regional Chairmen	Cindy Adams Kris Cabell Jane DeMerritt	Editorial Consultants	Diane Bakke Jackie Davis
	Charlene Gail Deanna Ganskow Nancy Nelson Pat Rauchenstein	Data Processing	Margaret Erickson Pat Krupa Arthur Whitmore
	Velma Steele Delphine Tramutt	Presale	Bonnie Eklund Mary Flowers Pat Krupa
Testing Chairmen	Kathleen Cook Anne Taylor		Kaye Schmitt Jean Stuck
Anecdote Researchers	Susan Chambers Jane DeMerritt Margaret Erickson JoAn Goodman Arlene Hansen Ruth Koons Marge Melle Nancy Nelson	Marketing/Distribution	Diane Bakke Susan Chambers Rosalind Grenfell Miles Hooley Marge Melle Nancy Nelson
(with special assistance from Rebecca Lintz and the Stephen H. Hart Library staff)		*(with special assistance from Peg Ekstrand, Carol Whitley, and the Historical Society's staff)*	
		Office Coordinator	Kaye Schmitt

INTRODUCTION

The Volunteers of the Colorado Historical Society are proud to bring you Across Colorado: Recipes and Recollections, *the product of more than three years' work. These recipes and anecdotes were contributed by hundreds of people from all across Colorado. The Volunteers sincerely thank each of you for your interest.*

The most difficult task of this project was selecting the very best recipes from the hundreds submitted—a true embarrassment of riches. In selecting recipes, our emphasis was on contemporary, fresh flavors, reflecting both urban and rural styles. The recipes have been tested and retested by volunteer cooks in their mile-high kitchens. Some recipes, primarily baked goods, may require a bit of experimentation for those of you making them at substantially different altitudes. Recipes were edited for ease of preparation; recipes contributed by restaurants were reformatted for home kitchens. The simplicity of the recipes should make them usable by cooks with a wide range of skill and inclination.

The Volunteers are deeply indebted to the staff of the Colorado Historical Society for their encouragement, especially to James Hartman, past president of the Colorado Historical Society, for starting us down the road; to Georgianna Contiguglia, President of the Society, for capturing the spirit of the book in her preface; to David Wetzel, Stan Oliner, and David Halaas for sharing their scholarly knowledge and reviewing for historical accuracy; and to the staffs of the Stephen H. Hart Library and the Photography Department. We are most grateful to Dr. Thomas J. Noel, Colorado's prominent historian, for his foreword as well as for his lifelong efforts to bring Colorado history to life.

The anecdotes and photographs are an exceptional feature of our book. Many of these "tiny tales" were sent to us by contributors; others came from the archives of the Colorado Historical Society. The search for photographs moved our book into a different dimension as we realized the vast potential that lay in the collections of the Society. The majority of the photographs in *Across Colorado* have never before been published.

The Volunteers owe a special debt of gratitude to the professional members of our project team: Ann Douden, designer extraordinaire; Fern Wilson, our dedicated and meticulous editor; Ruth Koons, our talented artist; and Margaret Erickson, writer of the region introductions and data processor.

All proceeds benefit the Volunteers and the Colorado Historical Society. The volunteer organization supports children's educational programs at the Museum, historic site preservation, artifact acquisition, and other projects that will further allow the Society to preserve and interpret the history of the state of Colorado. Please visit the Colorado History Museum in Denver and our other museums and properties throughout the state. We look forward to welcoming you.

Arlene Hansen
Project Director

Across Colorado

Palisade peach orchard, 1908

Across Colorado

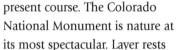
The Northwest Slope

"No one who leaves this valley will stay away forever—they will always return."

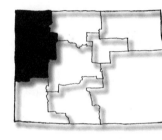

The Grand Valley of the Colorado River stretches out, lush with orchards—apple, peach, pear—vineyards, and fertile fields of tomatoes and corn. Above it rises the 10,000-foot-high island in the sky—Grand Mesa—the world's largest flattop mountain. Here sparkling lakes share space with thick stands of pine forests that are home to deer, elk, and bear. Streams meander end to end, linking lakes, providing trails for fishermen, marking the way for the wildlife.

Then the contrast. Monoliths, windows and spires, enormous craggy rocks, a maze of canyons and cliffs, all carved by the rushing waters of the Colorado River long before it knew its present course. The Colorado National Monument is nature at its most spectacular. Layer rests upon layer of sandstone, each a different shade of red and ocher touched with pink and orange, turning gold at sunset.

In 1776, Spaniards setting out from Santa Fe discovered a large Ute population along the rivers and in the valley. Canyons, mountains, and mesas still bear the names of these early explorers or the names given them by the Native Americans whose homeland they were.

Toward the end of the nineteenth century, the earliest settlers began to arrive and the Utes were forced to leave their mountain home. The railroads came bringing more settlers and soon the new arrivals began the development of irrigation canals. Lush green fields and abundant orchards replaced the sage and greasewood. Yet, desert country still edges the valley and the purple sage remains on its periphery.

Today tourism is a flourishing contributor to the economy of the Northwest Slope; many of the orchards have become vineyards, creating a new industry as the wineries of Colorado make their mark. Wild game is an important part of the local menu—venison or elk is the meat on many tables. Corn from Olathe is famous.

But the peach is probably the one thing that brings people back again and again to the Northwest Slope—the marvelous flavor of the Colorado peach and the "prophecy of the Utes," who, when they were forced away, said that "no one who leaves this valley will stay away forever—they will always return."

Across Colorado

The lower Grand Valley grew a bumper apple crop in 1911. Growers sent their apples to eastern markets in 1,800 railway cars.

Peach Festival

The first Western Slope peach festival, held in 1890, united the whole Grand Valley. Talented residents staged a valley-wide pageant that was "colorful and cultural." Soon each community tried to outdo the others in their fruit displays; Fruita and Palisade competed strongly for the most first prizes. The first festivals were so successful that they became annual events each September. By 1904, the festival became part of the Mesa County Fair and was held on the fairgrounds where Lincoln Park in Grand Junction is now located.

These early festivals grew into the Palisade Peach Festival, which is still held every year in August, featuring a barbecue, pancake breakfast, parade, and peach recipe contest.

Hot Crab and Jalapeno Dip

$1\frac{1}{2}$ teaspoons olive oil

$\frac{1}{2}$ medium red bell pepper, chopped

1   tablespoon chopped jalapeno pepper

1   14-ounce can artichoke bottoms, chopped and drained

1   cup low-fat mayonnaise

$\frac{1}{2}$ cup grated Parmesan cheese

$\frac{1}{4}$ cup thinly sliced green onion

1   tablespoon Worcestershire sauce

$1\frac{1}{2}$ teaspoons lemon juice

$\frac{1}{2}$ teaspoon celery salt

8   ounces crabmeat, drained

$\frac{1}{3}$ cup slivered almonds or pine nuts

Serves 6

Preheat oven to 375°.

Heat olive oil in medium skillet, add red pepper, and saute for 3 minutes. Transfer to large bowl. Add jalapeno pepper to same skillet and saute for 2 minutes. Transfer to same bowl as red pepper.

Add artichoke, mayonnaise, Parmesan, green onion, Worcestershire sauce, lemon juice, and celery salt to pepper mix. Stir to combine. Gently mix in crabmeat. Season to taste.

Transfer to 8-inch baking dish. Spread evenly and sprinkle nuts on top. Bake for 20 minutes until top is golden brown and bubbly. Serve warm with crackers.

This recipe can be doubled. It can also be prepared ahead of time, refrigerated, and baked just before serving.

The Colorado National Monument, probably Colorado's best kept secret, rises a few miles west of Grand Junction, covering more than 20,000 acres with 1,000-foot canyons and spectacular, isolated monoliths.

Across Colorado

His and Her Diary

James Samson Stephen began his diary en route from New Mexico to Mesa County, Colorado, in 1884. Nellie Nichols, seventeen years old, traveling with her family in the same party, continued the diary through 1885. Can you read romance between the lines?

James Samson Stephen and Nellie Nichols were married in 1888.

His Diary

James writes:

Tuesday, Sept. 15, 1884: Crossed the line of New Mexico and Colorado at 10 a.m. Camped in Los Animas County tonight.

Thursday, Sept. 17, 1884: Dan shot a prairie dog and fried him. I ate some of it and it was pretty good eating.

Sunday, Sept. 21, 1884: Camped on LaVeta Creek six miles from town. Dan caught 35 trout in a few hours. Got mouth organ today. Eat the mellon for dessert at dinner. Mrs. Schaffer and Nellie made pickles of mellon rinds.

Friday, Sept. 27, 1884: Pulled three miles of sand before we got to water today. Dan killed six rabbits this afternoon. Washed my feet tonight.

Wednesday, Oct. 1, 1884: Got a very nice doe in quarter of hour hunt. Put Bob [bird] in his cage. [He brought a bird with him in his wagon.]

Monday, Oct. 20, 1884: Pulled over the top of Grand Mesa.

Sunday, Oct. 26, 1884: Staked off the ranch today.

Thursday, Oct. 30, 1884: Put up the clothesline. Started work on bedstead.

Tuesday, Nov. 11, 1884: Finished the house all but Vega poles.

Wednesday, Nov. 12, 1884: We all worked at the house today.

By December 11, Stephen was back in Iowa. He left his diary with fellow traveler Nellie Nichols who continued it through 1885.

Her Diary

Nellie writes:

Monday, Jan. 5, 1885: Stormy all day. Could not wash. Pieced on Mama's log cabin quilt.

Thursday, Jan. 8, 1885: I pieced on the quilt. It is awful lonesome here.

Thursday, Jan. 15, 1885: Eva and Joe King came over in a sleigh.

Monday, Jan. 16, 1885: We washed today. I'm too tired to write.

Thursday, Jan. 29, 1885: Samp [James Samson Stephen] sent me his photo and a novel to read.

Wednesday, Feb. 4, 1885: Joe King brought us three eggs to make a cake for the dance on Friday night. Our hens don't lay yet.

Friday, Feb. 6, 1885: I got a letter from Samp. I also got a valentine. Don't know who sent it.

Tuesday, Feb. 17, 1885: There will be no school for awhile. Money played out. I went down to see the teacher. She goes to Grand Junction tomorrow.

Thursday, March 5, 1885: Kate laid her first egg.

Wednesday, July 22, 1885: Eva King and I banged our hair.

Monday, Aug. 10, 1885: I killed a bull snake in the house.

Sunday, Oct. 11, 1885: I wrote a letter to Samp this evening.

Wednesday, Dec. 2, 1885: Mr. Hampton was here for supper. He wants me to be the Post Mistress [Vega, Colorado].

Thursday, Dec. 3, 1885: Guess I will take the Post Office if I can get the appointment.

Hot Pepper Chutney

1	red bell pepper, cored and seeded
1	yellow bell pepper, cored and seeded
2–4	fresh jalapeno peppers 2 for a mild-hot flavor 4 for a HOT flavor
$\frac{3}{4}$	cup white wine vinegar
$\frac{1}{2}$	cup granulated sugar
$\frac{1}{2}$	cup packed light brown sugar
$\frac{1}{2}$	cup crystallized ginger cut into slivers (one 4-ounce jar)
$\frac{1}{2}$	cup golden raisins
2	cloves garlic, minced

(Wear rubber gloves when working with jalapenos.)

Makes 2½ cups

Cut red and yellow peppers into long strips and then into ¼-inch slivers.

Cut stems from jalapenos, cut in half, and then into ¼-inch slivers, including seeds. Stir peppers and remaining ingredients in a 2-quart microwave-proof casserole. Cook uncovered at full power in microwave for 20 minutes, stirring several times. Cook longer if you have a low-wattage oven.

Cool. Refrigerate overnight. Serve over cream cheese with crackers. Will keep for three weeks in refrigerator. This quantity is sufficient for three 8-ounce blocks of cream cheese and two boxes of crackers.

Homestead on the Western Slope

Across Colorado

Grand Junction's First Fourth

Miss Nannie stands in the doorway of her school and gazes at her students of assorted sizes.

In a letter to Grand Junction's *Daily Sentinel*, May 1, 1930, Mrs. Nannie Blain Underhill described that city's first Fourth of July celebration in 1882: "The question was 'Should Grand Junction celebrate the Fourth of July?' The answer: 'Certainly!' So the Town Board and the other town gentlemen arranged to have a dance at Armory Hall, the only building with a wooden floor."

However, Miss Nannie, the schoolteacher, was not in favor of a dance, and said she had no intention of attending a dance. What Miss Nannie did was most important because three young, unattached female friends were visiting her and they couldn't go to the dance without their hostess.

All available ladies were needed at the dance! Grand Junction gentlemen outnumbered them ten to one. The men of the town conspired to change Miss Nannie's mind. Two by two, they began calling very formally on the women, inviting them to the dance. Every five minutes a new duo would present themselves. Eventually Nannie took pity and consented to attend the dance with her guests, rather than offend all the gentlemen in town.

One participant observed of that first Fourth in Grand Junction: "All was quiet and orderly, no carousing, no drunkenness, no need for any officers to keep peace, no fireworks, no accidents." However, a close encounter with trouble did occur. Read on.

Across Colorado

Zucchini Appetizer

4 eggs, slightly beaten

½ cup vegetable oil

3 cups thinly sliced zucchini

½ cup chopped onion

2 tablespoons chopped parsley

1 clove garlic, chopped

1 cup baking mix, such as Bisquick

½ cup grated Romano cheese

½ teaspoon seasoned salt

½ teaspoon oregano

pepper to taste

Serves 10–12

Preheat oven to 350°.

Lightly grease a 9x13-inch pan. Mix eggs and oil together, then add vegetables. Mix in dry ingredients. Spread into pan. Bake until browned, 25–30 minutes. Cut into small squares or diagonal pieces. Good served hot or warm.

Miss Nannie Averts a Crisis

As Grand Junction's one and only schoolteacher, Nannie Blain was role model and social arbiter. She recounted an incident at that first Fourth of July celebration when her services as such were needed. In the summer of 1882 the Denver and Rio Grande Railway Company was constructing a roadbed through Grand Junction and a group of Utah men were doing the work. These men, she said, were patriotic and laid off work to celebrate the Fourth. They came to dance, but none of the girls would dance with them.

Nannie recounted that the visitors became angry and said, "We came here and paid our money and expected to dance." It looked as though there would be trouble. This was told to the schoolma'am [Nannie]. Nannie continued, "So when one of the men was introduced to the ladies and all of them declined to dance, I, without a word, arose and accompanied him [on the dance floor] . . . Thus, 'the day was saved,' and after that the visiting boys had no trouble in getting partners."

The Blains were a Grand Junction "first" family. Nannie was the first schoolteacher, her father planted the first fruit trees in the Grand Valley, and Nannie started the first Sunday School.

Across Colorado

Garnethurst in Delta

Garnethurst, a designated state historical site, has been a Delta gathering place for more than 100 years.

(Photo courtesy of Linda Loftis)

Garnethurst, a stately Victorian residence in Delta, has been a community focal point ever since Alfred Rufus "Judge" King built it in 1891. The Kings hosted visiting dignitaries, gave many parties, and even opened their home as the local graduation hall.

The Kings moved out in 1911. During World War I, Garnethurst became Delta's first hospital, run by two nurses, formerly of Denver's Mercy Hospital. In 1922, the Queen Anne residence reverted to a private home. Today Garnethurst is listed as a state historical site and in 1994 was a Colorado Preservation State Honor Award recipient.

Garnethurst is still a Delta gathering place. On the Saturday before Halloween, it hosts the Garnethurst Annual Pumpkin Bash. All guests are encouraged to bring their own pumpkin recipes. From soup to dessert, it's pumpkin, pumpkin, pumpkin!

Garnethurst is owned by Maxine Wheatcroft, whose daughter, Linda Loftis, received the 1994 Caroline Bancroft Award from the Colorado Historical Society for her extraordinary volunteer efforts to promote preservation projects in the city of Delta.

Try Garnethurst's Buffalo Pumpkin Chili in the Southwest Slope/Soups section.

Across Colorado

Miniature Pasties

	pie crust recipe or mix for 2 crusts
1/2	cup grated Cheddar cheese
1	tablespoon milk

Filling

1	cup diced cold roast beef
1/2	cup diced cooked potatoes
1/2	cup diced cooked carrots
2	tablespoons minced onion
1/4	cup sweet pickle relish
3	tablespoons salad dressing, such as Miracle Whip
2	teaspoons prepared mustard
	dash Worcestershire sauce

Makes 12 pasties

Heat oven to 425°.

In a large bowl make crust for two pies, adding cheese to dry ingredients. On a lightly floured board, roll out half of dough 1/8 inch thick. Using a 3-inch cutter, make 12 rounds. Line small-size muffin tins with the rounds. Roll out remaining half of dough and cut 12 rounds with a 2-inch cookie cutter.

Combine meat, vegetables, relish, dressing, and seasonings. Fill pastry-lined muffin tins with meat mixture. Brush edges with milk and seal on pasty tops. Make cuts for escaping steam. Bake 20 minutes. Cool 10 minutes.

Serve immediately or save for a camping trip or picnic. To save, wrap each pasty in foil and refrigerate or freeze. To reheat, place in oven at 350° for 25 minutes or in skillet on camp stove for 10 minutes. Unwrap and eat.

Read about Cornish pasties in the Colorado mines— see the Central Mountains/Salads and Vegetables section.

Across Colorado

A Tale of Two Rivers

It started about 1859 when Congress was wrangling over what to name the territory that became Colorado. San Juan, Idaho, Shoshone, Cibola, and Yampa Territory had strong supporters, but those who wanted Colorado Territory won. At this time the present Colorado River was called the Grand River, and the present Green River was called the Colorado River, which was indeed in Colorado Territory.

In 1876 when Colorado became a state, the border was realigned, and the state of Colorado did not contain the headwaters of the river bearing its name. In fact, the original Colorado River (now Green River and mostly in Utah) flowed only a few miles within the state, in the far northwest corner. For years, citizens and politicians decried this unhappy circumstance.

Finally, after much legislative bickering, in 1926 the name of the original Colorado was changed to the Green River and the Grand River (whose headwaters begin in Colorado up in Rocky Mountain National Park) officially became the Colorado River. The name Grand, however, lives on in the Grand Canyon, the Grand Valley, and Grand Junction, built at the confluence of the old Grand (now Colorado) and Gunnison Rivers.

The confluence of the Colorado and Green Rivers, west of the Colorado border, near Moab, Utah.

(*Time* magazine, August 23, 1954)

4UR Trout Mousse

3	10-inch trout
1	stalk celery
3	scallions
2	teaspoons whole black peppercorns
1/4	cup lemon juice
	water to cover bottom of skillet or poacher
2	8-ounce packages cream cheese
2	tablespoons lemon juice
1/4	teaspoon liquid smoke
1/4	teaspoon salt
1/4	teaspoon pepper
1	tablespoon chopped fresh dill
1	tablespoon chopped chives
1	clove garlic, minced
1/2	small red onion, chopped

Makes 3-4 cups

Poach trout with celery, scallions, peppercorns, lemon juice, and water to cover skillet bottom. Lay fish flat and simmer gently for 15 minutes. Remove fish, cool, and remove fish skin and bones.

Whip cheese until light and fluffy. Add other ingredients except fish. Beat in mixer until smooth, about 2 minutes. Add fish and mix on medium speed for 1 minute. Adjust salt and pepper to taste. Refrigerate. Will keep up to 1 week.

Serve as a spread on crackers. For a lighter mixture to serve as a dip, substitute 6 ounces cream cheese and 10 ounces sour cream for the 2 packages of cream cheese.

Read about early days at the 4UR Ranch in the South Mountains/Southwest Flavors section.

Across Colorado

The Rock That Burns

A train travels through the Grand Valley, approaching an oil shale mountain near Rifle.

Legend has it that a mother and daughter, living on a homestead near DeBeque, took their clothes to the creek to wash. They built a small wood fire under a kettle. They never added wood but the fire never went out—the rocks were burning!

Oil shale comes and goes as the topic of the day in DeBeque, Rifle, Parachute, Grand Junction, and other gathering places on the Western Slope. Many oil companies have carried out extensive work—beginning in 1902. Experimental plants have been installed. The economy has boomed time and again with the promise of oil production, then it has faded. Oil shale is still considered money in the bank— but a bank that is locked and no one can find the key.

Fast Fondue

1	clove garlic
1	cup dry white wine, such as Chardonnay
1	$10\frac{1}{2}$-ounce can Cheddar cheese soup
1	pound imported Swiss cheese, cubed or shredded
3	tablespoons cornstarch

Makes 4 cups

Rub small cooking pot with garlic. Simmer wine in pot and blend in soup. Combine cheese and cornstarch and stir into soup mixture. Heat until cheese melts, stirring frequently. Serve with crusty bread chunks.

The Green River Land and Townsite Company was one of many development companies that lured Easterners westward. This 1906 photograph shows the fledgling colony and Bookcliffs in the distance.

Across Colorado

Fruita's Moving Post Office

Fruita post office in the 1920s

Early-day towns and developments were highly partisan, jealous of each other, and forever promoting their own image. Fruita and Cleveland, located adjacent to each other about 25 miles west of Grand Junction, were two such settlements. Each tried to outdo the other. They both competed for the post office but Fruita won out. One night the small, one-room post office vanished from Fruita and appeared on Main Street in Cleveland. No mortals ever admitted to helping with the job. However, the Postmaster General in Washington, D.C., frowned on such ghostly activity and insisted that the post office be returned to Fruita.

Fruita eventually absorbed Cleveland.

Caponata (Eggplant Antipasto)

1	unpeeled medium eggplant (about 1 pound)
$2/3$	cup olive oil (divided use)
2	medium onions, diced
1	cup celery, diced
1	16-ounce can Italian tomatoes with juice
$1/3$	cup wine vinegar, red or white
1	tablespoon sugar
1	teaspoon salt
$1/4$	teaspoon pepper
3	dashes cayenne
14	ounces ripe or green olives, chopped, or a combination
2	tablespoons capers
1	tablespoon caper juice
2	tablespoons pine nuts
	juice of 1 lemon

Makes 5–6 cups

Cut eggplant into half-inch cubes. Salt lightly and let drain for 30 minutes. Heat $1/3$ cup olive oil in skillet. Saute eggplant 5 minutes. Remove eggplant from skillet. Saute the onions, adding the remaining oil. Add celery, tomatoes, and juice. Cook 15 minutes or until sauce is thickened and reduced. Stir in vinegar, sugar, seasonings, and eggplant. Cook, covered, about 10 minutes. Add olives, capers with juice, and pine nuts. Cook, covered, about 10 minutes longer. Add lemon juice to taste.

Chill well (best if made 24 hours in advance). Serve hot or cold as an antipasto with bread rounds, as a warm side dish, or as a cold salad.

The Lovett Log Cabin

Kate and Sam Lovett came to Cedaredge on Grand Mesa in 1889 from Taos, New Mexico, where Kate had been a teacher in mission schools and Sam had been a scout for Kit Carson. They built one of the first log cabins in the area, and it is still standing, a Colorado historical site.

The Lovett home has the distinction of having on its grounds two trees that are registered as state champions of their type, a white mountain ash and a white mulberry. Now named the Log Cabin Inn, the cabin today is a unique bed-and-breakfast.

Across Colorado

Long Trip to Denver

Grand Junction's handsome railway station, finished in 1906, was a beehive of activity in its early years. It still serves travelers today, but fewer of them.

In an interview with a historian gathering oral histories from early Grand Junction residents, one woman described her family's train trips to Denver.

She said that because the Moffat Tunnel had not been built, the trip took eighteen hours. The train went through Leadville, Salida, Canyon City, and Pueblo before coming into Denver. It was always an overnight trip.

However, the train trip was speedy compared to the old stage. In 1886, the stage wagon, full of passengers, baggage, and express, took two days to go from Grand Junction to Glenwood Springs. Every four hours its four-horse team was exchanged for a fresh crew. Passengers stayed overnight in Parachute.

Goat Cheese Crostini

1	1-pound loaf dense French bread, cut into 14–18 slices
6	ounces butter, room temperature
4	garlic cloves, crushed
4	ounces fresh goat cheese, domestic or French Montrachet, crumbled
9	oil-packed, sundried tomatoes, drained and cut into slivers

Makes 14–18 full-size crostini

Preheat oven to 350°.

Slice the bread and place on a large cookie sheet. Bake bread slices in hot oven for 5 minutes. Make garlic spread by combining butter and garlic. Remove bread slices from oven and coat with garlic spread, returning to cookie sheet. Top crostini (coated bread slices) with crumbled goat cheese and sun-dried tomato slivers. Bake at 300° for 10 minutes. Serve warm.

Variation: In place of or in addition to sun-dried tomatoes, use topping of ½ cup diced, pitted, black, brine-cured olives, such as Niçoise olives.

Excellent cut into halves as a cocktail or wine munchie, or good with grilled chicken salad or salmon and wild greens.

Maybell, Colorado

See the South Plains/Special Times section for the "way they do it in Maybell every Labor Day."

Across Colorado

Stagecoaches continued to carry passengers and freight between Meeker and Craig well into the 1920s because the towns were not connected by a railroad.

This six-horse stage, transporting hunters and their prey, was photographed in Meeker, probably about 1915.

Hanky Pankys

1	pound ground beef
1	pound Italian sausage
1	medium yellow onion, chopped
1–2	cloves garlic, minced
1	tablespoon dried parsley
½	teaspoon Tabasco
1½	cups processed cheese, such as Velveeta, cubed or shredded
1	package cocktail rye bread

Brown ground beef and sausage and drain. Add onion, garlic, parsley, and Tabasco. Mix well. Add cheese and stir until cheese melts. Spread on cocktail rye bread slices. Place on cookie sheet and broil until lightly browned. Serve hot.

Meat mixture can easily be made ahead of time, then refrigerated or frozen.

Makes about 36 hearty appetizers

Caviar Pie

2	8-ounce packages cream cheese
1	cup sour cream
¼	teaspoon Tabasco
1	tablespoon Worcestershire sauce
2	tablespoons lemon juice
4	hard-boiled eggs, chopped
½	cup chopped green onion
1	3- or 4-ounce jar caviar, black or red

Mix cream cheese, sour cream, Tabasco, Worcestershire, and lemon juice. Chill. Spread the cream cheese mixture on a decorative 8- or 9-inch plate. Top the cream cheese with an outer ring of chopped eggs, an inside ring of green onions, and spoon caviar gently into center. Serve with crackers or toast rounds.

Makes about 4 cups

Across Colorado

Excerpts from the Pioneer Press

Newspapers on the frontier set themselves up as guardians of the community's morals and pulled no punches in their reports of unseemly conduct. The following examples are from the *Grand Junction News*:

April 7, 1883: We would suggest that a certain sporting woman be compelled to lengthen her skirts or else ride on a country road. Such spectacles have a tendency to demoralize the young.

July 19, 1883: Has anyone noticed that of the twenty-five distinguished citizens who went a-Maying on Wednesday, exactly twenty-five claim to be the only sober man in the crowd?

The showpiece of the Moffat Road was David Moffat's private car, Marcia, built by the Pullman Company and completed in 1906. The car, named after Moffat's only daughter, is on display in Craig.

Hot Onion Dip

2	packages frozen chopped onions (12–16 ounces each)
3	8-ounce packages light cream cheese
2	cups grated Parmesan cheese
1/2	cup mayonnaise
	tortilla chips or crackers

Makes 6–7 cups

Preheat oven to 425°.

Thaw onions and squeeze to remove water. Stir onions, cheeses, and mayonnaise together. Place in a 2-quart bake-and-serve dish and bake for 15 minutes or until golden brown. Serve hot with tortilla chips or crackers. Recipe may be divided in half.

Herb Toast Sticks

4	ounces butter, melted
1/4	teaspoon dried thyme
1/4	teaspoon dried oregano
1	clove garlic, minced
1/2	teaspoon salt
1	teaspoon chopped parsley
	freshly ground pepper to taste
8	slices day-old bread, cut into strips

Makes about 32 strips

Preheat oven to 350°.

Mix butter and seasonings until well blended. Dip both sides of bread strips into the herb butter and place on baking sheet. Bake for 10 minutes, turning once. Serve hot or cold.

Across Colorado

General store in Rifle all
dressed up for the Christmas
season, about 1910.

Cherry Creek Dip

16	ounces light sour cream
2	tablespoons dry ranch dressing mix
$^1\!/_2$	teaspoon garlic powder
1	tablespoon onion flakes
2	tablespoons buttermilk

Mix all of the ingredients together. Allow to stand 1 hour before serving. Serve as a low-fat dip with fresh vegetables or as a side dressing for freshly steamed broccoli. Dip has about 20 calories per tablespoon and is full of flavor. Excellent with fresh veggies or pita chips.

Makes 2 cups

Shrimp Delight

$1^1\!/_2$	pounds large, cooked shrimp, deveined
1	6-ounce can water chestnuts
1	pint cherry tomatoes
$^1\!/_2$	medium head cauliflower, broken into flowerettes

Mix the sauce, then mix in other ingredients. Marinate for 8 hours or more. Serve in a clear glass bowl with cocktail picks. Easy and attractive.

Sauce

$1^1\!/_2$	cups mayonnaise
$^1\!/_2$	cup prepared horseradish
1	teaspoon dry mustard
1	tablespoon lemon juice

Serves 6–8

Across Colorado

The butcher shop in the prosperous town of Rifle, about 1910

Yuma County Cattlewomen's Dip

2	10$\frac{1}{4}$-ounce containers bean dip
3	medium avocados, mashed
2	tablespoons lemon juice
$\frac{1}{2}$	teaspoon salt
$\frac{1}{4}$	teaspoon pepper
$\frac{1}{2}$	cup mayonnaise
1	cup sour cream
1	package taco seasoning mix
1	pound hamburger, cooked, drained, cooled
$\frac{1}{2}$	cup sliced green onions
2	cups tomatoes, chopped
1	head iceberg lettuce, shredded
$\frac{1}{2}$	cup sliced ripe olives (optional)
8	ounces shredded Cheddar cheese

Serves 12–16

Prepare in layers in a large, shallow serving dish. Spread bean dip as bottom layer. Mix avocados, lemon juice, salt, and pepper. Spread on top of bean dip. Mix mayonnaise, sour cream, and taco seasoning mix. Spread on top of avocado mixture. Top these layers with the cooked hamburger. Sprinkle this layer with green onions, chopped tomatoes, shredded lettuce, sliced ripe olives (optional), and shredded Cheddar cheese, in order given. Serve with taco chips.

Across Colorado

Advice for Practical Housekeepers

Young pioneer wife demonstrating the wonders of her new cookstove

The following suggestions for homemakers are reprinted from Practical Housekeeping, *published by the Buckeye Publishing Company of Minneapolis in 1883.*

Testing the Oven. If the hand can be held in the oven only 20 to 35 seconds (or while counting 20 to 35), it is a "quick" oven, from 35 to 45 seconds is "moderate," and from 45 to 60 seconds is "slow." Sixty seconds is a good oven to begin with for large fruit cakes. All systematic housekeepers will hail the day when some enterprising Yankee or Buckeye girl shall invent a stove or range with a thermometer attached to the oven, so that the heat may be regulated accurately and intelligently.

Suggested Day's Menu. Breakfast: Waffles, broiled steak, fried apples. Dinner: Roast duck, apple sauce, brown stew, mashed turnips, sweet potatoes baked, prairie plum pudding with sauce, fruit cake, oranges. Supper: Light biscuit, whipped cream with preserves, sliced beef.

The Laundry. When inviting friends for visits of a week or more, try to fix the time for the visit to begin the day after the ironing is done. The girl feels a weight off her mind, has time to cook the meals better, and is a much more willing attendant upon guests. Do not have beefsteak for dinner on washing or ironing days—arrange to have something roasted in the oven, or else have cold meat. Do not have fried or broiled fish. The smell sticks, and the clothes will not be sweet; besides the broiler and frying pan take longer to clean. As for vegetables, do not have spinach, pease [sic], string beans, or applesauce.

All these good things take time to prepare, and can be avoided as well as not. Have baked white and sweet potatoes, macaroni, boiled rice, parsnips, sweet corn, stewed tomatoes, any canned vegetables in winter. For dessert, baked apples and cream, bread pudding, or something easily prepared.

English Muffin Wedges

1	cup chopped black olives
$\frac{1}{2}$	cup chopped green onions
$\frac{1}{2}$	cup mayonnaise
$1\frac{1}{2}$	cups Parmesan cheese
6	English muffins

Makes 48–72 wedges

Mix first four ingredients. Spread on muffin halves. Cut into 4–6 wedges. Broil until bubbly. Serve warm. Tasty and easy.

Roasted Garlic with Goat Cheese

4	heads garlic
$\frac{3}{4}$	cup chicken stock
1	14-ounce log goat cheese (Feta cheese may be substituted)
1	large loaf sourdough or country bread, cut in wedges, lightly toasted
	fresh thyme (optional)
	salt and pepper to taste

Serves 4–6

Preheat oven to 400°.

Cut off the upper part of garlic heads, exposing the cloves. Place heads in a small baking dish with the chicken stock, sprigs of thyme (optional), and some salt and pepper. Cover the dish tightly and bake about 1 hour or until garlic heads are very soft. Serve garlic with cooking juices spooned over and pass goat cheese and bread.

This is a great, easy appetizer. Let guests squeeze garlic pulp out of the cloves and onto bread wedges, crumbling the cheese on top. It is a bit messy as you squeeze the garlic cloves but tasty and fun!

Across Colorado

How to Dress an Old Lady

"An object of pride, a sort of show piece"

The grandmother, whose failing strength takes her partially out of the active cares of life, ought to be the object of tender consideration from everyone in the household; and it should be everyone's care to have her comfortable and well dressed; an object of pride, a sort of show piece, instead of a poor, pushed-aside, forlorn object to be kept out of sight. There is no arbitrary dictum requiring certain things, but custom restricts them to a narrow choice of color—brown, purple, black, and gray being the only ones allowed. Artistically considered, brown should be also excluded on account of its unbecomingness to the dull tints of hair, eyes, and complexion. The ideal dress for an old lady . . . is severely plain velvet, with soft tulle handkerchief folded across the breast, rich lace ruffles at the wrist to shade the withered hands, and a decorous cap, which makes no attempt to be a head-dress, but has protecting strings of lace or ribbon to tie loosely under the chin.

(From Practical Housekeeping, 1883)

Ever–Ready Garlic Spread

Quick Way

1	1-pound tub of soft margarine
$1/4$	teaspoon freshly ground black pepper
$1/2$–1	teaspoon Beau Monde seasoning or celery salt
5	medium-sized, fresh garlic cloves, crushed
	pinch dried basil

Mix all ingredients. Store in refrigerator and use to make garlic toast or toasted bread strips, whenever desired. Keeps at least three months.

Traditional Way

1	large, whole head garlic
	olive oil
8	ounces butter
8	ounces margarine
$1/4$	teaspoon freshly ground black pepper
$3/4$	teaspoon Beau Monde seasoning or celery salt
	pinch basil
	pinch thyme

Preheat oven to 300°.

Place head of garlic in a small, ovenproof dish. Bathe with olive oil. Cover with foil and bake for 2 hours. Remove from oven and cool. Squeeze roasted garlic from paper shell. Add roasted garlic to butter and margarine and blend well. Add seasonings. Refrigerate. Use as needed for garlic bread and toast, or toasted bread strips.

Makes about 2 cups

Across Colorado

Wild horses are part of the fauna in the Bookcliffs of the northwest slope, and the wild horse roundup is still a periodic event. This roundup took place in 1895.

Catching Horses, Wilson Creek Camp.

Shrimp de Wonderful

½	cup olive oil
1–2	tablespoons Creole seasoning
2	tablespoons fresh lime juice
2	tablespoons fresh parsley
1	tablespoon honey
1	tablespoon soy sauce
12–18	uncooked shrimp, peeled and deveined

Serves 6 as appetizer

Preheat oven to 450°. Mix all ingredients in 9x13-inch pan. Marinate 1 hour. Bake for 10 minutes. Serve with toothpicks.

This also may be served as a main course with fresh bread and a green salad.

Bachelors vs. Married Men

In 1882, in the days before Grand Junction was incorporated, Mesa County residents held their first county election for the school board. As related by the *Daily Sentinel* in its 1915 history of the county, there were two slates of candidates: one made up of bachelors and the other made up of married men.

The married men were soundly defeated. The *Sentinel* reported that "no sufficient reason was ever given for the overwhelming defeat suffered by the representatives of matrimonial felicity, though at one time it was whispered on the streets that the candidates' wives worked for the opposition, giving as a reason for doing so that 'a married man had no business fooling away his time with school marms.'"

Across Colorado

Before Mesa Verde became a national park in 1906, local groups used the Anasazi ruins as they pleased. Here a group of thespians, probably from the Colorado Cliff Dwellers Association, stages a pageant in Spruce Tree House.

Across Colorado

The Southwest Slope

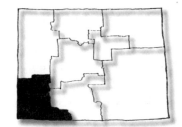

The

mystery

of the

ghostly, cliffside cities

remains—it continues

to lure visitors from

around the world,

haunting their

imaginations.

Magnificent. Mysterious. Melancholy. A land once teeming with the daily activity of thousands—then abandoned abruptly and left silently sleeping. How did that ancient civilization come into being? How and why did it flourish for centuries and then vanish? Remnants of ancient dwellings hang on many canyon walls throughout this region, known as the Four Corners area— where four states meet at one pinpoint.

The Anasazi (or ancient enemies) populated Colorado from the great Pagosa hot springs at the eastern edge to the dry deserty expanses of the west. In between was the green table—the Mesa Verde. The ghost cities, carved into cliffs, attest to the Anasazi's skills in design and masonry. The evidence of farming, the storage bins, and granaries suggest a system of cooperation, of communal care and concern.

Then the civilization vanished. Was it a great drought? Did enemies penetrate their secure community? Did internal factions decimate them? Or did a better way of life to the south call them away? Why did they leave without taking their possessions? There seem to be few answers and many questions.

Nomadic tribes probably roamed the region and hunters came and went; later the mountain men found their niche. Permanent settlement came in the mid-nineteenth century when the United States acquired the region after the Mexican War. Rumors of gold in the San Juans brought fortune hunters and serious prospectors. The narrow-gauge railroads linked mining camps; entrepreneurs built roads across seemingly impassable mountains. Towns were staked out and the area boomed—then prosperity faded and these cities, too, became ghosts. Many people moved on, but others stayed, waited for good times to return, and then wrought the changes that have brought the Four Corners into the twenty-first century.

However, the magnificent mountains, the temperate climate, and the mystery of the ghostly, cliffside cities remain—they continue to lure visitors from around the world. Today the steam engines that carried miners up the mountainside and the ore back down deliver tourists through canyons and beside rushing streams to a place where time stands still—where they can experience the way things were and lose themselves in the melancholy history of the ghost cities of the southwest slope.

The flavors of the Southwest— the blue beans of the Anasazi, enchiladas, tortillas, chiles, and the wonderful corn of the region enhance the visitors' adventures.

Across Colorado

Colorado Historical Society Saved Earliest Mesa Verde Collection

In 1889, after Richard Wetherill first saw Cliff Palace in Mesa Verde, he and his brother Al collected an assortment of artifacts and exhibited them with short lectures in Durango, Pueblo, and Denver. Al Wetherill reported that "the public didn't particularly care about being educated!" He said Durango was too small to be interested in anything but civic betterment, and Pueblo met them with indifference verging on ridicule. Denver also gave their story a cold shoulder.

However, when the Wetherills discovered a mummy of a child and sent it to Denver, interest in Mesa Verde caught on. The Colorado Historical Society became interested and bought the collection in 1890 through the generosity of three Historical Society members who signed personal notes for the cost. Thus, the Colorado Historical Society kept the first collection of Anasazi antiquities in the state of Colorado.

Mesa Verde Artifacts to Helsinki

In 1891, Swedish Baron Gustaf Nordenskjold visited Mesa Verde and collected, then shipped, 600 outstanding Anasazi artifacts back to Sweden for a tour of Europe. Residents of Durango staged enough of a protest for the county sheriff to impound the Baron's boxes briefly, but the district attorney could find no law against the removal of artifacts from public lands, so the Baron continued on his way. Today these artifacts reside in the National Museum of Helsinki, Finland.

Mesa Verde pottery

Mushroom and Spinach Soup

¼	cup vegetable oil
1	medium onion, minced
2	garlic cloves, minced
¾	pound mushrooms, sliced or quartered
6	ounces shiitake mushrooms, stemmed and sliced
1	teaspoon dried thyme
4	cups chicken stock
2	cups spinach leaves, sliced
1	tablespoon chopped parsley
	pepper

Serves 6

Heat oil in a large saucepan over medium-low heat. Add onion and garlic and saute until onion is tender, about 8 minutes. Add mushrooms and thyme, and saute about 5 minutes. Stir in chicken stock and bring to boil. Reduce heat, cover, and simmer 20 minutes. (Can be done to this point the day before, then cover and refrigerate. Bring to boil before continuing.) Add spinach and parsley to soup and stir until wilted. Season with pepper and serve with hearty bread.

Great served with a Chardonnay or a good Cabernet Sauvignon.

Quotable Quotes

From a Bride
"We've been married six weeks and I haven't eaten a piece of meat that didn't have a hole through it or a hook in it," complained a young bride who had come from the East to the San Juans.

Across Colorado

A Bead Bag for a Chicken

William Alva Short and Constance Belle Short homesteaded on the Florida (pronounced Flo ree' da) Mesa south of Durango about 1899 after the federal government removed the land from the Ute reservation and opened it to homesteading. Parties of Utes often stopped by and traded their beadwork for Constance's vegetables and chickens.

Today the vegetables and chickens are long gone, but the intricately beaded bags and belts make beautiful displays in shadow boxes in the Short descendants' homes.

Grandmother Short adapted her mincemeat recipe to the meat she had on hand—venison. The mincemeat is now a family tradition. Grandsons and granddaughters of the pioneer Shorts spend one day before Christmas every year mixing up mincemeat. Now they often adapt it back to beef.

See Grandmother Short's mincemeat recipe in the South Plains/Special Times section.

Ute women and children—the real "first families" of Colorado—on the Southern Ute reservation.

White Chili

2	cups dry white beans
2	bay leaves
8	cups chicken or turkey broth
1	tablespoon oil
1	onion, chopped
1	clove garlic, minced
$\frac{1}{2}$	teaspoon oregano
$\frac{1}{2}$	teaspoon thyme
1	$4\frac{1}{2}$-ounce can diced green chiles
2	cups cooked chicken or turkey, diced
1	teaspoon ground cumin
2–4	tablespoons fresh cilantro, minced
$\frac{1}{4}$	teaspoon cayenne pepper or 1 tablespoon red pepper flakes
	salt to taste

Serves 6–8

Place beans, bay leaves, and broth in a 3-quart stockpot. Simmer 3 or 4 hours until beans are tender. Remove about 1 cup cooked beans and mash them. Return to pot.

Saute onion, garlic, oregano, thyme, and green chiles in oil until onions are just soft.

Stir onion mixture into beans. Add remaining ingredients and return to a simmer.

Turn off heat and let stand 2 hours to blend flavors. Reheat and serve.

Across Colorado

First Visit to Two-Story House

W. H. Jackson, the "Photographer of the West," was in the party that made the first official visit to Mesa Verde in July 1874. This is his description: "It was growing dark, but I wanted to see all there was of it . . . we were 'stumped' for awhile in making the last hundred feet, but with the aid of an old dead tree and the remains of some ancient footholds, we finally reached the bench or platform on which was perched, like a swallow's nest, the 'Two Story House' of our first photograph. From this height we had a glorious view over the surrounding canyon walls, while far below our camp fire glimmered in the deepening shadows like a far-away little red star."

The Colorado Historical Society owns the world's largest collection of W. H. Jackson photographs.

A Hollywood crew shoots a silent film in Mesa Verde's Balcony House about 1926.

Garnethurst's Buffalo Pumpkin Chili

1	pound ground buffalo meat
1	16-ounce can solid pack pumpkin or 2 cups fresh pumpkin, steamed
1	onion, chopped
1	tablespoon chili powder
2	14½-ounce cans diced or crushed tomatoes
1	teaspoon salt
1	16-ounce can red kidney beans, undrained

Serves 6

Cook buffalo meat in a 3-quart saucepan over medium heat until meat loses its pink color. Stir in pumpkin, onion, and chili powder and simmer for 5 minutes. Add tomatoes and salt and bring to a boil. Cover and simmer for 20 minutes, stirring occasionally. Add beans and simmer uncovered for an additional 20 minutes, stirring often to prevent scorching.

Read about Garnethurst and its Pumpkin Bash in the Northwest Slope/ Appetizers section.

From Marietta Wetherill

"I married the right man. There's no doubt about it because I'll tell you in the first place I admired him for his knowledge; I admired him for being such a perfect gentleman; and learned to love him more than . . . I never could love any man as much." Marietta Wetherill wrote in her diary, about her husband Richard Wetherill, the discoverer of Cliff Palace and many other Anasazi ruins.

Marietta explored along with Richard, even in winter. She wrote, "We slept in that deep snow. We'd just take the shovels and shovel it off and Mr. Wetherill cut some brush and put it down and made our bed. And just put the tarp down and put the sleeping bags down and piled in, dead tired and hungry."

Reprinted from A Quilt of Words, *copyright 1988 by Sharon Niederman, with permission from Johnson Books, Boulder, Colorado.*

Across Colorado

Ridgway: Reborn with Movies

Ridgway, population about 400, is nestled in a notch between the San Juan Mountains and the Uncompahgre Plateau. Railroading created the town a century ago when rail-builder Otto Mears constructed the Rio Grande Southern Railway. Hollywood revived it in the 1950s and 1960s when it discovered the area's natural beauty.

Metro Goldwyn Mayer filmed *Tribute to a Bad Man*, with James Cagney, on one of the nearby mesas, then *How the West Was Won*, with Gregory Peck, James Stewart, Henry Fonda, and Debbie Reynolds. Another bonanza came in 1969 when Paramount sent a crew of over 250 people with John Wayne to make *True Grit*.

Everyone in town who wanted to be in *True Grit* worked as an extra for $16 a day, and carpenters, bricklayers, painters, and other laborers were put to work building sets and turning the town into the Old West. Today it is hard to tell the difference between the True Grit relics and the real ones.

Ridgway train station

Across Colorado

Fabulous Fish Stew

3	tablespoons extra virgin olive oil
1/4	cup finely chopped yellow onion
1	teaspoon minced garlic
1/2	cup chopped green pepper
1/2	cup chopped carrots
1/4-1/2	teaspoon red pepper flakes
1	bay leaf
1	teaspoon dried thyme
1	cup dry white wine, such as Chardonnay
1	28-ounce can whole or diced tomatoes
1	large red-skinned potato, cut into half-inch cubes
1	cup water
1 1/4	pounds deboned, skinned fish, such as grouper, halibut, monkfish, or cod
1/2	pint bay scallops or sliced sea scallops
1	cup heavy cream
1	teaspoon salt
1/4	teaspoon pepper
1/2	cup chopped fresh parsley

In a 3-quart saucepan, gently saute the onion, garlic, green pepper, and carrots in oil until the onion is translucent. Add red pepper flakes, bay leaf, thyme, wine, and undrained tomatoes. Bring to a boil. Rinse potatoes and add to pot. Cover and cook 10 minutes. Add water and cook for 10 minutes more. STOP here if you are not ready to serve; cover and hold at warm.

About 15 minutes before serving, cut the fish and sea scallops into bite-size chunks. Add to gently simmering broth. Cook for 3–5 minutes, or until fish and scallops are just cooked. Add cream, season with salt and pepper, and return to simmering point.

Sprinkle servings with parsley. Serve with generous amounts of garlic bread.

This is a rich, yet light, contemporary stew and is also excellent served over pasta.

Serves 4 as a main dish

Across Colorado

Galloping Goose Hatchery

The Galloping Goose was hatched in the Ridgway roundhouse.

The Galloping Goose was a novel idea conceived by the managers of the faltering Rio Grande Southern Railway to keep their railroad alive during the Depression. The first Galloping Goose produced in the Ridgway roundhouse was a gas-powered motor-car that carried passengers, freight, express, and the U.S. mail over the narrow-gauge rails with a one-man crew. This Goose weighed 5,300 pounds and replaced a train weighing 96 tons. When it behaved properly, it took flight at 45 miles per hour, but onlookers described its usual speed as "a waddle."

In all, eight "Geese" were hatched in Ridgway. Daily, a Goose made the trip between Durango, Ridgway, and points north for more than twenty years. However, in 1951 the Galloping Goose gave its last honk and was consigned to historical moments on TV, museum displays, and courthouse exhibits.

Look for a Galloping Goose outside the city hall of Telluride, on display in Dolores, and three Galloping Geese at the Colorado Railroad Museum in Golden. Sadly, no Galloping Goose remains in Ridgway.

Cream of Asparagus Soup

3	pounds fresh asparagus (stalks should be the diameter of a dime)
3	tablespoons butter
$\frac{1}{2}$	cup diced onion
1	cup chopped fresh leeks, white part only (do not substitute—leeks are essential)
2	cups chicken stock or canned broth, warmed
2	cups half-and-half
	salt and pepper to taste
	lemon juice (optional)
	sour cream and chives for garnish

Makes 2 quarts

Rinse asparagus and trim off bottom $1\frac{1}{2}$ inches of stalk. Cut asparagus into 1-inch lengths. Melt butter in a 12-inch skillet. Add asparagus, onion, and leeks. Saute over medium heat for 4–8 minutes. Season with salt and pepper. Cover skillet, reduce heat to medium low, and cook for 15–20 minutes or until asparagus is tender. Stir often; do not allow to brown. Place vegetables in the work bowl of a food processor. Process until completely pureed. Add chicken stock and process 30 seconds longer.

Pour soup into a 3-quart saucepan. Add half-and-half. Warm over low heat. Adjust seasoning. A squeeze of lemon juice may be added for balance. Serve warm, topped with a dollop of sour cream and a sprinkle of chives. For fewer calories, replace some of the half-and-half with milk. Can be made in advance and can also be frozen.

Schoolteacher on the Ranch

A young schoolteacher described the kitchen/dining room of the ranch house where she boarded in Dolores County in 1897: *"There was a long homemade table with benches around it. The walls of the room were papered with newspaper and many times later I saw cowboys on stormy days walking around the rooms that were papered, reading them. They would be quite disgusted at the thoughtlessness of the one who did the papering when they found one bottom side up."*

Across Colorado

Two miners pose in the kitchen corner of their cabin in the San Juans.

Miner, Diarist, Cook

George W. Howard explored the San Juan Mountains for gold in 1860–1861, then became a permanent settler in La Plata County, and is the namesake of Howardsville. His diary from 1872–1873 survives:

May 12, 1872:

I thought I would try to get some fresh meat for a change, so shouldered my gun and sallied forth in quest of "whom I might devour," but after a three-hour fruitless search for "whom," I returned to camp and put on my trusty pot of beans . . .

July 4, 1872:

Not knowing how to celebrate the glorious fourth [of July] in this isolated region other than by "feasting," I cooked up a big pot of beans, had some boiled and some baked, and for pastry I made a great big kind of apple pie, filling my bread pan nearly half full. I made some sauce for it, with condensed milk well sweetened, and added a little whiskey to it for flavoring.

Boulder Squash Soup

1½   pounds acorn squash

1½   pounds sweet potatoes

3   tablespoons olive or vegetable oil

2½   cups chopped onion

7   cups chicken broth (low sodium can be used)

½   teaspoon garlic salt

       salt and pepper to taste

3   tablespoons sliced, fresh chives

Peel squash (microwave for 5 minutes to soften) and cut into cubes. Peel sweet potatoes and cube. In a 6-quart stockpot, cook onions in oil until translucent. Add squash and potatoes and cook 5 minutes. Add chicken broth and simmer for 1½ hours or until cubes of vegetables are tender.

Puree in blender when cool.

Serve hot or cold. Season to taste. Garnish servings with chives. A dash of curry powder can be added.

Serves 8 – 10

Mushroom Barley Soup

1   large onion, diced

¾   pound sliced mushrooms

3   tablespoons butter

2   tablespoons flour

8   cups chicken or beef broth

1   cup medium-size barley

2   cups milk

1   cup half-and-half

       salt and pepper

In a stockpot, saute the onion and mushrooms in melted butter until onion is translucent. Add flour and cook, stirring, for 3 minutes. Stir in the chicken or beef broth and barley. Bring liquid to a boil. Simmer mixture for 45 minutes, covered. Add milk and half-and-half and cook at a bare simmer, covered, for 30 minutes. Season with salt and pepper to taste.

This easy and delicious soup is equally good preceding an elegant dinner party or for lunch on a cold winter day. Can be made ahead and frozen.

Serves 8-10

Across Colorado

Food for Snowbound Miners

In autumn, the miners of the San Juans said goodbye to their families and to the "girls" of the towns and climbed to the remote and high boardinghouses where they would live, work, and be trapped by snow for the next six months.

Keeping these snow- and ice-captured miners productive and happy was a challenge to the mine superintendent. A good cook who would provide pie for breakfast and meat and potatoes for dinner was a necessity. But in addition to quantities of "plain" foods, an occasional change added to the men's contentment. A good cook in the cookhouse was a top priority to keep the mine functioning.

Tobogganing in the San Juans

Miners often used their scoop shovels as a fast means of transportation to town after work. Seated on the scoop of the shovel and holding the handle between his legs, the miner would streak down the snowy mountainside on his one-man toboggan.

Miners' boardinghouse at Alta where the Gold King was a producing mine until 1948.

Old Plantation Black Bean Soup

3	cups black beans
2	quarts chicken stock or water
8	ounces bacon, diced
1	medium onion, chopped
1	large green pepper, cored, seeded, and diced
3–4	stalks celery, diced
3	cloves garlic, minced
2	teaspoons salt
1	teaspoon dry basil
1	teaspoon dry oregano
½	teaspoon dry thyme
¼	cup wine vinegar
4½	ounces canned or frozen tiny shrimp
	sour cream

Serves 6 – 8

Wash, pick over, and soak beans overnight in a large pot. Drain. Add remaining ingredients except the shrimp and sour cream. Bring to boil. Lower heat and cook on a slow simmer for 4–6 hours. Beans should cook gently in the pot. Stir occasionally and add more liquid if necessary. When beans are very tender, take an old-fashioned potato masher and mash the beans. Check for seasoning, and reheat briefly. Ladle soup into bowls, and top with a generous dollop of sour cream and a garnish of tiny shrimp.

This soup is even better the second day.

This was the favorite soup served at the Old Plantation Restaurant in Estes Park for thirty-one years. Robert Burgess, who operated the Old Plantation with his family from 1961 to 1992, says that they always served Black Bean Soup with Jalapeno Cornbread (see the North Mountains/Breads section).

Her first duty: "to preside over the house as its queen"

Notes of a Missionary Priest

On mountain hospitality—"The prospector's cabin on the trail was left unlocked. You might step in, cook your dinner and go on, or if tired, unroll your blankets and rest to your heart's content. If the owner was at home it was all right, if not the conditions of hospitality were the same, and these were 'come in, help yourself and go rejoicing on your way' . . . the owner of the cabin, free with his money, bacon or bunk, deemed it an honor to entertain his caller, however poor."

On the role of women—"As women have enlarged opportunities of usefulness they must equip themselves for their new duties. But they must not forget that they are women, and that their first duty is to preside over the house as its queen." (From *Notes of a Missionary Priest* by J. J. Gibbons)

Across Colorado

Colorado Potato-Leek Soup

4	leeks
5	large white potatoes
3	tablespoons butter
$\frac{1}{2}$	medium onion, diced
8	cups chicken broth
	salt to taste
	white pepper to taste
	chopped chives for garnish

Serves 8

Cut the green tops off the leeks. Wash white part and chop coarsely in food processor. Peel potatoes and dice into 1-inch cubes. In a stockpot, melt the butter and cook leeks until softened. Add potatoes, onion, salt, pepper, and broth and bring to a boil. Reduce heat and simmer uncovered for 30 minutes. Let cool. Puree soup in food processor, then return to pot and heat. Serve with a garnish of chopped chives.

This is a perfect soup for Colorado's quickly changing weather because it can be served hot or cold. It can be made ahead and rewarmed, and it freezes well.

Ute Indian Museum

The Ute Indian Museum in Montrose contains the memorable history of Colorado's Ute Indians on the site of Ute Chief Ouray's last home. The museum offers one of the most complete collections of artifacts from the Ute people and exhibits of Chief Ouray and family members. On the grounds is a monument to Chief Ouray. Exhibits and dioramas also pertain to the early exploration in the western part of the state. The Ute Museum is a property of the Colorado Historical Society.

Across Colorado

Two varieties of miners' cabins

San Juan Hardships

Silverton residents experienced many snow blockades in the early years when avalanches would close for weeks all trails and the railroad into the isolated San Juan Mountains. One winter all that was left in town was flour, dried apples, and beans. During another snow blockage, Mrs. Alice Corbin Dyson was the only lady in town with any sugar left. As a result, a social was held at her house, so that she could make the cakes and provide sugar for coffee and tea.

Alice Corbin had come from New England in 1879 to marry her eastern beau, James Dyson, Silverton's leading surveyor. In 1880 she became the tenth person that year to take over the job of teaching the one-room Silverton school. She even returned after her first term, the only teacher who had ever done so.

Tortellini Soup

2	pounds mild Italian sausage
1	cup chopped onion
1	green pepper, chopped
5	cups beef broth
1	cup water (omit for thicker soup)
2	16-ounce cans tomatoes
1	8-ounce can tomato sauce
3	tablespoons parsley, minced
$\frac{1}{2}$	teaspoon dry basil
$\frac{1}{2}$	teaspoon oregano
1	8-ounce package dry cheese tortellini
1	medium zucchini, thinly sliced
1	cup uncooked noodles, such as small shells or elbow shapes

Serves 8 – 10

Cut sausage into 1-inch pieces. Place in a 3-quart stockpot and brown with the onion and green pepper. Drain fat. Add all ingredients except tortellini, zucchini, and noodles. Cook 40 minutes at medium to low heat. Add tortellini and cook 25 minutes longer. Add zucchini and noodles and cook an additional 10–15 minutes. Serve with garlic bread. Can be frozen and reheated.

Hearty fare for your favorite snowboarder.

"Riders of the Purple Sage"

One of the country's first and most famous western writers, Zane Grey, had a ranch at Dove Creek in Dolores County, where he wrote *Riders of the Purple Sage* in 1912. Again and again, *Riders of the Purple Sage* was made into a western movie, and it always became a box office hit.

Across Colorado

Silverton—Surviving Town in San Juan County

San Juan County has a long mining and railroad history: In 1900 approximately 5,000 residents lived in the county's numerous small mining towns, which were served by four railroads. All of those towns, except Silverton are ghost towns now. The last mine in the county closed in 1991. Most of San Juan County's present population of 550 (the least populated county in the state) live in Silverton, which is now served by just one railroad, the Durango and Silverton Narrow Gauge—but only in the summer.

The Silverton, Gladstone & Northerly Railroad Company served the mines of the San Juan Mountains.

Picnic Gazpacho

6	fresh tomatoes, skinned and quartered
1	large red onion, diced
1	large cucumber, peeled and cubed
1	large green pepper, diced
2	cloves garlic, minced
2	cups tomato juice
1	teaspoon Tabasco (or to taste)
1/4	cup red wine vinegar
	salt and pepper to taste

For garnish, cut the following fresh vegetables into spoon-sized pieces:

1	yellow squash
1	zucchini
1	peeled cucumber
1/2	yellow pepper

M a k e s   3   q u a r t s

Place the fresh vegetables in the bowl of a food processor. Process until the vegetables are blended and smooth (15–20 seconds). Pour processed vegetables into a glass or stainless steel bowl. Stir in tomato juice. Season with Tabasco, wine vinegar, salt, and pepper. Adjust seasonings to your liking. Remember that the garlic and Tabasco will be more pronounced after the gazpacho stands. Add garnish vegetables. Mix. Refrigerate for 4–8 hours before serving. Recipe can be halved. Will keep for 3–4 days.

Excellent picnic fare poured from a chilled thermos jug and served with chunky homemade croutons or garlic toast.

Portable Soup

Miss Leslie's New Cookery Book, published in Philadelphia in 1857, suggests a going-away gift: "If you have any friends going the overland journey to the Pacific, a box of portable soup may be a most useful present to them!

"This is a very good and nutritious soup, made first into a jelly, and then congealed into hard cakes resembling glue. A piece of this glue, the size of a large walnut, will, when melted in water, become a pint bowl of soup."

The directions:
"To make portable soup, take two shins or legs of beef, two knuckles of veal, and four unskinned calves' feet. Put the whole into a large clean pot that will hold four gallons of water . . . "
The recipe continues for several paragraphs, not reprinted here because most modern-day cooks will have a problem finding the unskinned calves' feet, a large enough pot, and the 8 hours required boiling time, skimming all the while.

Across Colorado

Recipes Fund Tennis Courts

Economic crises leave their marks on communities. One such crisis occurred in Ridgway in 1984 when the town lacked the funds to finish construction of its tennis courts. Several active community members decided to publish and sell a cookbook, with family recipes and memories that would tell the story of Ridgway's past.

Exactly ten weeks from the idea's conception the cookbook was published—212 pages of recipes and old-time recollections. Each section is prefaced by the legend of one pioneer family.

Ridgway Recipes and Remembrances is now in its fifth printing. The cookbook has funded two new parks and maintains them, has finished a community center, has organized an Arts and Crafts Festival, and still sells like hotcakes.

Residents and visitors swam in Ridgway's indoor pool of hot mineral spring water until the 1940s.

North African Lamb Soup

2	tablespoons vegetable oil
6	ounces finely ground raw lamb
1	large onion, diced
2	cloves garlic, crushed
1	teaspoon salt
1	tablespoon curry powder
¹/₄	teaspoon ground black pepper
2	teaspoons ground allspice
1	tablespoon mild chili powder
1	6-ounce can tomato paste
1	tablespoon sugar
1	fresh green chile, seeded and chopped
3	cups water
1	16-ounce can beef broth
1	16-ounce can garbanzo beans
¹/₃	cup dry couscous
1	tablespoon chopped fresh mint
1	tablespoon chopped fresh parsley
	lemon slices
	pita bread

Place oil in large stockpot over medium heat. Add lamb and brown. Add onion, garlic, salt, curry powder, black pepper, allspice, and chili powder. Cook until onion is translucent. Add tomato paste, sugar, green chile, water, broth, and garbanzo beans. Stir well. Simmer gently for 1 hour. Add couscous, mint, and parsley. Simmer 10 minutes longer. Remove from heat, cover, and let stand for 5 minutes.

Serve with lemon wedges and warm pita bread.

For an authentic North African taste, dry-roast 1¹/₂ tablespoons coriander seeds and 1¹/₂ teaspoons cumin seeds until they change color. Add 3–4 crushed cardamom pods. Add these spices in place of the curry powder.

This is a great cold-weather soup with an addictive blend of flavors, hearty enough for après-ski.

S e r v e s   6

Across Colorado

Silverton Rhubarb Festival

Celebrating the Fourth of July
in early Silverton

Silverton, high in the San Juan Mountains, has only fourteen frost-free days each year. This limits the crops that residents can grow, but it does not limit their rhubarb. Few homes are without at least one rhubarb plant, and it thrives in alleys and vacant lots, hardy survivors of the original roots planted by the early miners and their wives.

Each year on the Fourth of July, the Public Library sponsors the Silverton International Rhubarb Festival, complete with rhubarb pie and rhubarb ice cream for sale, a pie-eating contest, and a rhubarb recipe competition.

Copper Creek Mushroom Soup

1½	cups chopped onions
4	tablespoons butter (divided use)
12	ounces fresh mushrooms, sliced
1½	teaspoons dry dill weed
2	cups chicken stock or canned broth (divided use)
1	tablespoon soy sauce
1½	tablespoons paprika
3	tablespoons flour
1½	cups milk
½	teaspoon salt
¼	teaspoon pepper
2	teaspoons lemon juice
	dash of nutmeg
½	cup sour cream

Serves 4

Saute onions in 2 tablespoons butter. Add mushrooms, dill, ½ cup chicken stock, soy sauce, and paprika. Cover and simmer for 10 minutes.

Melt remaining 2 tablespoons butter in another pan. Whisk in flour and cook for 5 minutes on low heat, stirring constantly. Add milk and cook over low heat for 10 minutes until thick. Add mushroom mixture and remaining stock. Cover and simmer 10–15 minutes. Before serving, add salt, pepper, lemon juice, and nutmeg. Garnish each bowl with a dollop of sour cream.

This mushroom soup recipe was contributed by an associate of the Creede Repertory Theatre, which is celebrating its 31st season in 1997. Read about it in the South Mountains/Southwest Flavors section.

Cold Treatment at Grand Imperial

A more recent likeness of Silverton's Grand Imperial Hotel

The Grand Imperial Hotel in Silverton was sometimes not so grand. Built in 1882, the original structure had a mansard roof, three stories, arch windows, lower level, saloon, dining hall, sample rooms, public rest rooms, suites, stores, and, initially, the offices and courtrooms of San Juan County.

In 1921, Henry Freckner, a thrifty miner, bought the hotel for taxes. Freckner was famous for squeezing the dollar and for his economies at the Grand Imperial. One winter night a wayfarer, trying to go through Ophir Pass on foot, froze to death. At the same time a group of construction workers were staying at the hotel. The next morning they huddled around the potbellied stove in the lobby, trying to get warm. Freckner walked in from the street and asked if they had heard about the man who had frozen to death. One patron immediately asked, "Which room was he in?"

Today the Grand Imperial Hotel in Silverton is one of the premier historic hotels of Colorado with an overflow clientele of skiers, tourists, and history buffs.

HOTEL GRAND.

A. W. DANES, PROP.

Three-Story Brick Structure Centrally Located, In Post-Office Block. Rooms Well Ventilated. Incandescent Light, Everything First-Class. Commodious Sample Rooms.

SILVERTON, — COLORADO.

Hungarian Cold Cherry Soup

1	pound ripe Bing cherries, washed and stemmed
	rind of 1 lemon
	rind of 1 orange
$\frac{1}{2}$	stick cinnamon
2	cloves
$\frac{1}{4}$	cup sugar
	pinch salt
	water

Thickening

1	egg yolk
2	tablespoons cornstarch
$\frac{1}{2}$	cup sour cream, at room temperature

Serves 4

Place cherries, lemon rind, orange rind, cinnamon, cloves, sugar, and salt in a 2–3-quart saucepan. Add water to cover fruit, plus 1 inch of depth. Simmer uncovered for 45 minutes. Cool to room temperature. Strain soup. Discard cinnamon, cloves, and fruit rinds. Pit cherries and set aside. Mix thickening in a small bowl. Whisk thickening into cherry liquid and blend well. Bring cherry liquid to a simmer over low heat. Add pitted cherries and stir. Heat soup several minutes longer, or until smooth and lightly thickened. Chill thoroughly before serving, at least 6 hours.

Recipe can be successfully doubled or tripled.

The perfect summer treat. This soup can be made only for a few weeks during the summer when fresh cherries are available. Simple but elegant fruit soups are popular in Europe.

Lavish Praise for Ouray

Crofutt's *Grip-Sack Guide of Colorado*, Volume I, dated 1881, describes the town of Ouray in purple prose: "The little park in which it [Ouray] is situated is

Street scene in Ouray, 1890. W. H. Jackson

nearly round, and only about one-fourth of a mile in diameter. On all sides the cañon walls and mountains rise, range upon range, peak overshadowing peak all grooved and furrowed by the hand of the Great Maker, from the tiniest wrinkle to a chasm of most gigantic proportions, from the smallest depression and most rugged ravine to one of the grandest cañons of the world. Coupled with this wild scene are cascades, towering pines, leafy shrubs and creeping vines, with mosses, ferns, and delicate tinted flowers; which with the towering walls, are of every color, shade and hue, sandwiched in, as it were in the wildest profusion. In the centre of this great circle, this grand amphitheatre of nature, compared with which the Colosseum of Rome was an infant, is located the city of Ouray."

Ouray Miners' Prayer

In 1881, the main concern of residents of Ouray was to get a railroad. Crofutt's *Grip-Sack Guide of Colorado*, Volume I, described the situation well: "If the miners of Ouray pray at all, it is for the coming of the 'Iron Horse'; they consider the completion of the railroad to their city the one thing of paramount importance." The railroad arrived in Ouray about one year later and called its last "all aboard" in 1953.

Good Green Soup

1	pound dried split green peas, rinsed
2	10-ounce packages frozen green peas
2	red-skinned potatoes, diced, unpeeled
2	carrots, scraped and cut into $^{1}/_{2}$-inch slices
8–10	cups broth (chicken, turkey, beef, or vegetable)
$1^{1}/_{2}$	pounds smoked ham shanks or ham bone
$^{1}/_{4}$	teaspoon dried thyme
	salt
	pepper

Serves 6–8

Place all ingredients in a 5-quart stockpot. Simmer for 2–3 hours over low heat, stirring occasionally. Remove ham shanks from soup and allow to cool. Trim meat from shanks and return meat to soup. Soup can be served immediately, chilled and reheated, or frozen in quart containers.

This soup is especially good with biscuits that have been sprinkled with Cheddar cheese.

Ruth Van Sant

Across Colorado

Cultivated Dandelions

When the first miners and settlers arrived in the San Juan Mountains, there were no dandelions, so they say. These green plants with the bright yellow blossoms that pepper the town lawns were painstakingly collected from Colorado meadows elsewhere and planted in the San Juans by central Europeans, particularly those from Tyrol. Tyroleans missed the bitter greens used in their home country for salads in the spring, and they discovered that dandelions filled the empty niche.

Dandelions were particularly suited for the San Juans' high altitudes, which discouraged successful harvest of lettuce and other greens. Then, too, as any immigrant knew, the blossoms of the dandelion, when properly prepared, made a soft and delicious wine.

Proprietress, customers, and horse pose in front of the general store and Black Wonder mill in the mining town of Sherman.

The Spa of Choice

Trimble Hot Springs, about nine miles north of Durango, was once a favorite spa of the Native Americans. It later became the site of the Trimble Hot Springs Hotel. The legend goes that once a week, the call houses of Durango would close down for a night out at the Trimble Hot Springs Hotel. The Durango madams would rent one of the swimming pools and it would be closed to everyone else.

Vegetarian Chili

2	cups tomato juice
¾	cup bulgur
3	small, dried smoked ancho chiles
2	tablespoons oil
1	large onion, diced
3	celery stalks, cut in ¼-inch dice
3	carrots, cut in ½-inch dice
5	tablespoons chili powder
4	large garlic cloves, minced
1½	teaspoons salt
½	teaspoon freshly ground black pepper
1	teaspoon cumin
1	teaspoon dried basil
½	teaspoon dried oregano
1½	cups green pepper, cut in ½-inch dice
1	28-ounce can whole tomatoes
1	1-pound can kidney beans, drained and rinsed
1	1-pound can garbanzo beans, drained and rinsed

In a 1-quart saucepan, bring tomato juice to a boil. Add bulgur and dried chiles. Remove from heat and set aside.

In a 6-quart stockpot, heat oil. Add all ingredients except canned tomatoes and canned beans. Saute over medium heat for 10–15 minutes. Stir in bulgur mixture and canned tomatoes. Mix well. Cook for 1 hour on medium-low heat. Add canned beans and cook for 30 minutes more. Add water if chili is too thick. Remove chili pods before serving.

Chili is best made a day in advance. Can be frozen. The smoked dried chiles give the chili a beautiful aroma that stirs memories of South of the Border.

Makes 3–4 quarts

Across Colorado

Silver Miners Meet Silver Tongue

A huge crowd in Telluride cheers William Jennings Bryan as he delivers the Fourth of July oration in 1908.

"You shall not press down upon the brow of labor this crown of thorns; you shall not crucify mankind upon a cross of gold," rang the voice of William Jennings Bryan, July 4, 1908, as he thundered his famous speech from a platform erected in front of the Sheridan Hotel in Telluride at its Independence Day celebration. His message mesmerized Telluride's silver miners.

Hot Cheese Soup

1	10-ounce package frozen chopped broccoli
1	cup diced onions
3	cups sliced carrots
2	cups chopped celery
12	ounces margarine
2	16-ounce cans cream of chicken soup
3	16-ounce cans chicken broth
1	pound sharp Cheddar cheese, grated
1	pound processed cheese, such as Velveeta, cubed
1	15-ounce can stewed tomatoes with green chiles
1	teaspoon salt
	pepper to taste

Serves 6 – 8

Cook broccoli according to package directions. Saute the onions, carrots, and celery in the margarine. Put in soup pot. Mix in the other ingredients and simmer about 30 minutes until the flavors are blended.

If you do not enjoy "hot" foods, use a can of stewed tomatoes and a small can of diced green chiles to taste.

Across Colorado

Steamboat Springs ladies take to the slopes in the early 1900s.

Across Colorado

The North Mountains

The beautiful hay meadows and herds of grazing cattle remind visitors that this is still cowboy country and home on the range.

Out of Colorado's north mountains flow the streams that grow into the mighty rivers that water huge populations both east and west of the Continental Divide. Small trickles become the North Platte, then turn into a great waterway as the Platte joins the Missouri and Mississippi. West of the Continental Divide, the Colorado begins its run to the Gulf of California, providing a playground along its banks and in its waters as well as power for western cities and irrigation for their food supplies.

In times long past, lush green parks developed along the base of the north mountains. Much later, North Park, Middle Park, and the Yampa Valley became the summer hunting grounds for Colorado's earliest inhabitants.

After the first gold strike in Gregory Gulch, prospectors swarmed into the canyons and across the face of the mountains; then they drifted off to the north and discovered minerals where none were thought to exist. Deposits were rated only fair but there was enough excitement for the *Grand Lake Prospector* to report "enough ore in these hills to support thousands for years to come." The assessment was overly optimistic. None of the gold mines showed lasting promise and many mining towns and camps became silent ghosts. Other minerals took up the slack—the coal of the Oak Creek area has been worked for many years.

Settlers came and found the high meadows superb cattle range. Ranching became a way of life in Colorado and a fad for the younger sons of European nobility.

Contrasts abound in the north

mountains. Estes Park has been a favorite resort since the days when the Stanley brothers of Stanley Steamer fame built the imposing Stanley Hotel. Today Central City and Black Hawk echo a new kind of entertainment. Trail Ridge Road and Grand Lake provide unlimited and unparalleled scenery. Trapper's Lake, Lake John, and high mountain streams offer prime trout fishing.

Denver skiers flock to Winter Park, and Steamboat Springs prides itself on growing and grooming Olympians. However, the beautiful hay meadows and herds of cattle remind visitors to the many dude ranches that this is still cowboy country and home on the range.

When you are in North or Middle Park, try the mountain honey, sample some of the game in season, grill the trout you catch over an open fire, and have some of the best beef in the world.

Across Colorado

A Crash in Central City

Washington Hall in Central City is now the home of the Gilpin County Art Association.

The oldest continually used public building in the state of Colorado is Washington Hall in Central City. Across the street from the famed Central City Opera House, it began its existence as the county jail.

On Saturday night, March 18, 1871, Republicans gathered in the hall to nominate candidates for city office. Between 300 and 400 men jammed the room in the upper story, crowding around the chairman's table. Never intended to support such weight, the floor collapsed, sending lighted lamps, furniture, and men into the jail area below. Several fires started from the lamps but were extinguished with hats, coats, and carpeting. Men crawled out first-story windows or climbed the collapsed floor to escape through the hall's door. The local hook and ladder company arrived. Amazingly, no one died and the only injuries were minor.

Castle Marne Royal Scones

3/4	cup currants
1/4	cup liqueur of your choice
3 1/4	cups all-purpose flour, sifted
3/4	cup sugar
2 1/2	teaspoons baking powder
1/2	teaspoon baking soda
3/4	teaspoon salt
3/4	cup firm butter, cut into 1/2 -inch bits
1	cup buttermilk

Makes 12–16 scones, 2 inches in diameter

Preheat oven to 425°.

Soak currants in the liqueur (orange is especially nice). Set aside. In a large bowl, stir together dry ingredients. Using a pastry blender, cut butter into dry ingredients until the mixture resembles coarse meal. Drain currants and stir into flour mixture. Make a well in flour mixture and add buttermilk. Stir until dough pulls away from sides of bowl. Gather dough into a ball, turn out onto a floured surface, and pat lightly into a circle 1 1/2 inches thick. Cut with a 2-inch cookie cutter. Place 1 1/2 inches apart on lightly greased cookie sheet. Bake for 12 minutes or until lightly browned. Serve warm with jam or lemon curd.

Really excellent. Goes together in a flash.

Castle Marne, a Denver bed-and-breakfast, serves these scones daily at tea time.

Across Colorado

The Legend of Grand Lake

Grand Lake has long been a summer playground.

In summertime the Plains Indians and the mountain tribes often met in the parks atop the Continental Divide, sometimes trading goods and sometimes settling old scores. One meeting of the Utes with a Plains tribe, before the coming of the white man, is remembered as the "Legend of the Lake."

As a strong Plains war party approached from the west, Ute warriors on the shores of Grand Lake boarded their women and children onto a huge raft and shoved them off to safety—toward the middle of the lake. The affair already was going badly for the Utes when, at the height of the battle, a strong wind came from the northwest, created huge waves, and capsized the raft. The women, children, and battle were lost. From that time on, the Utes avoided Grand Lake and called it "bad medicine."

Lipton Cup Regatta

Shortly after the founding of the Grand Lake Yacht Club (the world's highest yacht club) in 1905, English tea baron Sir Thomas Lipton was wined and dined by several of the club's members. They convinced him that their annual regatta needed a trophy. He donated a solid sterling silver cup, which was appraised at $500,000 in 1985. Each year members of the Grand Lake Yacht Club compete for the prestigious Lipton Cup while spectators cheer them on.

Simple Sweet Scones

$2\frac{1}{2}$ cups all-purpose flour

1   tablespoon baking powder

$\frac{1}{2}$ teaspoon salt

8   ounces cold, unsalted butter, cut into 12 pieces

$\frac{1}{4}$ cup sugar (use $\frac{1}{2}$ cup for slightly sweeter scones)

$\frac{2}{3}$ cup milk

Makes 12 or 16 triangular or 18 round scones

Preheat oven to 425°.

Mix flour, baking powder, and salt in a large bowl. Using a pastry blender, cut butter into dry ingredients until mixture resembles coarse meal. Add sugar; toss to mix. Add milk and stir with a fork until a soft dough forms. Form dough into a ball, turn onto lightly floured board, and knead very gently 10–12 times.

To make triangular scones, cut dough in half. Knead each half lightly into a ball and turn smooth side up. Pat or roll into a 6-inch circle. Cut each circle into 6 or 8 wedges. Place wedges on an ungreased cookie sheet—slightly apart for crisp sides, touching for soft sides. Bake about 12 minutes or until medium brown on top. Place on a linen or cotton cloth and cool completely before serving.

To make round scones, roll dough to 12x5$\frac{1}{2}$ inches. Cut 15 scones with a 2-inch cookie cutter. Reroll scraps and cut again until all dough is used.

Variations
Sweet Whole Wheat Scones: Use 1 cup of all-purpose flour and $1\frac{1}{2}$ cups whole wheat flour. Bake about 15 minutes at 375°.

Lemon Scones: Add 1 tablespoon freshly grated lemon peel to flour mixture. In a small bowl, mix 2 teaspoons fresh lemon juice with 2 tablespoons sugar. Top each scone with $\frac{1}{4}$ teaspoon of the mixture before baking.

This scone recipe comes from the Denver English-Speaking Union.

Across Colorado

Princess Redfeather

Tsianina Redfeather, part Cherokee and part Creek, was born on Oklahoma reservation land in 1882. Her ancestors had been uprooted between 1820 and 1842 and forced to march the "Trail of Tears" to Oklahoma territory. Tsianina had a beautiful voice and studied music in Denver and New York. Composer Charles Wakefield Cadman discovered her and gave her the stage name Princess Redfeather. She toured with his group all over the world, making Cadman's songs, "Indian Love Call" and "Land of the Sky-Blue Water" famous.

In 1922, Dr. D. O. Norton, who was developing resort property 50 miles west of Fort Collins, heard Princess Redfeather sing and decided to name his mountain village Red Feather Lakes in her honor. Princess Redfeather died in 1985 at the age of 103.

Tsianina Redfeather probably never saw Colorado's Redfeather Lakes, named for her. (Photo courtesy of Arlene Ahlbrandt)

Irish Soda Bread Scones

3¼	cups all-purpose flour
½	teaspoon salt
½	teaspoon baking soda
2	tablespoons sugar
1½	cups buttermilk (or 1 tablespoon vinegar stirred into 1½ cups milk)
1	egg beaten with 2 teaspoons water (egg wash)
½–1	cup sharp Cheddar cheese, grated

Makes 12 scones

Preheat oven to 450°.

Blend first four ingredients together in large bowl. Add buttermilk and mix in gently with a wooden spoon or spatula. Turn dough out onto a floured surface and knead gently. Shape into rectangle about ¾ inch thick. Brush with egg wash. Cut into 12 pieces or use a cookie cutter of your choice. Dip top of each piece in grated cheese. Bake on ungreased cookie sheet for approximately 10 minutes.

During Boulder's Colorado Shakespeare Festival, this has been one of the favorite recipes for the annual "Rocky Mountain High Tea" held each year by the Festival's guild on Shakespeare's birthday.

Across Colorado

The "Mad Ladies" of Steamboat Springs

Students at the Perry-Mansfield Dance Camp express the joy of the dance amid the scenic glories of the Rocky Mountains, probably about 1915.

After Charlotte Perry and Portia Mansfield graduated from Smith College in 1910, they celebrated by coming to Colorado on a bear hunt. It was their first and last bear hunt, but they fell in love with the mountains and returned in 1914 to establish the Perry-Mansfield Dance Camp outside of Steamboat Springs. The local ranchers and homesteaders laughed at them and dubbed them "the crazy ladies." Their school of the performing arts alumni, among whom are Agnes de Mille, Julie Harris, and Dustin Hoffman, agree that the women had a "divine madness."

Charlotte and Portia employed miners from Oak Creek to build their first lodge in return for wages plus meals, but after the first week the men said they were quitting because the food was so bad. In tears, the girls consulted the mine owner to find out what they had done wrong—they had prepared the best roast beef, roasted potatoes, crisply cooked fresh vegetables, and fancy desserts.

The mine owner laughed and advised them to prepare everything swimming in greasy gravy, to cook vegetables until they were mush, and always to have thick, heavy pies. Portia and Charlotte talked the workers into staying one more week and changed the menu. The men remained until the job was done, happy with the "improved" cooking.

Across Colorado

Miner's Dream Cheese Biscuits

2	cups all-purpose flour
1	tablespoon baking powder
$^1/_4$	teaspoon salt
4	ounces cold butter, cut into 8 pieces
1	cup extra sharp Cheddar cheese, coarsely shredded
$^2/_3$	cup milk

Makes 16 biscuits

Preheat oven to 425°. Grease two heavy-duty cookie sheets.

In large bowl combine flour, baking powder, and salt. Using a pastry blender, cut in butter until mixture resembles coarse meal. Add cheese and milk and mix gently with a fork. (Do not overmix.)

Turn dough out onto a floured surface and knead 3 or 4 times. Pat into a $^1/_2$-inch-thick circle. Cut biscuits using a 2-inch cutter. Re-form dough and continue cutting until all dough is used. Place biscuits on cookie sheets. Bake for 12–14 minutes. Serve hot.

This is a great improvement on the "saleratus biscuit," the diet staple of early miners, which was made of flour, water, and the leavening agent saleratus.

Brown Bread

2	cups buttermilk
1	egg
$^1/_2$	cup molasses
1	teaspoon baking soda
1	teaspoon salt
2	cups whole wheat flour
$^1/_2$	cup white flour
$^1/_2$	cup raisins (optional)

Makes 3 loaves (soup can size)

Preheat oven to 350°. Grease three soup cans or small bread pans.

Place all ingredients in a bowl and mix well with a wooden spoon. Pour into prepared cans.

Bake for 40–45 minutes. Cool slightly. Remove from cans and cool on rack. (It may be necessary to cut bottom out of can to remove easily.) Bread improves when allowed to sit overnight.

This recipe was in the 1912 edition of The Golden Circle Cookbook, *which was issued by the Golden Circle of the First Presbyterian Church in Fort Collins.*

Across Colorado

A Debt to the English

Sunday scene in Middle Park

The story of the livestock industry in Larimer County would not be complete without mention of the contribution made by the Englishmen who came here in the infancy of the cattle business. They brought with them the love of good cattle and horses, as well as the knack of gracious living. In the Livermore area it was the English who planned and worked to get daily mail service and a telephone line decades before these services were customary in rural communities. Most of these Englishmen were unmarried when they came, and as bachelors they played many pranks for their own amusement and staged the inevitable horse races.

Cowboy country

PHOTO BY REV. HANDEL.

Across Colorado

Oatmeal Muffins

1	cup regular oatmeal (not instant)
1	8-ounce carton yogurt (plain, lemon, peach, and maple are good)
1	cup + 2 tablespoons flour
1	teaspoon salt
1½	teaspoons baking powder
½	teaspoon baking soda
1	egg
½	cup dark brown sugar
¼	cup cooking oil

Makes 18 medium muffins

Preheat oven to 400°. Grease 18 muffin cups or use paper liners.

Pour yogurt over oatmeal and set aside. Sift together flour, salt, baking powder, and soda. Add egg and brown sugar to oatmeal and yogurt and mix well. Stir in sifted dry ingredients; then add oil and mix well. Spoon into prepared muffin cups and bake 15 minutes.

Very healthful and delicious.

Across Colorado

Unladylike Lady Moon

"She was distinctly a frontier type. A very, very rough diamond." This was U.S. Forest Ranger Gilbert Hunter's description of Katy Lawder who married English

Sidesaddle horsemanship in ranch country

baronet and Colorado cattle baron Cecil Moon. Over in England,

when the death of a relative made Cecil Lord Moon and heir to the family fortune, his mother came to the Moon ranch in the Red Feather Lakes area to investigate.

Mama Moon hired a Miss Ballou who lived in Fort Collins and had been raised in New England to teach Lady Moon basic manners. Apparently, the lessons didn't take. Throughout her marriage to Lord Cecil Moon and for years after, Lady Moon's eccentricities scandalized the proper folk and delighted Ranger Hunter, who was

assigned to the Poudre district where Lady Moon operated her combination 2,100-acre ranch, moonshine factory, and haven for wayward outlaws and animals.

A Colorado First

When a rift developed between the Lord and Lady Moon, they divorced. Lord Moon left the country for New Zealand and Lady Moon was left with the ranch. Even though the Lord had inherited all the Moon estate, he brought suit against his former wife for alimony and won. Thus Lady Moon became the first woman in Colorado (and maybe the country) to pay alimony.

(Adapted from Hardships & Hope: Fascinating Pioneer Women of Northern Colorado. *Published by Midland Federal Savings, 1977.)*

Cranberry Muffins

1½	cups flour
¾	cup sugar
½	cup wheat germ
1	tablespoon freshly grated orange peel
1½	teaspoons baking powder
½	teaspoon baking soda
½	teaspoon salt (optional)
	juice of 1 fresh orange
3	tablespoons oil
1	egg
1	cup chopped cranberries
½	cup chopped nuts

Makes 12 muffins

Preheat oven to 400°. Lightly grease 12 muffin cups or use paper liners.

Combine flour, sugar, wheat germ, grated orange peel, baking powder, baking soda, and salt. Add enough water to orange juice to make ¾ cup and combine with oil and egg. Add to flour mixture and mix gently. Stir in cranberries and nuts. Pour into muffin cups and bake for 20 minutes.

Across Colorado

Estes Park—for Cattle and Climbers

Mr. and Mrs. Joel Estes

Ready for mountain climbing, 1920s

"The cattle should do fine here." Joel Estes uttered those words in 1859 and Estes Park was on its way to being settled. Estes and his family moved to the valley in 1860. Visitors to the homestead were few—mountain men, Indians, and explorers were long gone.

In 1874, however, the challenge of climbing Longs Peak attracted William Byers, editor of the *Rocky Mountain News*. Byers and his two companions stayed with the Estes family while attempting to climb the peak. Byers was so enamored with the scenery, he wrote a story in the *News* and proclaimed the area "Estes Park," in honor of his host. Joel Estes is best remembered for his determined and successful crusade to establish Rocky Mountain National Park.

Near Estes Park, 1900

Pork & Beans Fun Bread

1	cup raisins
1	cup boiling water
3	eggs
1	cup vegetable oil
2	cups sugar
1	16-ounce can pork and beans
3	cups all-purpose flour
1	teaspoon cinnamon
½	teaspoon baking powder
1	teaspoon baking soda
½	teaspoon salt
1	teaspoon vanilla extract
1	cup chopped nuts

Makes 2 loaves

Preheat oven to 325°. Grease two 3x9-inch loaf pans.

Pour boiling water over raisins and mix well. Set aside. Using an electric mixer, blend eggs, oil, sugar, and pork and beans until beans are broken. Add flour and remaining dry ingredients to bean mixture. Stir in vanilla and nuts. Drain raisins and add, stirring to mix well.

Pour batter into prepared loaf pans. Bake for 50–60 minutes, or until toothpick inserted into center of loaf comes out clean. Cool 10 minutes, then remove to rack.

Here's the fun part! See if anyone can guess the ingredients. Almost no one trying the bread for the first time can identify the beans. This also makes a good holiday bread, similar to banana or date loaves.

Across Colorado

"Work and Babies"

Susan Miner Johnston and her husband Tom settled in Hot Sulphur Springs in 1879, then in Grand Lake. They had five children. Her biographer, Mary L. Cairns, described Susan's life in Middle Park:

"An occasional dance was the only recreation that the region afforded. At these times they bundled up the babies and went, sometimes miles and miles away. The dances began at 7 p.m. and would last until morning. On these rare occasions, all the pleasure possible must be crowded into a few brief hours. In the intervals there was work, babies and work, work and babies. But when a neighbor needed help, Susan was the first to go, sometimes riding horseback on a side saddle, with her smallest child tucked in front."

Nana Bread

²/₃	cup sugar
¹/₃	cup shortening
2	eggs
1³/₄	cups flour
1¹/₄	teaspoons baking powder
³/₄	teaspoon salt
¹/₂	teaspoon baking soda
2	tablespoons milk
4	ripe bananas, mashed
¹/₂	cup chocolate chips
1	teaspoon vanilla extract

M a k e s   1   l o a f

Preheat oven to 350°. Grease and flour a 3x9-inch or 4x8-inch loaf pan.

Cream shortening and sugar. Add eggs and mix. Combine dry ingredients and add to egg mixture alternately with milk. Stir in mashed bananas, chocolate chips, and vanilla extract.

Pour into prepared loaf pan. Bake 1 hour or until a wooden toothpick inserted into center of loaf comes out clean. Cool, wrap, and store overnight in refrigerator.

A very moist, quick, and easy breakfast bread. Children love it!

Across Colorado

The Story on the Sign

The account of Lord Gore's travels is posted atop Gore Pass.

Altitude 9000 Feet

Here in 1884 passed Sir St. George Gore an Irish baronet bent on slaughter of game and guided by Jim Bridger. For three years he scoured Colorado, Montana, and Wyoming accompanied usually by forty men, many carts, wagons, hounds and unexampled camp luxuries. More than 2000 buffalo, 1600 elk and deer, 100 bears were massacred for sport. A trail by 1866, a wagon road by 1874, this modern highway opened in 1956.

Lordly Mountain Living

Lord Gore, an Irish baronet for whom the Gore Range is named, spent two summers in Middle Park (1854–1856) accompanied by famed scout Jim Bridger.

It is said he lived in a striped silk tent with a brass bed and down-filled mattress with linen coverings.

He traveled with trunks of clothes, barrels of delicacies, leather-bound books, wines and liqueurs, pewter mugs, a bathtub, hand-carved and inlaid rifles, packs of hounds, a collapsible raft, a fur-covered commode, and a retinue of servants.

Jalapeno Cornbread

1	cup all-purpose flour
3/4	cup cornmeal
1	tablespoon baking powder
1	tablespoon sugar
1	teaspoon salt
1	large egg
1	cup buttermilk
3	tablespoons melted shortening
1/2	cup whole kernel corn, drained
1/2	cup diced green chiles

Serves 4–6

Preheat oven to 400°.

Mix flour, cornmeal, baking powder, sugar, and salt. Add the unbeaten egg and buttermilk. Stir until lightly mixed. Add melted shortening, corn, and diced chiles. Pour into a greased 8x8x2-inch pan. Bake for 30 minutes, or until golden brown.

The Old Plantation Restaurant in Estes Park served this cornbread with its Black Bean Soup during the years that it was a popular eatery for both tourists and locals. For the Black Bean Soup, see the Southwest Slope/Soups section.

Across Colorado

Lillian Gish in Central City

In 1932, led by Territorial Governor John Evans's daughter, Anne Evans, a group of Denver leaders revived the glory days of the elegant old opera house in Central City. They brought famed stage and silent motion picture star Lillian Gish to open the first Opera Festival in the title role of *Camille*.

A countless array of distinguished performers have appeared at the opera house since 1932, in both stage and opera performances. These include Cyril Ritchard, Julie Harris, Helen Hayes, Katharine Cornell, George Gobel, and Nanette Fabray in plays, and operatic singers Sherrill Milnes, Samuel Ramey, Catherine Malfitano, and Beverly Sills early in their careers.

Orchestra entertains from the balcony as ladies wait for matinee doors to open, 1937 season.

Across Colorado

Cumin Pine Nut Cornbread

1	cup all-purpose flour
3/4	cup cornmeal
1 1/2	teaspoons cumin seed
1	teaspoon baking powder
3/4	teaspoon salt
1/4	teaspoon cayenne pepper
1	cup milk
1/4	cup vegetable oil
1	large egg
1/2	cup finely minced red bell pepper
1/2	cup piñon nuts

Makes 16 mini muffins

Preheat oven to 400°. Grease mini muffin pan or use mini paper liners.

Mix dry ingredients in large bowl. Whisk milk, oil, and egg in small bowl to blend. Add milk mixture to dry ingredients and stir just until evenly moistened. Fold in red pepper and piñon nuts. Pour batter into prepared pan. Bake about 18 minutes or until golden on top and tester inserted into center comes out clean.

Across Colorado

At the Baldpate Inn

The Baldpate Inn, nestled on the side of Twin Sisters Mountain near Estes Park, is famous for its longevity (since 1917), as the setting for that old mystery drama, The Seven Keys to Baldpate, and for its Key Room with more than 15,000 keys. The unique collection includes the keys to Westminster Abbey, Fort Knox, Jack Benny's dressing room, submarines, jail cells, and medieval castles. In 1997, the Baldpate Inn, with bed-and-breakfast accommodations, celebrates its eightieth season.

At the Stanley

The cover of an early brochure entices visitors to the Stanley Hotel in Estes Park.

More recently, the Stanley has received attention as the setting for the Stephen King thriller, The Shining.

Oatmeal Bread

1½	cups regular oatmeal
3	cups water (divided use)
1	package dry yeast
5½–7	cups flour (divided use)
6	tablespoons molasses
3	tablespoons cooking oil
2	teaspoons salt

Makes 3 loaves

Preheat oven to 375° when ready to bake. Grease three 8-inch loaf pans.

Cover oatmeal with 2½ cups boiling water and set aside to cool to lukewarm. Soften yeast in ½ cup warm water for 10 minutes. In large bowl, mix together 1½ cups flour, yeast, and oatmeal mixture. Let batter rise for 1 hour.

Add molasses, oil, salt, and enough of the remaining flour to the batter to make a firm but soft dough. Kneading can be by machine or by hand. If by hand, turn out onto floured surface and knead until smooth and elastic. By machine, knead for 6–7 minutes.

Divide dough into 3 loaves and place in prepared pans, or shape into round loaves and place on large, greased cookie sheet. Let rise for 30–60 minutes. Bake for 35–40 minutes. Cool slightly, then remove to wire racks and cool completely.

A delicious, moist bread that keeps well and is good for sandwiches or toast. The amount of flour depends on method used and weather. If mixed by machine, little or no hand kneading is necessary.

Across Colorado

Return to the Alpenaire

The owner and manager of the Alpenaire Inn at Estes Park tells of two recent guests who had returned to Estes to relive a vacation they had taken together fifty-two years ago. The two women had stayed in a small boardinghouse in 1943, which they could not find. One of their most interesting recollections was their journey and arrival in Estes Park. They had traveled by bus from their home in Minnesota and eventually arrived several days later in Lyons, early in the morning. There they were met by the RFD mailman, who spent the rest of the day delivering the mail between Lyons and Estes Park before he delivered the girls to the boardinghouse.

See the Alpenaire's recipe for venison chops in the South Plains/Special Times section.

Christmas Dinner on the Yampa

Thomas H. Iles, a cook for a group of trappers on the Yampa River, described in an early Routt County newspaper the food he prepared for Christmas 1874.

On Christmas morning, he fed the men fried grouse and gravy, biscuits baked in a Dutch oven, and black coffee. But the Christmas dinner was a real masterpiece for campfire cooking: porcupine stew and dumplings, a steamed pudding, hot biscuits, and coffee. Taking the place of the hard sauce and brandy was a thin syrup made of brown sugar and thickened with flour.

Ice Box Yeast Rolls

1	package dry yeast
1	cup warm water
$\frac{1}{2}$	cup butter, regular margarine, or shortening at room temperature
$\frac{1}{4}$	cup sugar
1	teaspoon salt
1	egg
3	cups all-purpose flour
2	tablespoons melted butter

Makes 24 rolls

Preheat oven to 375° before baking rolls. Grease one or two 9x9-inch pans depending on number of rolls to be baked.

Dissolve yeast in warm water. In mixer bowl, cream together butter, sugar, salt, and egg. Add yeast and mix well. Add flour, working into a soft dough. Place dough on a floured surface and knead gently for 2 minutes. Place dough in a greased bowl, turning once to grease top, then cover with plastic wrap and place in refrigerator. Let rest for at least 8 hours or up to 3 days.

When ready to use, pull off golf ball–size bits of dough. Place 12 dough balls in one pan, sides touching. Brush with 1 tablespoon melted butter. Repeat with remaining dough or refrigerate for later use. Let rise for 1 hour or until doubled in bulk. Bake for 15 minutes and serve hot.

Soft and simple with old-fashioned taste.

Food for a Pioneer Dinner

From the *Steamboat Pilot*, December 26, 1940: "Logan and John Crawford went to Denver Tuesday morning to spend Christmas and the remainder of the week with their sister, Mrs. Lulie Pritchett and family. They took along food for a pioneer dinner, several dinners in fact. The package contained six wild ducks, six beaver tails, a roast of elk meat, jelly made from wild berries and several other things that will be reminders of old times when they and their parents pioneered in Routt County."

The parents, Mr. and Mrs. James Harvey Crawford, founded Steamboat Springs in 1875. Mr. Crawford was fond of telling about the old frontiersman who said, "Where good beaver tail on table, push everything else back!"

Eating at the Roundup

J. H. Payson, who operated a cattle ranch from 1888 to 1905 in the Livermore vicinity, described a calf roundup: "We started on the calf roundup May 3 and were gone 16 days. Mr. Alford said to me before we started work, 'Never be the last man to saddle' and I never forgot that advice. The roundup butchered a beef about every other day, generally a two- or three-year-old heifer or a dry cow. Never a steer. One of the boys would rope the animal, then someone would shoot it and then the cooks would take over . . . Bread, meat and coffee were the regular standbys with plenty of canned tomatoes and sometimes spuds. Sugar wasn't rationed and we had worlds of that."

Shepherd's Bread

3½	cups warm water (divided use)
3	tablespoons sugar
3	packages dry yeast
8	cups all-purpose flour (half of flour may be whole wheat)
1	tablespoon salt

M a k e s   1   l a r g e   l o a f

Preheat oven to 350° when ready to bake bread. Grease 4–5-quart Dutch oven and lid or large covered casserole and lid.

Mix ½ cup warm water, sugar, and yeast in a small bowl. (Above 6,500 feet altitude, use 2 packages of yeast.) Let stand in a warm place for 10–15 minutes, or until bubbly.

In a large bowl mix 4 cups flour with the salt. Add yeast mixture and 3 cups warm water. Mix well. Add enough of remaining flour to make a stiff dough. Turn out onto a floured surface and knead until smooth—about 10 minutes.

Place in a large greased bowl. Turn once to grease top. Cover and let rise 45–60 minutes or until doubled in bulk.

Punch dough down and shape into a ball. Place dough in prepared pan and cover with lid. Let rise about 20 minutes. Dough should start to lift lid. Bake for 65 minutes. Remove lid and bake 10 minutes longer to brown top. Remove from pan and cool on wire rack.

This is a version of Basque Shepherd's Bread. Half whole wheat flour gives it a more homespun flavor.

Across Colorado

Dishwashing Laws

Dorothy Wither (1903–1987) was the main force in establishing the Tread of Pioneers Museum in Steamboat Springs. She saved her 1917 Steamboat Springs High School Domestic Science Work Book with its strict rules for dishwashing:

1. Collect the dishes.
2. Scrape them off.
3. Pile dishes of a kind together. Place dishes to be washed first nearest the dish pans.
4. Use hot soapy water for the dishes and hot clean water for rinsing.
5. The order in which dishes should be washed:
   a. glassware
   b. silverware
   c. cups and saucers
   d. small dishes
   e. plates
   f. remaining china dishes
   g. cooking utensils
6. Wash towels and dish cloths immediately after using.

Where Was the Steamboat?

According to most accounts, Steamboat Springs got its name in 1875 when three French trappers riding horseback along the Yampa River heard a chugging sound they thought was a steamboat. It turned out to be some hot springs that continued to chug until 1908, when a railroad builder blasted out the rock chamber over it.

Axial Basin Wheat Bread

1½	cups whole milk
½	cup clear honey
6	tablespoons margarine or butter, melted
1	tablespoon salt
1½	cups water
2	packages dry yeast
7–8	cups whole wheat flour

Makes 3 loaves

Preheat oven to 375° when ready to bake bread. Grease three 4½ x 8½-inch loaf pans.

Heat milk, margarine, honey, and salt until margarine is melted. Pour into a large bowl, add water, and cool to room temperature. Add yeast and 3 cups flour. Let stand until bubbly. Beat for 5 minutes with mixer. Gradually blend in 4 cups of flour. Using a dough hook, knead dough 6–8 minutes, or turn out onto floured surface and knead for 8–10 minutes until dough is smooth. If dough is very soft, add another cup of flour, a little at a time, while kneading.

Place in large greased bowl, turning once to coat top. Cover with plastic wrap and set in a warm place. Let rise until double in bulk, 1–2 hours.

Divide dough into 3 equal portions. Form into loaves and coat with butter. Place in prepared pans. Let rise in warm place for approximately 1 hour, or until double. Bake for about 35 minutes. Remove from pans and cool on wire rack.

The original recipe was made with homegrown wheat. This bread can be frozen and makes great toast.

Across Colorado

Advice Today's Bride Will Never Need

"Never fail, new bride, when baking, to take out some of the sponge to use as starter on the next baking day. If for some reason you forget, this is what you must do:

"Peel a nice sized potato and cut it into small pieces. Boil it in a pint of fresh water until it disintegrates. A potato masher will hasten the process. Sift several tablespoons of good white flour to remove impurities, lumps, and weevils. Stir sifted flour into the potato water until there are no lumps (use an egg beater, if necessary). Pour this thin batter onto a large platter or cookie pan which will not rust. The object is to expose as much surface to the air as possible. If the day is warm and there is a gentle breeze, carry the platter outside, otherwise your kitchen will have to do. Look at the platter from time to time. If it begins to work, you have caught some kind of start. The more bubbles the better. But if it just lies there dead all day, feed it to the livestock and start over again tomorrow.

"The only test of a good starter is to bake with it. Make just one loaf of white bread. It's an encouraging sign if the bread rises. If it both rises and smells good, you have probably begun a starter that will be treasured by many a cook. If it fails to rise or smells bad, feed it to the chickens and try again. It may make delicious bread or a loaf the flavor of swamp water. After a series of failures, go to town and get a start from someone else. Or write home to Mother. She can dry a spoonful of her starter to powder and send to you. Such powders will live up to a hundred years."

—*Advice from Great Grandmother Lucema Elizabeth Carlton Sprague, who lived from 1868 to 1913 and spent most of her adult life cooking for railroaders in the southern mountains of Colorado.*

Rosemary Garlic Bread

1²⁄₃	cups warm water
¹⁄₃	cup warm milk
1¹⁄₂	teaspoons salt
¹⁄₄	cup sugar
¹⁄₃	cup dried rosemary, crushed (that's right—¹⁄₃ cup)
1¹⁄₂	tablespoons garlic powder
3	ounces butter or margarine, softened
1	egg
2	packages dry yeast
5¹⁄₂–6	cups all-purpose or bread flour

Serves 8–10

Preheat oven to 375° when ready to bake bread. Grease baking sheet.

In large bowl, mix water, milk, salt, sugar, rosemary, garlic powder, margarine, and egg. Add yeast and blend well. Add flour ½ cup at a time, beating well after each addition. Add enough flour to form a soft dough that does not feel sticky to the touch. Turn out on a floured surface. Knead for 5 minutes or until dough is smooth. Place in greased bowl, cover with plastic wrap, and let rise in warm place until doubled. Punch down; divide into two or three pieces depending on the size and shape desired. Shape dough into two 9x13-inch rectangles or three 9-inch rounds and place on prepared baking sheet. Cover with plastic wrap and let rise until doubled. Bake for 18–20 minutes, or until bread sounds hollow when tapped. For a softer crust, brush top with butter after removing from oven. Cut into squares or wedges.

The River Run Inn in Salida, formerly famous as the "Poor Farm," serves this soft and tasty bread. Read about the early residents of this structure in the South Mountains/Southwest Flavors section.

Across Colorado

The Mess Wagon

Making pies

Foccacia Alla Genovese

1	package (2$\frac{1}{2}$ teaspoons) dry yeast
2$\frac{1}{2}$	cups warm water
2	tablespoons olive oil
1	tablespoon salt
20	chopped fresh sage leaves or other herbs (optional, but delicious)
6–7	cups flour
	olive oil for brushing dough

Toppings (your choice):

chopped herbs

minced onions

crushed garlic

minced green pepper

chopped olives

kosher salt

Makes three 9- to 10-inch rounds

Preheat oven to 400° when ready to bake. Grease large baking sheet.

Stir yeast into warm water; let stand until creamy (about 10 minutes). Stir in olive oil, salt, sage, or other herbs, if used, and 2 cups flour. Whisk until smooth. By HAND: Add more flour, 1 cup at a time, stirring until soft dough forms. Knead 7–10 minutes, until velvety and smooth, adding more flour if dough feels sticky. By MACHINE: Attach dough hook, start machine on low, at first adding 1 cup of flour at a time, then $\frac{1}{2}$ cup at a time. Push dough down occasionally with a rubber scraper. In 5–10 minutes, dough will form a ball and feel velvety and elastic.

Place dough in a lightly oiled bowl, cover with plastic wrap, and let rise for 1–1$\frac{1}{2}$ hours, or until doubled in bulk.

Roll out or pat dough to about $\frac{1}{2}$-inch thickness and cut into desired shapes and sizes. This amount of dough will make three 9- to 10-inch rounds, or two 10x15-inch rectangular shapes, or 25–30 individual 3-inch rounds. Cover and let rise for about 30 minutes.

Dimple dough vigorously with fingertips and brush with olive oil, letting some oil pool in indentations. Add desired toppings and sprinkle with kosher salt.

Let foccacia rise 10 minutes or bake immediately—the result seems to be the same. Bake 20 minutes or more, depending on size of foccacia. Cool on racks.

Foccacia should be eaten freshly baked or frozen and reheated. Great to have as snacks, or slice them for wonderful sandwiches.

Across Colorado

Steamboat Springs railroad
station

Across Colorado

Party Sandwiches

3   loaves quick bread

3   varieties flavored cream cheese
     spreads

Makes 40–60 party sandwiches

To produce a quick bread, such as banana bread or zucchini bread, that does not have a cracked or humped top, all you need are two loaf pans of the same size. Use one pan for batter, then invert the other pan on top of the batter-filled pan. Place in oven and bake as directed by your recipe. Remove the top pan after 25 minutes of baking. Continue baking as directed by recipe. A nice Pullman-style loaf of quick bread is the result, and is especially useful when you wish to make party or tea sandwiches.

Make three loaves of quick breads, using your favorite recipes and the inverted pan method. A nice selection is one banana bread loaf, one loaf flavored with orange juice, and one gingerbread or date loaf. Chill loaves thoroughly. Cut each loaf into 20 neat slices. Spread 40 slices with flavored cream cheeses. Stack in three layers. Chill. Trim crusts and cut sandwiches into squares, triangles, or fingers. Store sandwiches on wax paper-lined trays covered with plastic wrap. Can be made 4–6 hours in advance. Keep refrigerated.

Prior to the 1970s, party sandwiches enjoyed a great vogue. Today they are chiefly served at bridge luncheons or bridal parties, but they are always well received at potlucks and other gatherings.

Across Colorado

One hundred years ago, a hazardous wagon road wound down Glenwood Canyon, following the turbulent Colorado River.

Across Colorado

The Central Mountains

Once again the mountains are being carved by people, but no longer on the inside.

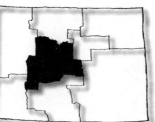

It all began about 70 million years ago when molten minerals burst through fissures in the granite and gneiss mountains, creating seams of gold and silver. Then rushing waters crumbled the rocks, releasing nuggets and sands of gold that washed into the mountain streams. Eons later came men who saw the shining flakes, found the nuggets, and knew there had to be a source—the man who found it would be rich beyond his wildest dreams! The Colorado gold rush was on!

They came from east and west, most with little more than their fantasies and the clothes they wore. Some had a pick and shovel, many worked for their supplies, or they promised a piece of the find to anyone who offered them a stake. A few lucky ones made fortunes with little more invested than a sack of beans, a slab of bacon, and a few crude tools.

Towns grew wherever there was a strike. Oro City, a sprawling camp in California Gulch, was home to postmistress Augusta Tabor and her entrepreneurial husband, H.A.W., who may never have lifted a shovel but made millions supplying miners' basic needs, then claiming a share of the strike.

Towns came and went as the fortunes of the miners boomed, then crashed. The population of Oro City moved up the hill and Leadville was born. Men who made no fortunes there pushed on and some struck it rich along Castle Creek and on Smuggler Mountain, giving rise to the town of Aspen. Breckenridge had its day. Gone are the once booming camps of Independence and Ruby, Holy Cross City and Gold Park, Kokomo and Quartsville.

Today a different prosperity has come to the central mountains.

Once again the mountains are being carved by people, but no longer on the inside. Instead the slopes are crisscrossed with sweeping trails, first cleared of trees and brush, then carefully groomed for skiers. Breckenridge booms again and Aspen is winter wonderland for the world famous. New playgrounds—Vail, Copper Mountain, Keystone—are meccas for skiers.

Elegant restaurants and chic little eateries catering to the most sophisticated palates have supplanted the staples of the mining era—beans and pork bellies, jerked beef, cornbread and biscuits, and lots of boiled coffee. But however tastes have changed, the cold and clear mountain air, the sparkling outdoors, and strenuous physical exercise still give sojourners in Colorado's central mountains healthy and hearty appetites.

Across Colorado

Gold News Travels Fast

The Clear Grit Mine in Leadville

How the news of a small gold find in Colorado exploded throughout the eastern United States is a puzzle. Traders may have heard the story that two brothers from Georgia had found gold dust in Cherry Creek and carried the news back to Kansas City. Perhaps an adventurer, when he returned to St. Louis, exaggerated tales he had heard of gold nuggets. Suddenly the cry "Pikes Peak or bust" spread like wildfire throughout the land, although Pikes Peak had little to do with gold.

Albert Richardson, a Boston newspaperman who traveled by stagecoach to Colorado with Horace Greeley in 1859, had this to say about the "Pikes Peak" phenomenon: "Thus far no gold has been discovered within sixty miles of Pikes Peak, but the first reports located the diggings near that mountain, and 'Pikes Peak'— one of those happy alliterations which stick like a burr in public memory—was now the general name for this whole region."

Richardson also wrote, "During our journey from Leavenworth we have doubtless passed ten thousand emigrants."

About 100,000 gold seekers left the eastern United States for Colorado in the spring of 1859. Of these, probably 50,000 reached their destination. Of that 50,000, at least one-half were "go-backs." They gave up and went back home after a few weeks.

Blue Cheese Salad Dressing

4	ounces blue cheese
4	tablespoons mayonnaise (regular or light)
1	cup sour cream
$1/4$	teaspoon freshly ground black pepper
$1/4$	teaspoon garlic powder
$1/2$	teaspoon garlic salt
$1/8$	teaspoon onion powder
2–4	tablespoons milk or cream to thin

Serves 4–6

Using a fork, mash together the blue cheese and mayonnaise. Add remaining ingredients and blend. Let rest 4–8 hours. Before using, check consistency and add milk or cream as desired. Dressing can be kept refrigerated for several days.

Across Colorado

Barney Ford in Breckenridge

One of many historic buildings in Breckenridge is the Victorian house at 111 East Washington. Still a private home, it was built in 1882 by Barney Ford, an escaped slave who migrated to Colorado with gold fever and stayed to become one of the state's most prominent residents.

Barney Ford, pioneer for civil rights

Over the years Ford made and lost several fortunes with mining, restaurant, hotel, and other business enterprises in Breckenridge and Denver. A pioneer civil rights leader, he successfully lobbied against statehood for Colorado until voting rights for black men were guaranteed. A commemorative stained glass window in the State Capitol honors him. Ford Elementary, a Denver public school in Montbello, bears his name, as does the Barney Ford Heights housing development.

Breckenridge ladies go skiing in 1889.

Creamy Caesar Salad Dressing

4	ounces cream cheese, at room temperature
1	cup sour cream
$^{1}/_{4}$	cup extra virgin olive oil
$^{3}/_{4}$	cup salad oil
1	teaspoon salt
$^{1}/_{2}$	teaspoon freshly ground black pepper
$^{1}/_{2}$	teaspoon sugar
2	tablespoons red wine vinegar
2	tablespoons apple cider vinegar
1–2	tablespoons anchovy paste (available in tubes)
$^{1}/_{2}$	cup grated imported Parmesan cheese
4	medium cloves garlic, crushed
$^{1}/_{4}$	cup milk to thin dressing as needed

Makes 2 $^{1}/_{2}$ cups

Blend cream cheese and sour cream in a small bowl. In another bowl whisk together oils, salt, pepper, sugar, and vinegars until emulsified. Beat in cream cheese–sour cream mixture until well blended and creamy. Add anchovy paste, Parmesan cheese, and garlic. Beat well.

Allow to rest 4–8 hours before using. Thin dressing with milk as needed. Dressing will keep for one week and recipe can be halved. Serve dressing on hearts of romaine lettuce, allowing approximately 1 $^{1}/_{2}$ cups of torn romaine for each serving. This dressing has all the elements of the traditional Caesar dressing without the raw egg. Great on a buffet.

Across Colorado

Not Doomed to Drown

Fay and Lenore Bryant built the Arapahoe Cafe in the old town of Dillon in the early forties. When the Denver Water Board announced plans for a major reservoir on the Blue River, which would flood the area, both the town and the cafe were doomed to disappear under the rising waters of Lake Dillon.

Many local citizens abandoned their homes and businesses to the bulldozer or moved them to Frisco, Breckenridge, or the valley below the dam, which later became Silverthorne. A few hearty souls, however, including the Bryants, determined to see a new Dillon built among the pines on the shores of the new lake. In 1960, the Arapahoe Cafe, along with the Community Church (now the Dillon Historic Museum) and a scattering of private homes, was moved up the hill to the site of the new town. This move explains why the floors of the Arapahoe Cafe are a bit uneven and the walls somewhat out-of-square.

Today the Arapahoe Cafe is one of the historic landmark sites in Dillon.

Newcomers arrive in old Dillon, about 1890.

Across Colorado

August Garden Salad

1	pound fresh, ripe tomatoes cut into wedges
1	zucchini, cut into 3x$\frac{1}{4}$-inch sticks
1	yellow squash (yellow zucchini) cut into 3x$\frac{1}{4}$-inch sticks
6	sundried tomatoes, packed in oil, cut into slivers
2	tablespoons extra virgin olive oil
2	tablespoons balsamic vinegar or red wine vinegar
$\frac{1}{2}$	teaspoon salt
	freshly ground black pepper
	Bibb lettuce

Serves 4

Place fresh tomatoes, zucchini sticks, yellow squash sticks, and sundried tomato slivers in a glass bowl. In a small bowl whisk together olive oil, balsamic or red wine vinegar, salt, and pepper. Blend well. Pour over vegetables. Toss gently. Allow to rest for 1 hour at room temperature or 4–6 hours in refrigerator. Serve on Bibb lettuce leaves.

Across Colorado

The Buffalo Bar

Change and adaptation—that's the story of the West and of the magnificent rosewood and burl bar at the Buffalo Restaurant in Idaho Springs. Built in Chicago in the 1860s, this bar has been assembled, disassembled, and reassembled, time and again.

The backbar (a gigantic mural with sidepieces of turned spindles and beveled mirrors), the bar, the floor-to-ceiling cooler, and the huge breakfront were brought out in sections on a wagon train from Chicago for the Cosmopolitan Hotel in Telluride during the boom days of the 1880s. Fire destroyed most of the hotel but the bar was saved. The pieces were then brought back to Denver.

The bar became the centerpiece for the Belle Starr Room (named for a famous Denver madam) of the Windsor Hotel on Larimer Street. Before the wrecker's ball demolished the Windsor in 1960, the matching pieces (now somewhat the worse for wear) were bought at auction and taken to Idaho Springs. Refurbished and with a mirror replacing the original mural, the bar, breakfront, and cooler found a new and fitting home in the 1888 Mercantile Building, which is the heart of the Buffalo Restaurant.

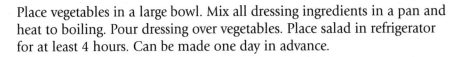
Buffet Salad

2	16-ounce cans French-style green beans, drained
1	16-ounce can peas, drained (reserve liquid)
1	16-ounce can corn, drained
1	small jar chopped pimentos
1	diced green pepper
1	diced onion
4	stalks celery, chopped

Dressing

2	tablespoons liquid from peas
$\frac{1}{2}$	teaspoon salt
3	tablespoons salad oil
$\frac{3}{4}$	cup sugar
$\frac{1}{2}$	cup white vinegar
$\frac{1}{2}$	teaspoon paprika

Serves 8–12

Place vegetables in a large bowl. Mix all dressing ingredients in a pan and heat to boiling. Pour dressing over vegetables. Place salad in refrigerator for at least 4 hours. Can be made one day in advance.

Across Colorado

Famed Marble from Marble

A huge block of marble dwarfs a man sitting beside it.

The town of Marble, on the Crystal River, boomed for more than forty years as the value of its marble deposits was realized; then it became a ghost town when the last marble quarry closed in 1941. Today it is a favorite spot of history buffs, fishermen, and vacationers. The marble laid on the floors throughout the state capitol in Denver was quarried at Marble. Marble marble was also used for the Lincoln Memorial in Washington, D.C. in 1915 and the Tomb of the Unknown Soldier in Arlington National Cemetery in 1931. At that time, the block of white marble used for the Unknown Soldier's tomb was the largest single block of marble ever quarried in the world.

Thanksgiving Cranberry Salad

1	pound fresh cranberries, ground or finely chopped
1	cup sugar
1	6¼-ounce bag mini marshmallows
1	cup pecans, chopped
1	8¼-ounce can crushed pineapple, drained
1	cup heavy cream, stiffly whipped

Combine cranberries with sugar and let stand in refrigerator 2 hours or overnight. Blend in marshmallows, nuts, and pineapple. Mix well. Gently fold in stiffly whipped cream. Serve immediately or refrigerate for up to 8 hours. Recipe can be doubled.

Makes 4–8 servings on a buffet

Butternut-Apple Bake

2	pounds butternut squash
2	large baking apples
½	cup packed brown sugar
1	tablespoon flour
½	teaspoon mace
1	teaspoon salt
¼	cup butter, melted

Preheat oven to 350°.

Peel squash and remove seeds. Slice squash into pieces ½ inch thick. Arrange in a 7x11-inch baking dish. Core apples and slice ½ inch thick. Place on squash. Combine sugar, flour, mace, and salt with melted butter. Dot on squash and apples. Cover pan with foil and bake 1 hour.

Note: This recipe was contributed by a member of the Short family, whose great-grandparents homesteaded in the Durango area in the 1880s. See the story about Grandmother Short in the Southwest Slope/Soups section.

Serves 6

Across Colorado

Redstone Revival

The Cleveholm Manor

Mrs. John Osgood

Called "Cleveholm Manor," the palatial castle at Redstone was built at the turn of the twentieth century by John C. Osgood, a wealthy industrialist.

Planning an ideal village for the miners in his nearby coal mine, Osgood also built the town of Redstone with forty Swiss cottages (each unique) for miner families, a forty-room inn for bachelor miners, and a miners' clubhouse. Osgood had widespread mining interests and was the first president of Colorado Fuel and Iron Company (CF&I). But after ten years, his empire crumbled.

Now, more than eighty years later, many of Osgood's structures are again alive and well. The miners' cottages are lived in (especially in the summer), the bachelor's inn is the prospering Redstone Inn resort, the manor is the Cleveholm Manor Bed and Breakfast, and all of the village of Redstone has been named a state and county historic district.

Marinated Eggplant Salad

2	medium-sized eggplants, unpeeled
4	cloves garlic, minced
$1/3$	cup plus 2 tablespoons extra virgin olive oil (divided use)
1	tablespoon coarse salt
2	medium-sized onions, finely diced
	juice of 1 lemon
$1/2$	cup fresh basil, finely cut
	freshly ground black pepper to taste

Serves 4–6 as a salad

Serves 8–12 as part of a composed salad

Preheat oven to 350°.

Wash eggplants and cut into $1/2$-inch cubes. In a large bowl, toss the eggplant cubes with the garlic, $1/3$ cup olive oil, and salt. Put mixture in a 9x13-inch cake pan lined with aluminum foil. Bake for $1/2$ hour or until tender but not mushy. In the meantime, on medium heat, saute the finely diced onions in 2 tablespoons olive oil until lightly browned, approximately 15 minutes. In a large bowl, toss together the eggplant mixture, onions, lemon juice, basil, and pepper. Serve at room temperature or chill until ready to serve. This recipe can be halved.

This salad is excellent for a "composed salad" platter. Line a large platter with lettuce. Heap marinated eggplant salad in the middle. Surround it with 3 or 4 other salads; for instance, carrots, lightly steamed, chilled, and marinated in raspberry vinaigrette; cucumber, black olives, red peppers, or other vegetables marinated in vinaigrette; and steamed and marinated beets with walnuts.

Across Colorado

"The First Time I Saw Redstone"

"The first time I saw 'the castle' at Redstone was from above as we climbed the surrounding mountains. It looked well-preserved but deathly still and uninhabited, as seemed its neighbor, the town of Redstone. The year was 1960. We hiked on down the mountain and circled this lonely manor, touching the perfectly matched stonework of its exterior. Each seam was the same width as the next, each stone precisely laid against the adjoining one. We learned later that Italian masons were imported to do the work.

"A lone workman appeared around a corner and greeted us. He said, 'Go on in and look around. Everyone else does.' We found the unlocked door and entered. No electricity, so we turned on our flashlights and explored. I best remember the gold leaf ceiling of the library, reflecting in the flashlight beams, and my sudden gasp as the gold glittered above us. In the library we found first editions; in the pantry a complete set of china, gold rimmed and bearing the crest of the royal family of Spain.

"I have returned to the castle several times since that first visit and tracked its evolution. Now it is the Cleveholm Manor Bed and Breakfast and still grand. But the aura and majesty of the structure has not been duplicated since that day when we discovered it, dusty and ghostlike—just waiting in loneliness for its original owners to return."
—*as remembered by one Historical Society volunteer*

Mango Salad

2	ripe mangoes
1	large navel orange
1	small red onion or 2 scallions
1	head Bibb lettuce
1–2	ounces Asiago cheese, block type (may substitute Parmesan)
	fresh mint leaves

Dressing

⅓	cup olive oil
1	large clove garlic, crushed
1	heaping tablespoon honey
1	tablespoon poppy seeds
2	teaspoons ground ginger
¼	teaspoon cayenne
¼	cup cider vinegar

Serves 4

At least one hour before serving, make the dressing. Combine all dressing ingredients except the vinegar in a Mason jar. Microwave 1 minute on high, uncovered. Let cool slightly, then add vinegar while still warm. Cover and shake well.

Peel and slice mangoes into a mixing bowl. Pare orange down to orange flesh and pop sections from their sleeves. Cut four very thin slices of red onion, or chop scallions very finely. Add oranges and onion to mangoes and toss with the dressing. Place lettuce on individual plates. Arrange mango and orange mixture on lettuce leaves. Pare 3 or 4 curls of Asiago cheese over each plate. Garnish with sprigs of mint.

The Asiago cheese adds a special flavor to this salad, which is an excellent starter for a rich meal or could be served with a tomato-based entree.

Across Colorado

Leadville's Ice Palace

To prop up its sagging image and economy after the Panic of 1893 and the fall of silver, the citizens of Leadville built an ice palace that opened January 1, 1896. The structure was a magnificent, Norman-style affair that covered five acres. It had ice walls eight feet thick separating grand staircases, a restaurant, ballrooms, banqueting rooms, and a skating rink. Special trains came from Denver with tourists.

Sadly, the winter of 1896 was unusually mild, the sun took its toll on the south side, frequent chinooks chinked the ice blocks on the north, and the train trip from Denver was a long one. Leadville business leaders claimed the palace a success; it remained open until its scheduled closure on May 1; but that was the last ice palace they ever built.

Spicy Spiral Salad—Thai Style

3	tablespoons crunchy peanut butter
6	tablespoons soy sauce
2	tablespoons vegetable oil
2	tablespoons sesame oil
1	tablespoon white vinegar
¼	cup chopped green onion
1	tablespoon minced fresh gingerroot
2	tablespoons minced garlic
1½	tablespoons crushed Szechwan peppercorns (optional)
1	tablespoon chile puree with garlic (bottled)
8	ounces spiral pasta, cooked and cooled

Serves 4

Whisk all ingredients except pasta until blended. Pour over pasta and toss to coat. Chill several hours.

If you like a spicier flavor, use more chile puree. Excellent with grilled chicken breasts.

Pony Express to
Leadville
COMMENCING SATURDAY, APRIL 5, 1879,
24 HOURS SAVED.

This company will deliver letters in Leadville or Denver 24 hours in advance of the regular mail.

All letters must be paid in a government pre-paid envelope.

We have twenty saddle horses for this route, and have employed competent carriers. Will connect daily at Webster with the railroad. Mail will arrive about 9 p. m. at Leadville.

This company will not transport currency or articles of value.

Mail closes at Denver with Clarence Zerega, Agent, at Cigar Stand, American Hotel, at 7:15 o'clock a. m.

PONY EXPRESS CO.,
L. C. WHEELER,
SUPERINTENDENT.

Across Colorado

Leadville ladies visit mid-street. Mrs. Jerome, wife of the owner of the Hotel Jerome in Aspen, is second from left.

Leadville Weather

Doc Holliday made an astute appraisal of Leadville weather that residents and tourists have quoted over the years. He said, "Leadville has ten months of winter and two months of late fall." At an altitude of 10,188 feet, Leadville is the highest incorporated city in the United States—which may explain why summer never comes.

Across Colorado

Strawberry Spinach Salad

6	cups fresh spinach, washed and torn into bite-sized pieces
2	cups fresh strawberries, washed and halved
$^1/_2$	teaspoon sesame seeds

Dressing

$^1/_4$	cup salad oil (not olive)
2	tablespoons red wine vinegar
$1^1/_2$	teaspoons sugar
$1^1/_2$	teaspoons fresh dill weed
$^1/_8$	teaspoon onion powder
$^1/_8$	teaspoon garlic powder
$^1/_8$	teaspoon dry mustard
	salt and pepper to taste

Serves 4 – 6

Place dressing ingredients in a Mason jar with lid. Shake well to blend. Refrigerate briefly.

Toss together the spinach, strawberries, and sesame seeds. Reshake dressing well and toss with salad ingredients, adding the dressing slowly so that you have the amount of dressing you desire.

This is a bright and sprightly salad served in a clear glass bowl, very appropriate for spring. Delicious, too. Children love it.

Across Colorado

Milk—an Aspen Gold Mine

Children go for a donkey ride in early Aspen.

Some fortunes were made in mining towns with resources other than gold. Arthur Foster tried his luck in Leadville, then moved to Aspen in the 1870s. From there he wrote his mother in Maine, "I traded a span of ponies for six cows with their calves. There was no milk in Aspen, so I brought them here soon afterward. A friend traded his team for the same that I did and came into town. I was all fixed up for business so I proposed to him to put the stock together as it would be cheaper running them. We soon found we could not supply the town so we got eight more cows . . . That gave us all we wished to do." *(From a letter written by Arthur B. Foster as quoted in* Pioneers of the Roaring Fork *by Len Shoemaker.)*

Saving Souls on the Frontier

The Reverend Jacob Rader, an itinerant Methodist minister, arrived in Aspen in the 1880s to preach fire and brimstone and attack the vices of gambling halls and saloons. He didn't make a big dent on the miners' sinful ways, but he did impress Emma Bourquin, one of Aspen's first schoolteachers, so much that she married him. Later Rev. Rader turned his attentions to another collection of souls that needed his ministrations possibly more—the Colorado State Legislature. He served in the legislature as both chaplain and elected representative.

Shrimp-Rice Salad

3	cups cooked shrimp, chilled
2	cups cooked rice, chilled
8	ounces water chestnuts, sliced
1	cup celery, sliced
$\frac{1}{2}$	cup black olives, sliced
$\frac{3}{4}$	cup green onions, chopped

Dressing

$1\frac{1}{4}$	cups mayonnaise
1	tablespoon lemon juice
1	teaspoon soy sauce
$\frac{1}{4}$	teaspoon ginger
$\frac{1}{4}$	teaspoon curry powder

Serves 6 – 8

Blend dressing ingredients in a small bowl. Mix salad ingredients and toss with dressing. Chill. Good for brunch or lunch and great to take on a picnic.

Tunnel Closes, Pizzas Sell

When the Eisenhower Tunnel was completed, Front Range skiers cheered loud and long. No more driving over Loveland Pass with its blowing snows, icy curves, and potential avalanches. Winter driving problems were solved! Or so Coloradans believed. But Mother Nature has the last laugh and to this day adverse winter conditions can make mountain roads impassable and the tunnel closes a few times each winter.

As always, one man's blizzard is another man's bonanza. In the early seventies, enterprising employees at a Silverthorne restaurant saw opportunity in the closed tunnel and the lines of cars with no place to go. They dressed warmly and made runs to the waiting cars, taking orders for "gourmet pizzas." Then they would run to yell the orders through the kitchen window, run back to take more orders, take them to the kitchen window, get their first orders to deliver, and do it again and again. Gourmet pizzas lightened the moods of anxious and tired skiers, soothed hot tempers, and probably averted accidents. Soon gourmet pizzas became famous. Busloads of ski clubs from Kansas and Nebraska began to load up on gourmet pizzas before heading for home.

See the Gourmet Pizza recipe in the Denver Metro/Main Dishes section.

Across Colorado

Hotel Jerome in Aspen in the 1930s

Childhood in Early Aspen

Fleeta Lamb Cooper, born in Aspen in 1888, related many memories of the early mining town in an oral history. She remembered that "some of the finest plays came then because Aspen was a big mining camp and my mother would dress up in these beautiful dresses and a big hat and go to her seat . . . and the usher would come and ask my mother to take the hat off."

Fleeta recalled going with her mother to the brand new Hotel Colorado when it opened in Glenwood Springs and staying for six weeks. As children do, she remembered the inequities. At dinnertime, she ate with the other young ones in a room called "the ordinary" because children were not allowed in the formal dining room.

Baked Barley

1	8-ounce can mushrooms, drained
6	tablespoons butter (divided use)
1	medium onion, chopped
$\frac{1}{2}$	cup medium pearled barley
2	teaspoons chicken bouillon crystals
$\frac{1}{2}$	teaspoon pepper
	salt to taste
1	14$\frac{1}{2}$-ounce can chicken broth

Serves 6 – 8

Preheat oven to 325°.

Over medium heat, saute mushrooms in 3 tablespoons butter until browned. Remove to 2-quart casserole. Saute onions in remaining butter until transparent. Add dry barley. Stir until barley is coated; add to mushrooms. Sprinkle with the bouillon crystals and pepper. Add salt to taste. Pour chicken broth over all and bake, covered, for 1 hour or until liquid is absorbed. Remove lid and let brown a few minutes.

An unusual side dish.

Rice Pilaf Josephine

1	large onion, chopped
4	ounces butter
1$\frac{3}{4}$	cups rice, uncooked
2	14-ounce cans beef broth or consommé
1	cup sliced fresh mushrooms
1$\frac{1}{2}$	cups sharp Cheddar cheese, grated
$\frac{1}{2}$	cup sliced almonds

Serves 8 – 10

Preheat oven to 325°.

Saute onion in butter until onion is translucent. Add rice, consommé or broth, mushrooms, and cheese. Mix well. Place mixture in greased 3-quart casserole and sprinkle with almonds. Cover. Bake 45 minutes or until liquid is absorbed and rice is tender.

Excellent with grilled lamb or sauteed veal chops.

Across Colorado

Skiing Loveland

eatery. Her chili was spicy and always on the menu. Early-day skiers prized its warming qualities, and warming qualities were definitely needed on those windy slopes of the Continental Divide before the days of GORE-TEX™.

Seibert had trained at Camp Hale as a ski trooper in World War II and was wounded in Italy. He went on to become one of the founders of Vail.

Tenth Division troopers do their calisthenics on skis during World War II at Camp Hale, near Leadville.

Loveland Ski Area is the oldest continuously operating ski area in Colorado. The original portable rope tow was installed in 1936–1937, run by a Model-T engine. Rope tows were all the area offered until 1956, when a stock company with six directors put in the first chairlift and hired a manager, Pete Seibert.

The operation used a Forest Service building in its parking lot as a headquarters and the manager's mother established an

Corn Festival Casserole

4	tablespoons butter or margarine
1/4	cup milk
1	8-ounce package cream cheese at room temperature
2	15-ounce cans corn, drained (frozen corn may be used)
1	small can green chiles, chopped
1/2	teaspoon garlic salt or garlic powder

Preheat oven to 350°. Butter a 1-quart glass casserole.

Melt butter or margarine in a small saucepan. Add milk and cream cheese. Stir until cream cheese is blended and mixture is smooth. Place corn, chiles, and garlic salt in a bowl. Pour cream cheese mixture over corn. Stir well. Pour into casserole. Bake 20–30 minutes or until bubbly.

Serves 4 – 6

Crustless Zucchini Quiche

3	cups zucchini, thinly sliced
1	onion, finely chopped
2	small cloves garlic, minced
1/4	cup oil
1/4	cup Parmesan cheese, grated
4	eggs, lightly beaten
1/4	cup fresh parsley, chopped

Preheat oven to 350°.

Mix all ingredients in a bowl. Pour into a greased 9x13-inch pan. Bake for 30 minutes or until top is browned. Allow to cool slightly before serving.

Nice with seafood.

Serves 4 – 6

Across Colorado

English Delicacies at the Mines

Anne Ellis came from Missouri to Colorado as a child in the 1880s. In her book, *Life of an Ordinary Woman*, she recounts her coming of age in the mining camps and towns of central Colorado. Her story of the mining frontier is vivid proof that she was an extraordinary woman. She had only a few years of grade school education, but she learned from everyone and everything, and then recorded it all, first from a child's, then a young woman's, point of view.

Ellis recalled that a colony of Englishmen, all educated, lived nearby, and that some of them were remittance men. Anne would hang around their cabin, and they would lend her books and treat her with food sent from England. Through them she made her first acquaintance with chocolate, orange marmalade, and Worcestershire sauce.

Miner's cabin

Across Colorado

Quick Mushrooms Saute

1	pound very fresh white mushrooms, no more than 1$\frac{1}{2}$ inches in diameter
3	tablespoons butter
	salt and pepper
1$\frac{1}{2}$	teaspoons, or slightly more, Maggi liquid seasoning
2	tablespoons heavy cream

Cut mushrooms into quarters. Melt butter in a 10- or 12-inch skillet over high heat. Add mushrooms and saute rapidly, stirring/tossing often. Mushrooms will cook in 5–8 minutes. Flavor with Maggi seasoning, a seasoning often used by restaurants. At the last moment add cream. Serve immediately. Excellent with grilled steaks.

Note: Two or 3 tablespoons of dry Spanish sherry can be substituted for the Maggi seasoning. Do not use cooking sherry.

Serves 4

Sweet Potato Souffle

5	eggs
4	ounces margarine, melted
1	teaspoon vanilla
$\frac{1}{2}$	cup sugar
$\frac{1}{2}$	teaspoon allspice
$\frac{1}{2}$	teaspoon cinnamon
1	can sweetened condensed milk
1	cup pecans, chopped
4–5	cups sweet potatoes, cooked, drained, and mashed

Preheat oven to 350°. Grease a 9x13-inch casserole dish.

Beat eggs. Blend in melted margarine, vanilla, sugar, allspice, cinnamon, condensed milk, and pecans. Stir in sweet potatoes. Pour into casserole dish. Bake for 35–40 minutes.

Serves 6

Across Colorado

Cornish Pasties in Colorado

"Pastry rolled out

like a plate,

Piled with turmut,

tates and mate,

Doubled up and

baked like fate,

That's a Cornish

Pasty."

Welsh and Cornish miners brought their skills, foods, and customs to the mines of Colorado. Pasties were the complete meal that the miners took to work in a cotton "morsel bag," which was boiled regularly by the wife to keep it snow white.

Pasties are turnovers that are usually filled with meat, but when times were hard and meat was scarce, they were filled with potatoes and called Tiddy Oggies ("tiddy" being the name for potato), not to be confused with Piddy Oggies, which came from Somerset, England, and were filled with pork and cheese.

Legend says that the miner always threw the very last bit of his pasty to pacify the invisible Tommyknockers, the little people who lived in mines and played harmful tricks on miners. Another theory is that there was so much arsenic involved in mining, with no way to wash hands, that the bit of pasty the miner held was thrown away because it was probably poisonous.

Potato Puff

4	large red potatoes, peeled, boiled, cooled, and grated
$^1/_2$	cup chopped fresh parsley
1	onion, grated
$^1/_2$	green pepper, diced
$^1/_2$	teaspoon salt
$^1/_4$	teaspoon pepper
1	cup sharp Cheddar cheese, grated
$^1/_2$	cup margarine, melted
3	eggs, beaten
1	cup milk

Serves 6–8

Preheat oven to 350°.

Blend all ingredients. Place in greased 2-quart casserole. Bake uncovered 40–45 minutes.

Sophistication in Georgetown

Adolphus François Gerard, alias Louis Dupuy, opened the Hotel de Paris in Georgetown in 1875. Hotel de Paris was certainly the most urbane hotel at that time in Colorado. Born in Alençon, France, Gerard tried to transplant the sophistication of his native land to the wilds of Colorado.

The building was replete with excellent cabinetry and wood carving. Imported furnishings from Europe were hauled fifty miles into the mountains by wagon from the railroad in Denver. The hotel boasted steam heat, Haviland china, rich carpets, elaborate decorations, and the menu of a gourmet.

Across Colorado

Georgetown Loop

During the summer, the Colorado Historical Society operates its steam-powered train over the reconstructed Georgetown Loop, an amazing arrangement of loops and trestles by which ore trains traversed the 700-foot change in elevation between the two mining towns of Georgetown and Silver Plume. The track crosses over four bridges, including the spectacular Devil's Gate bridge, crosses over itself once, and makes three and one-half circles to attain the necessary altitude. The Loop is a tortuous four miles of twists and turns, although Georgetown and Silver Plume are only slightly more than one mile apart as the bird flies.

Across Colorado

Dijon Potatoes and Leeks

$\frac{1}{2}$ cup leeks, sliced in $\frac{1}{2}$-inch pieces

$1\frac{1}{2}$ pounds new red potatoes, unpeeled, quartered

1 cup water

$\frac{1}{2}$ cup dry white wine

1 tablespoon Dijon mustard

1 bouillon cube (chicken or beef)

Serves 4–6

Spray large skillet with cooking spray. Saute leeks until tender. Remove to side dish. Add potatoes, water, wine, mustard, and bouillon cube. Cook covered, 6 minutes. Uncover and cook 20 minutes longer or until potatoes are tender. Add leeks and pepper to taste.

Fresh Summer Squash Saute

2 tablespoons butter

1 tablespoon extra virgin olive oil

1 large red onion, diced

6 small, fresh yellow squash, cut into $\frac{1}{4}$-inch rounds

salt and pepper

$\frac{1}{2}$ teaspoon garlic powder, or to taste

$\frac{1}{2}$ cup Parmesan cheese, freshly grated

Serves 4

Melt butter with olive oil in a 10- or 12-inch skillet over medium-high heat. Add diced onion and saute until onion is translucent. Add yellow squash slices and mix well. Lower heat and cover skillet. Saute for 8–10 minutes or until squash is cooked but still firm. Season with salt, pepper, and garlic powder. Sprinkle with Parmesan cheese just before serving.

Across Colorado

Healy House and Dexter Cabin

In the summer, costumed guides portray the Victorian lifestyle of the 1878 boarders who lived at the Healy House in Leadville. On the grounds of the Healy House is the Dexter Cabin, which looks like an ordinary log cabin but is furnished inside with fine woodwork and hardwood floors. Built by James V. Dexter, one of the state's early millionaires, the cabin contains many of his belongings. The Colorado Historical Society owns and maintains both of these properties.

Across Colorado

Twice Baked Potatoes North Ranch

4	large Idaho baking potatoes
2–4	tablespoons butter at room temperature
	salt and pepper
$\frac{1}{2}$	teaspoon garlic salt
$\frac{1}{2}$	teaspoon garlic powder
2–4	tablespoons cream or half-and-half
6	scallions, finely minced
$\frac{1}{2}$	cup Cheddar cheese, grated
1	tablespoon sour cream
$\frac{1}{4}$	cup Parmesan cheese, grated
	crumbled bacon bits (optional)
	paprika

Serves 4

Preheat oven to 400°.

Scrub potatoes and wrap in aluminum foil. Bake for 1¼ hours or until tender. Remove potatoes from foil and allow to cool slightly. Slice off the top third of the potatoes. Scoop out potato from skin, without piercing skin. Mash potato pulp with a potato masher. Add remaining ingredients and mix, allowing some chunks to remain. Stuff potato mix back into skins, mounding on top. Sprinkle a bit of additional Cheddar on top and add a dash of paprika. Place potatoes in a 9x13-inch glass dish. Bake at 350° for 25 minutes and serve immediately.

Potatoes can be made one day in advance. Cover with plastic wrap and refrigerate. To serve premade potatoes, heat in microwave oven for 8–10 minutes or in 300° oven for 30 minutes. A wonderful do-ahead food with steaks or for a cookout.

Across Colorado

Grand Dame of Historic Hotels

Hotel Colorado and the Glenwood hot springs pool and lodge in the late 1890s

President Theodore Roosevelt (right) dines in Meeker during one of his hunting trips to Colorado.

Two stone stairways rise from the center of the Hotel Colorado in Glenwood Springs. They are long and broad and beg for the sweeping skirts and wasp waists of yesteryear. An elevator also was available to guests when the hotel opened in 1893, powered by smooth hydraulic hoists, it was a much heralded invention.

A greater wonder, however, was the second elevator located in the kitchen. This carried food from the "freezer" in the basement, where over 300 tons of ice chilled the hotel's supply of perishables. The ice was cut from the Colorado River in winter and stored in the caves above Glenwood.

Old registers of Hotel Colorado bear famous names, such as Armours, Goulds, Mayo Brothers, David Moffitte [sic], Lulu Long, Diamond Jim Brady, and Evelyn Walsh McClain [sic]. In 1905 the hotel became the "Little White House" where the Secretary of State tended to business while President Theodore Roosevelt went off on bear hunts in the Colorado mountains. It is said that when the President came back to the hotel from a hunt, empty-handed and depressed, the hotel staff made and presented him with the first "Teddy" bear.

Across Colorado

Jack Frost Baked Squash

¼	cup butter
2	cups finely minced onions
¼	teaspoon ground nutmeg
¼	teaspoon salt
¼	teaspoon pepper
½	teaspoon cinnamon
⅓	cup dry white wine, such as Chardonnay
2	yellow delicious apples, peeled, cored, and sliced very thinly
2	tablespoons brown sugar
2	teaspoons currants or raisins
2	teaspoons balsamic vinegar or red wine vinegar
2	acorn squash, sliced in half and seeds removed

Serves 4

Preheat oven to 350°.

In a 12-inch skillet melt butter and add onions, nutmeg, salt, pepper, and cinnamon. Saute until onion is translucent. Add wine, apple slices, brown sugar, and currants. Cover and cook over low heat for 5–10 minutes or until apples are soft. Add vinegar. Place squash halves in a 9x13-inch pan. Fill squash cavity with onion-apple mixture. Fill pan with ¼ inch hot water. Cover pan with foil. Bake for 50–60 minutes or until squash is cooked. Test for doneness by piercing squash with a fork. Squash should be soft.

Can be reheated but not frozen.

Across Colorado

The eight daughters and one son of the Vidal family ran their ranch outside of Gunnison after they lost their parents. They also performed in the first movie made in Colorado, in 1910. One daughter had gone to San Francisco when this picture was taken.

Squash Menkhaven

2	medium zucchini or yellow squash, sliced
3	slices bacon, diced
1	medium onion, chopped
1	green pepper, chopped
1	cup grated Cheddar cheese (divided use)
1	cup corn
	chopped canned green chiles to taste
½	cup milk
1	tablespoon butter
½	teaspoon ground cumin
2	garlic cloves, crushed
	salt and pepper to taste
1	tablespoon fresh basil or ¼ teaspoon dry basil, crumbled

Serves 4 – 6

Preheat oven to 350°.

Cook squash in small amount of salted water, being careful not to overcook. Drain. While squash cooks, saute bacon, onion, and pepper. Drain fat. Add drained squash, ¾ cup of cheese, and remaining ingredients to bacon mixture. Simmer for 5 minutes. Place in casserole dish, cover, and bake for 20 minutes. About 5 minutes before casserole finishes baking, top with remaining grated cheese.

This squash casserole was "Queen" Menke's recipe and is still served at Menkhaven. "Queen" Menke was the mother of the Menke sisters and ran the kitchen at Menkhaven. She was quite the organizer and expected the guests to arrive for dinner on time while the food was still hot. She would lock the dining room door, forcing nonpunctual guests to come through the back door and enter the dining room through the kitchen. Queen would scold but would always serve them a hot meal.

(See the story about the Menke sisters in the South Mountains/Southwest Flavors section.)

Bear Stories

Mamie met Grant Ferrier when she was riding her horse to school and they were married more than sixty-seven years, all of them spent in the valley of the North Fork of the Gunnison River. They both told stories about the early days on the North Fork, including these bear tales:

At one of Grant's summer camps a bear kept getting into the tent and creating havoc in the cupboard and supplies. One day the bear came into the tent when Grant's helper Loal was there. Loal hit the bear in the face with a dishpan, ending that bear's visits and the camp's bear trouble.

Another year, another bear kept coming into the cabin, hitting the

stove, and scattering ashes all over. Then he found the store of canned foods. This bear learned to puncture the cans and drink out all of the liquid—one smart bear who never met a dishpan.

Summer Squash Casserole

4   cups fresh yellow squash, sliced
$\frac{1}{4}$–$\frac{1}{2}$ inch thick (4–6 squash)

2   tablespoons oil

1   cup chopped onion

1   green pepper, chopped

1   cup sour cream

1   can cream of mushroom soup, undiluted

     salt and pepper to taste

4   tablespoons butter or margarine, melted

4   cups dry cornbread stuffing or day-old homemade cornbread, crumbled

Serves 10–12

Preheat oven to 400°. Oil a 9x13-inch baking dish.

Simmer summer squash in salted water until tender. Drain and mash with a potato masher or fork. Heat oil in a 9-inch skillet. Add onion and green pepper and saute until onion is translucent. Remove skillet from heat. Add mashed squash, sour cream, and soup to onion mixture. Season with salt and pepper and blend. In a bowl, toss cornbread crumbs with melted butter or margarine. Cover the bottom of baking dish with half the crumbs. Pour squash mixture over crumbs. Top with remaining crumbs. Bake for 30 minutes.

Across Colorado

The Great Sand Dunes dominate the landscape of the San Luis Valley.

Across Colorado

The South Mountains

Today the Hispanic influence clings to the San Luis Valley and the south mountains—in the soft-sounding Spanish names, in the architecture, in colorful holiday customs, and in spicy Hispanic foods.

After the Great Sand Dunes had settled at the base of the Sangre de Cristo Mountains but before the settlers came across LaVeta Pass, the Ute, Apache, and Comanche roamed this land, hunting, fishing, and gathering. Then late in the seventeenth century, strangers appeared from the south. Columns of light-skinned men, armored and helmeted, tramped through the dust, blazing a trail for those with long black robes and tonsured heads. They were the expeditions sent north from La Villa Real de la Santa Fe to establish a new route to Monterey, and along the way, to convert the native population.

To encourage settlement, the Spanish and Mexican governments offered huge land grants to the intrepid Hispanic colonists who would venture here to live. They came and brought with them the knowledge of irrigation and their Spanish culture.

The plans of the Mexican government to dominate the Southwest halted in 1848 with the treaty that ended the war between the United States and Mexico. Today the Hispanic influence clings to the San Luis Valley and the south mountains, in the soft-sounding Spanish names—Sangre de Cristo, San Luis, Rio Grande, Conejos, Costilla—in the architecture, in colorful holiday customs, and in spicy Hispanic foods.

The first church in Colorado, Our Lady of Guadalupe, rebuilt and repaired, occupies its original site and still holds Mass in the tiny village of Conejos. Ruins of early settlements—one-story adobe structures built with common walls around a plaza—attest to the need for protection. Later, more elaborate establishments—Fort Massachusetts and Fort Garland—became military garrisons, trading posts, and sanctuaries.

During the nineteenth century, sheep became an important enterprise in the San Luis Valley. More recently potatoes, barley, sugar beets, and other vegetables add to the agricultural basis of the region. Throughout South Park and the Upper Arkansas Valley, the prospect of riches gleaned from the mountains—gold, silver, lead, and other minerals—lured fortune hunters and more serious settlers alike. Many stayed on and became the forefathers of today's ranchers and river runners.

Great steaks, roast beef, lamb chops, and potatoes fixed any way you like dominate menus in the valleys and mountains of south Colorado, but you won't want to miss the frijoles, tamales, and chile con carne—spicy or mild.

There Is No Night in Creede

BY **CY WARMAN**

Here's a land where all are equal
Of high or low birth—
A land where men make millions
Dug from the dreary earth.
Here meek and mild-eyed burros
On mineral mountains feed.
It's day all day in day-time
And there is no night in Creede.

The cliffs are solid silver
With wondrous wealth untold.
And the beds of running rivers
Are lined with purest gold.
While the world is filled with
   sorrow,
And hearts must break and bleed,
It's day all day in the day-time
And there is no night in Creede.

Cy Warman arrived in Creede in 1880. In time, he became a locomotive engineer for the Denver and Rio Grande Railroad, which hauled ore from mines, often hung on cliff faces. From poetry and railroading he turned to journalism. Warman edited the *Creede Chronicle* and later the *New York Sun*.

Abandoned mine in Creede

Indian Fry Bread

3	cups unsifted all-purpose flour
1	cup unsifted whole wheat flour
2	tablespoons baking powder
1	tablespoon cooking oil
1½	teaspoons salt
2	tablespoons sugar
1¾	cups warm water

Serves 6

Combine flour, baking powder, oil, salt, sugar, and water. Mix well, using hands if necessary. Let dough stand at room temperature for 30 minutes. On well-floured surface, knead dough till smooth and elastic.

Break off dough in small pieces and roll out to serving-size pieces ⅛ inch thick. Make a slit in center with tip of knife.

Fry bread in moderately hot cooking oil, ½ inch deep, until brown on both sides, turning once. Serve with Navajo Taco Sauce.

An authentic recipe from a pioneer family in Durango.

Navajo Taco Sauce

1½	pounds ground beef
1	6-ounce can tomato paste, diluted with 2 cans water
1	15-ounce can chili beans with sauce
1	package dry taco seasoning mix
6	rounds Indian fry bread, flour tortillas, or tacos
2	cups shredded lettuce
1	cup shredded Cheddar cheese
1	cup chopped green onions

Serves 6

Crumble meat into heated skillet. Cook over moderate heat until meat loses its redness. Drain off fat. In a bowl, combine tomato paste with water, beans, bean sauce, and dry taco mix. Using potato masher, mash beans well. Add bean mixture to the ground beef. Bring to boil, reduce heat, and simmer, covered, about 20 minutes.

Place a round of Indian fry bread, a flour tortilla, or a taco on each plate. Mound lettuce on top of fry bread, tortilla, or taco. Top with beef mixture and cover with cheese and onions.

Across Colorado

The Menke Sisters—Act I

The Menke sisters performing their Hawaiian act. (Photo courtesy of Cynthia Whiteside)

Three beautiful girls boarded the Denver and Rio Grande narrow gauge in their hometown in 1916 and journeyed to New York City to pursue vaudeville careers. The girls were Ella (known as "Dutch"), Gladys, and Hazel Menke, and the hometown was Antonito in Colorado's San Luis Valley. The girls had grown up in Antonito, had been sent to Denver's Loretto Heights College for their high school education, then on to Thomas Normal School in Detroit. Their Detroit apartment had been close to a vaudeville house, so they spent much of their time watching glamorous performers. After they developed an act of their own, they returned home to convince their father that they should go into show business.

In New York, the Menke sisters soon became headliners. However, Dutch, never as smitten with the stage as her sisters, dropped out of the act after a couple of years, but Hazel and Gladys played the vaudeville circuit for the next fifteen—sharing billing with top performers of the day—young Donald O'Connor, the Marx Brothers, Morey Amsterdam, Martha Raye, the Ritz Brothers, George Burns—they knew them all. Hazel and Gladys continued on tour until their father became critically ill. Then they packed their trunks and headed back to the San Luis Valley. But their show doesn't end here.

Across Colorado

Mexican Krich

10	eggs
1	16-ounce container cottage cheese
1	teaspoon baking powder
1	teaspoon salt
10	drops Tabasco sauce
½	cup flour
8	ounces Monterey Jack cheese, shredded
8	ounces Cheddar cheese, shredded
1	4-ounce can diced green chiles
	salsa

Serves 6–8

Preheat oven to 400°.

Beat eggs and add remaining ingredients. Mix well and pour into a 9x13x2-inch pan. Bake 15 minutes at 400°, then lower oven temperature to 350°, and continue baking for 20–25 minutes or until mixture is set. Remove from oven and allow to rest 5 minutes. Cut into sections and serve with salsa.

Cooked sausage or diced ham may be added before baking or served as an accompaniment.

Menkhaven—Act II

When Gladys and Hazel ended their vaudeville days, they found that sister Dutch had plans for their future. Dutch had watched sportsmen from all over the country wade the Conejos River for some of the best trout fishing in the world. Always ready to take chances, the sisters with their spry mother, called Queen, opened a resort, Menkhaven on the Conejos, in 1931—the middle of the Depression. Mother Queen cooked and the sisters served meals in the big dining room for fifty guests, and sometimes they entertained with their old vaudeville routines.

The Menkes sold their resort in 1947 but the huge log lodge with its rustic cabins still gives haven to guests—often the same ones year after year—who are fascinated by its history and in love with the beauty and fish of the Conejos. The cabins at Menkhaven retain their original names—for the Menke sisters' oldtime friends. You can sleep in the beds of the Martha Raye cabin, the Mills Brothers, the Bob Hope, the Ritz Brothers, or cabins named for other celebrities.

See the Central Mountains/Salads and Vegetables section for Queen's Menkhaven Squash.

Across Colorado

Antonito—Best Place in the World

Interior of second Warshauer
mansion, built in 1913

Fred Warshauer emigrated from Germany in 1879 to become the "King of Conejos County," according to the *La Jara Enterprise* of May 31, 1912. The *Antonito Ledger* called him "the Sheep Baron." Fred Warshauer married an Antonito girl (she was Queen Menke's sister) and built two mansions in Antonito. The first one burned to the ground in 1911. The second one is still standing and is on Colorado's register of historic residences.

In 1912, when Fred's nephew, Kurt Warshauer, graduated from the University of Berlin, his father gave him a trip around the world for a graduation present. Young Warshauer got as far as Antonito to visit his uncle—and stayed. He said he had found the best place in the world. He also found the woman he wanted to marry. Her name was Ruth McEntire.

Capirotada or Torrejas (a Southwest Sweet)

2$\frac{1}{2}$ cups bread cubes

1   egg

vegetable oil for deep fat frying

$\frac{1}{4}$ cup sugar mixed with 1 teaspoon cinnamon

$\frac{3}{4}$ cup pine nuts

$\frac{1}{2}$ cup citron, finely chopped

Sauce

2   cups sugar

$\frac{1}{8}$ teaspoon cream of tartar

1   cup water

$\frac{1}{2}$ teaspoon cinnamon

Serves 6

Preheat oven to 350°.

Brown bread cubes thoroughly in the oven (15–20 minutes). As cubes brown, prepare sauce. Combine sugar, cream of tartar, cinnamon, and water in saucepan and heat gradually to boiling. Boil until the syrup threads. Set aside, keeping hot.

Separate the egg and beat the white until stiff; add the yolk and beat again. Dip the browned bread cubes in the egg and fry in deep fat. Drain on paper towel, then pile on a hot platter. Sprinkle with sugar and cinnamon mixture, then add pine nuts and citron. Pour hot sauce over all and serve immediately.

Leona Wood, the granddaughter of Josefa Jaramillo Carson and Kit Carson, gave this recipe of her grandmother's to the Volunteers of the Colorado Historical Society in 1963 for our first cookbook, Pioneer Potluck.

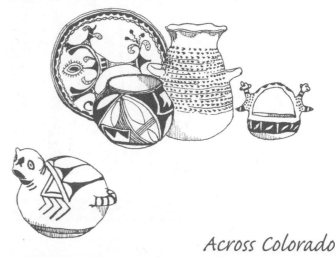

Drawings based on artifacts in the Colorado Historical Society collections

Across Colorado

Our Lady of Guadalupe Church

Our Lady of Guadalupe
Church, built in 1858 in
Conejos, is the oldest church
in Colorado. Reconstructed, it
continues to hold Mass.

Mexican Cornbread

8	slices bacon
1	cup yellow cornmeal (masa)
1	cup flour
2	teaspoons baking powder
1	teaspoon salt
1	teaspoon sugar
$\frac{1}{8}$	teaspoon chili powder
1	cup milk
2	eggs
$\frac{1}{4}$	cup vegetable oil
$\frac{1}{4}$	cup diced green chiles
$\frac{1}{2}$	cup Cheddar cheese, shredded
1	8$\frac{1}{2}$-ounce can cream-style corn

Makes 12 slices

Preheat oven to 350°. Grease a 9x13-inch pan.

Cook bacon until crisp, then drain, cool, crumble, and set aside. In large bowl, mix dry ingredients. In another bowl, whisk together milk, eggs, and vegetable oil. Stir ingredients together and mix until well blended. Carefully fold in chiles, cheese, and bacon bits. Stir in the corn. Pour into prepared pan. Bake 30–40 minutes.

Across Colorado

Cumbres & Toltec Scenic Railroad

This excursion train leaves its station in Antonito and travels over the Denver and Rio Grande narrow-gauge tracks in a twisting, turning climb on the Continental Divide to Chama, New Mexico, carrying thousands of tourists each year. Spiked down in 1880 as the San Juan Extension of the Denver and Rio Grande, the Cumbres & Toltec was built to serve the rich mining camps in the San Juan Mountains. Today it is a main economic base of the town of Antonito and Conejos County.

Fresh Salsa

6	large, ripe, fresh tomatoes
8	scallions, finely chopped
4	tablespoons fresh cilantro, finely minced
3	fresh, fire-roasted Anaheim chiles, diced (or use canned)
1	clove fresh garlic, minced
	salt, pepper, Tabasco sauce

Makes 3 cups

Peel tomatoes, using a small, sharp paring knife. Chunk tomatoes and gently blend in remaining ingredients. Season to taste with salt, pepper, and Tabasco. Refrigerate until well chilled. Serve with warmed tortilla chips or over any southwest-style dish.

The essence of the Southwest.

Food to Ride the Rails

Lois Brady Young (1895–1962) lived in Durango, Chama, and Alamosa, where she was in the restaurant business as owner, manager, and chef. Her establishment was always near the railroad tracks and her diners were the trainmen before, after, and mid-shift. She also prepared packed lunches for the men in the engines and in the cabooses.

One of Lois's lunches was probably on the ride with her husband, a veteran conductor, when his Denver and Rio Grande Western passenger train was swept away in a snow slide on Cumbres Pass. The train slid a great distance down the mountain, but miraculously, no one was hurt.

Across Colorado

Manassa Pioneer Days

Of the 1,000 residents of Manassa today, about 50 percent are Hispanic and most of the others are Mormon. The ancestors of the Hispanics were there to greet the Mormons' ancestors when they arrived about 1877. During Manassa's Pioneer Days each summer, the population swells to about 12,000 when people from all over the country come back for reunions.

Two early-day Mormon arrivals were the John Dempseys, parents of heavyweight champion of the world, Jack Dempsey, who was born in Manassa in 1895 and became known as the Manassa Mauler. Dempsey's last trip to his hometown was in 1966 when he attended Pioneer Days. Dempsey died in 1983.

The Menkes, the Warshauers, and Jack Dempsey were all friends.

The Menke girls used to have reunions with Jack when they were billed in the same city. The Warshauers often had dinner with Jack in New York as they were on one of their frequent trips to Europe.

Jack Dempsey and his parents

Across Colorado

Pico de Gallo

4	ripe medium-sized tomatoes, finely chopped
$\frac{1}{2}$	medium white onion, finely chopped
$\frac{1}{2}$	green pepper, finely chopped
1	bunch fresh cilantro, finely chopped
$\frac{1}{4}$	teaspoon salt
$\frac{1}{2}$	teaspoon dried oregano
2	teaspoons sugar
2	tablespoons white vinegar
	juice of $\frac{1}{2}$ lime

Makes 2 $\frac{1}{2}$ cups

Place tomatoes, onions, green pepper, and cilantro in bowl. Sprinkle with salt and oregano. Dissolve sugar in vinegar, pour over vegetable mixture, and mix thoroughly. Squeeze juice of half a lime over all ingredients and let stand in refrigerator for 30 minutes. Serve atop Mexican food, baked potatoes, or with chips as an appetizer. Lime-chile tortilla chips are excellent with this mixture.

Across Colorado

Home Design in Culebra

Nathaniel P. Hill was traveling with Territorial Governor William Gilpin in 1864, when they stopped for the night at Culebra, a village about 20 miles south of Fort Garland. In his letters, Hill described the architecture of Culebra and the home furnishings of his host:

"After a day's travel over an arid plain, destitute alike of water and vegetation, we have arrived at the model specimen of a Mexican [Hispanic-type] town known as Culebra. It contains a thousand inhabitants . . . The population is entirely Mexican and the place [although in Colorado Territory] possesses all the characteristics of the Mexican towns. It contains only adobe houses, extending along for half a mile on either side of the road and all joined together . . .

"We are staying at the house of Amidor Sanchez, one of the old and rich men of the place. He is 101 years old, and was born in the house in which he now lives . . . The house is splendid in its way. The walls are covered with calico. Instead of carpets, they use cowhides, dressed with the hair on. The floor is entirely covered with them. A cushioned seat extends entirely around each room, and the walls are well covered with small paintings, most of which represent the crucifixion or some event in the life of Christ. The house contains eight rooms, each about 12 x 20 feet."

Hill was a chemistry professor from Brown University who came to Colorado and developed an improved smelting process for separating gold from other ores. Later he was elected a U.S. senator from Colorado.

Chorizo and Vegetable Soup

1	pound white beans (dry)
2	cups water (from beans)
2	tablespoons olive oil
2	cloves garlic, chopped
1	medium onion, chopped
2	chorizo sausages, sliced
2	large carrots, sliced
1	red pepper, chopped
2	stalks celery, chopped
2	cups chicken broth
2	tablespoons oregano
	salt to taste

Serves 8

Cook white beans according to package directions. Drain, reserving 2 cups water. In a large stockpot, heat olive oil and saute garlic and onions until onions are translucent. Add chorizo and cook until sausage is browned. Stir in remaining ingredients, including cooked beans and reserved liquid. Season with salt. Stir well and cook over low heat for 30–60 minutes or until flavors are well blended.

Time enhances the flavor.

Across Colorado

Creede Repertory Theatre

Established in 1966 by the Junior Chamber of Commerce as an economic development project, the Creede Repertory Theatre has grown to become the largest employer in Mineral County during the season. The theater draws thousands of visitors each summer to enjoy up to seven plays produced in true rotating repertory format on one stage.

The productions encompass a variety of musicals, comedy, drama, and shows for children, most of them reviewed in the metropolitan (Denver) press. Operating in a recently renovated theater on the two-block main street, the theater will celebrate its thirty-first season in 1997.

Historic view of Wagon Wheel Gap near Creede

Buckhorn Exchange Red Chili with Buffalo and Sausage

1	pound buffalo meat, ground
1	pound breakfast-style pork sausage
3	cups water (divided use)
1/2	cup onion, cut in 1/4-inch dice
1/2	cup celery, cut in 1/4-inch dice
1	medium green pepper, cut in 1/4-inch dice
1/4	cup red chili powder
2	tablespoons ground cumin
1	tablespoon salt
1	tablespoon ground black pepper
1	tablespoon sugar
3	tablespoons dry minced garlic
1	4-ounce can green chile strips
1	15-ounce can kidney beans, undrained
1	15-ounce can pinto beans, undrained
1	28-ounce can diced tomatoes
2	tablespoons vinegar
1	tablespoon Worcestershire sauce
2	beef bouillon cubes
1	chicken bouillon cube

Place ground buffalo meat and pork sausage in a large skillet and add 1 cup of water. Cook until meats are browned. Use a potato masher to crumble meat as it cooks. Drain fat. Add the onion, celery, green pepper, chili powder, cumin, salt, black pepper, sugar, garlic, and green chiles to skillet. Blend well and simmer for 15 minutes. Add the remaining ingredients and bring to a boil. Add 2 cups of water and simmer for 30 minutes.

Serves 6 – 8

See the Denver Metro/Main Dishes section for stories about the historic Buckhorn Exchange.

Across Colorado

Lost Starter a Calamity

Great Grandmother Sprague spent most of her adult life cooking for railroaders and passengers in the eating room of various stations from Monarch Pass through Hesperus, Vance Junction, and Mancos—all while raising a family of six children.

Once, when snowed in at Vance Junction for several weeks, Great Grandma Sprague accidentally baked all of her dough without removing a starter. Being marooned with no means of leavening flour was a serious matter. However, she had given some of her sourdough starter to an old prospector who lived in a mining shack between Vance and Ophir. After miles on snowshoes, Great Grandma Sprague was back with a bit of that crucial starter, and baked goods were once again plentiful in the depot at Vance Junction.

Bowl of the Wife of Kit Carson

4	cups rich chicken broth
1	cup cooked chicken or turkey, cut into bite-sized pieces
1	cup garbanzo beans, cooked
1	cup chipotle pepper, chopped
1	cup cooked rice
4	pinches dried oregano
1	cup Monterey Jack or Muenster cheese, cubed
1	avocado, sliced

Serves 4

Heat broth to boiling and add chicken, garbanzos, chipotle pepper, rice, and oregano. Stir well and bring to a simmer. Serve in large individual bowls, adding cheese cubes and avocado slices just as the bowl is served.

This superb "dry" soup requires a special smoked chile pepper called the chile chipotle adobado, available from Mexican groceries in cans.

Sam Arnold serves "The Bowl of the Wife of Kit Carson" at his restaurant, The Fort, in Morrison. Kit Carson's granddaughter, Leona Wood, told Arnold that she remembered eating this "bowl" as a youngster.

Across Colorado

Hot Springs at 4UR Ranch

Fishing for trout on the Rio Grande at Wagon Wheel Gap.

When the Ute Indians wanted "big medicine," they went to the hot springs at Pagosa Springs, but for "little medicine" they soaked themselves in the hot waters that are now part of the 4UR Ranch, located at Wagon Wheel Gap, about ten miles southeast of Creede. At one time a foot trail connected the two natural spas.

The 4UR has a colorful story. In the 1870s there was a comfortable hotel with thirty pools of bubbling water that ranged in temperature from icy to near boiling. In the 1890s, railroad tycoon William J. Palmer purchased the hotel and built the Wagon Wheel Gap Hot Springs Resort—his own guest ranch, a small establishment of gentility and relaxation. The 4UR remains a place for relaxation. Julia Childs, President Dwight D. Eisenhower, and Walt Disney are among the notables who have fished and vacationed here.

Try the 4UR Trout Mousse in the Northwest Slope/Appetizers section.

Black Bean Chili

4	cups dried black turtle beans
2	tablespoons olive oil
5–6	cloves garlic, crushed
1	pound bulk sausage
2	teaspoons cumin
$2\frac{1}{4}$	teaspoons salt
2	teaspoons basil
$\frac{1}{2}$	teaspoon oregano
1	tablespoon lime juice
2	medium bell peppers, chopped
$\frac{1}{2}$	cup tomato puree
2	4-ounce cans green chiles
	black pepper to taste
	red pepper flakes to taste
	sour cream
	salsa
	Monterey Jack cheese, grated

Serves 8–10

Soak beans for several hours or overnight. Drain and simmer in fresh, boiling water for 3 hours, or until beans are tender. Drain, reserving 2–3 cups of the cooking liquid. Saute in olive oil the garlic, sausage, seasonings, lime juice, and bell pepper until tender. Add sausage mixture, tomato puree, green chiles, black pepper, and red pepper flakes to beans and water. Simmer over very low heat for about 45 minutes. Serve with sour cream, salsa, and Monterey Jack cheese.

Across Colorado

Wolf Creek Pass Opens

When the road over Wolf Creek Pass was completed in 1916, more than 1,000 people attended the ribbon-cutting celebration, feasting on free elk meat and coffee. The new road was hard-packed dirt, steep, and narrow but it afforded a shortcut from the San Luis Valley to Durango and Farmington, New Mexico.

Eighty years later, even with snow tires and four-wheel drive, Wolf Creek Pass is a hazardous trip in bad weather.

Crossing Wolf Creek Pass in 1939

Hacienda Pork and Green Chiles

2	tablespoons vegetable oil
4	pounds boneless pork loin, trimmed of fat and cut into $1/2$-inch cubes
$1/3$	cup finely minced, fresh garlic
5	tablespoons flour
2	$14\frac{1}{2}$-ounce cans beef broth
21	green chiles (Anaheim or Hatch's), fire-roasted and diced
2	teaspoons salt
	freshly ground black pepper

Makes 3 quarts

Heat oil in a 5-quart stockpot over medium heat. Add pork cubes and garlic. Cook for 20–25 minutes, or until pork is cooked. Blend in flour and cook 5 minutes longer. Add broth and chiles. Season with salt and pepper. Simmer gently for 1–1½ hours. Chile will be mildly hot. Add more chile or jalapenos for greater fire. Serve in soup bowls with sour cream and warmed flour tortillas. Can be used as green chile sauce over burritos or enchiladas. Can be frozen or will keep one week in refrigerator.

A wonderful way to savor the autumn flavor of fire-roasted green chiles.

Across Colorado

Branding Cattle, Female Version

When Fritz Becker died, his three daughters took over the chores of the ranch he had homesteaded in 1875 near Salida. Pictured are Catherine, Emma, and Harriet branding the cattle in 1894.

Across Colorado

Tulum Chili

1	pound bulk chorizo sausage
1	pound ground round
1	onion, chopped
1	apple, peeled and diced
4	ounces green chiles, chopped
2	ounces jalapenos, chopped
1	14-ounce can stewed tomatoes
1	6-ounce can tomato paste
1	bottle Carta Blanca beer
1	tablespoon chili powder
1	tablespoon molasses
½	teaspoon hot sauce
1	15-ounce can chili beans
1	cup sharp Cheddar cheese, grated

Serves 6–8

Chop chorizo and brown in a large stockpot. Remove sausage and brown ground round, onion, and apple in the remaining fat. Add all remaining ingredients except beans and cheese and bring to a boil. Lower heat and simmer for 2 hours. Add beans and simmer 1 hour longer. Serve garnished with grated cheese.

Originated in Tulum, Mexico. HOT!

Across Colorado

Historic Fish Stories

Descendants of the Brandon family, early settlers of Custer County, heard many fish stories from their forebears. Now hear these and long for the early days:

• A young Brandon boy hiked over the mountains to Cotten Lake where he caught eleven huge trout weighing from five to nine pounds each—a catch too big to carry. He laboriously packed nine of the monsters in snow and cached them, then carried two home. The next day, with help from younger brothers and sisters, he retrieved them all.

• What did the Brandons do with so many fish? Just ahead of winter, the family would catch several gunnysacks full of fish and clean them. Mrs. Brandon then salted the fish down in five- and ten-gallon crocks for winter use. After soaking in fresh water for a day or two, the fish were delicious.

• The Brandons found the high lakes in the Sangre de Cristo Range full of rainbow trout, natives, and brookies. Trout weighing ten and eleven pounds were not uncommon, with the average catch from three to six pounds.

Rio Grande Stew

2	pounds beef stew meat, cubed (chicken may be substituted for beef, but do not brown)
2	tablespoons oil
3	cups water
1	10$\frac{1}{2}$-ounce can beef broth
$\frac{1}{2}$	cup chopped celery
$\frac{1}{2}$	cup chopped onion
2	cloves minced garlic
1	tablespoon oregano
1	tablespoon coriander
2	teaspoons cumin
2	bay leaves
1$\frac{1}{2}$	teaspoons salt
	pepper
3	carrots, cut into chunks
1	7-ounce box frozen corn
1	15-ounce can garbanzo beans
1	small head cabbage, cut into 8 wedges

Salsa

1	16-ounce can diced tomatoes
$\frac{1}{2}$	cup diced onion
1	4-ounce can green chiles, diced
1	clove garlic, minced
$\frac{1}{4}$	cup chopped parsley
$\frac{1}{2}$	teaspoon salt

Serves 4

Brown stew meat in oil. Add water, broth, celery, onion, garlic, and seasonings. Simmer for 2 hours. Skim fat. Add carrots, corn, beans, and cabbage. Simmer 30 minutes. Taste for seasoning.

Mix together all salsa ingredients. Spoon salsa over individual servings of stew. This is a great après-ski meal.

Across Colorado

The Poor Farm

When this large, brick structure in Salida opened in 1891, it was dedicated to providing a roof over the heads of indigent, elderly men who were described as "once rich men who had succumbed to a life of drink and ended up paupers." The thirty residents were expected to work the soil, grow the crops, tend the cows, make the butter, and produce their own food.

The Poor Farm ceased operations as a poor farm in the early 1940s. The building was used as a Grange hall, then the whole place was abandoned to become a chicken coop. In 1982 the building was transformed to a bed-and-breakfast. Recently new owners changed its name to the River Run Inn because they believed potential customers might be frightened by its longtime designation, the Poor Farm. After all, "Who wants to go to the poor farm?" Answer: Only those who enjoy historic settings, relaxation, and rich trout fishing on a beautiful stretch of the Arkansas River.

Try the River Run Inn's Rosemary Garlic Bread in the North Mountains/Breads section.

River Run Inn

Across Colorado

Four Corners Pintos and Rice Salad

4	cups chicken stock
2–4	tablespoons butter
2	cups long-grain white rice
2	15-ounce cans pinto beans, drained and rinsed
1	bunch scallions, sliced
½	cup finely minced onion
1	bunch fresh cilantro, chopped
1	teaspoon black pepper
1	teaspoon ground cumin
6	ounces pine nuts (optional, but very nice)
	prepared salsa to taste
6	cups arugula/chicory or wild greens mix
2	pint baskets cherry tomatoes
6–10	fresh, fire-roasted Anaheim chiles (optional)

Serves 6 – 10

In a 2-quart pot, combine chicken stock and butter. Bring to a boil. Stir in rice. Cover pan and reduce heat to low. Cook for 25 minutes or until rice is done. Remove from heat and cool. Place cooled rice in a large bowl. Add pinto beans, scallions, onions, cilantro, pepper, cumin, and pine nuts. Mix well. Taste and add enough salsa to make rice mixture flavorful and moist. Refrigerate for several hours. Serve on a bed of chopped arugula or greens, garnished with tomato halves and chile strips.

Can be served in one large bowl for a buffet. Very low fat, high flavor.

Across Colorado

Through the Years with the Tuesday Evening Club

Members of the Tuesday
Evening Club in Salida
socialized for many years.
Their series of group pictures
record changing styles as
well as their passage from
youth to maturity.

Adobe Chicken Salad

- 1 carrot, diced
- 1 cup whole-kernel corn, drained
- 1 medium zucchini, chopped
- 1 tomato, chopped
- 1 bunch green onions, sliced
- 1 avocado, sliced or chunked
- 1 can black beans, drained
- 1 pound grilled chicken, sliced or chunked

Dressing

- 1/2 cup picante sauce
- 1 tablespoon fresh lemon juice
- 2 tablespoons olive oil
- 1/2 teaspoon ground cumin
- 1/2 teaspoon garlic salt
- 2 tablespoons fresh cilantro, minced

Serves 4

In a large bowl, mix all salad ingredients. Mix dressing ingredients and pour over salad. Chill for several hours.

A great luncheon salad. Serve with fresh fruit and cornbread.

Across Colorado

In the Easter parade, circa 1908

Poncha Springs on July 4, 1908

Number, please?

Chimichangas

1–1½	pounds hamburger or ground turkey
2	teaspoons taco seasoning or chili powder
½	teaspoon ground cumin
½	teaspoon oregano
¼	cup diced green chiles
¼	cup salsa or picante sauce
¼	cup sour cream
2	tablespoons vinegar
2	green onions, chopped
	salt to taste
¼	cup margarine
6	flour tortillas

Garnishes

Cheddar cheese, grated

tomatoes, chopped

lettuce, shredded

guacamole

salsa

sour cream

Serves 6

Preheat oven to 450°.

Brown hamburger. Drain. Add next nine ingredients and simmer 10 minutes.

Melt margarine in microwave oven. Lay tortillas on waxed paper and brush both sides with melted margarine. Spoon ⅓ cup filling onto center of each tortilla and fold, envelope style. Place seam side down in 9x13-inch pan. Bake for 20–25 minutes. Sprinkle with grated cheese. Return to oven to melt cheese. Serve with additional cheese and other garnishes of your choice.

A romantic moment in Salida, 1908

The proposal

Across Colorado

Stagecoach Etiquette

After the Civil War, stagecoach companies sprang up all over the West. Rules like these were posted at stage stops:

1. Abstinence from liquor is requested, but if you must drink, share the bottle. To do otherwise makes you appear selfish and unneighborly.

2. If ladies are present, gentlemen are urged to forgo smoking cigars and pipes as the odor of same is repugnant to the gentle sex.

3. Gentlemen must refrain from the use of rough language in the presence of ladies and children.

4. Buffalo robes are provided for your comfort during cold weather. Hogging robes will not be tolerated and the offender will be made to ride with the driver.

5. Don't snore loudly while sleeping or use your fellow passenger's shoulder for a pillow.

6. Firearms may be kept on your person for use in emergencies. Do not fire for pleasure or shoot at wild animals as the sound riles the horses.

7. In the event of runaway horses, remain calm. Leaping from the coach in panic will leave you injured, at the mercy of the elements, hostile Indians and hungry coyotes.

8. Forbidden topics of discussion are stagecoach robberies and Indian uprisings.

9. Gents guilty of unchivalrous behavior toward lady passengers will be put off the stage. It's a long walk back. A word to the wise is sufficient.

Have a good trip!

(From the stagecoach exhibit at Fort Garland Museum.)

WPR Frittata

6	corn tortillas
6–7	ounces green chiles, diced
4	cups Jack cheese, grated
10	eggs
$^3/_4$	cup half-and-half
$^1/_2$	teaspoon ground cumin
$^1/_2$	teaspoon onion salt
$^1/_2$	teaspoon garlic salt
$^1/_2$	teaspoon black pepper
$^1/_2$	teaspoon salt
	picante sauce

Serves 6–8

When ready to bake, preheat oven to 350°. Spray a 9x13-inch casserole with canola oil.

Spread half of the diced green chiles on the bottom of the casserole and top with three of the tortillas torn into 1x1-inch squares. Add 2 cups of the cheese. Repeat layers (chiles, tortillas, cheese). Whisk eggs and half-and-half together, add seasonings, and mix well. Slowly pour egg mixture over entire top layer in casserole. Cover with foil and refrigerate overnight.

When ready to bake, uncover casserole and bake for 45 minutes or until lightly browned and bubbly. Cut into serving-size pieces and pass picante sauce.

This recipe comes from the West Pawnee Ranch Bed and Breakfast in Grover, Colorado.

Across Colorado

Fort Garland

From the west barracks, the Sangre de Cristo Range towers above Fort Garland. (Photographed about 1909)

Named for Brigadier General John Garland, Fort Garland was built in 1858 to replace Fort Massachusetts, which was 6 miles farther north. The new Fort Garland was closer to the white settlements in the San Luis Valley, yet still guarded the approach from the east over the Sangre de Cristo Mountains. The fort served as a threatening gesture and as a refuge and social center for settlers rather than a base for military operations. It was maintained until 1883, when the command was moved to Fort Lewis in the San Juan basin. Located in the village of the same name, Fort Garland is 25 miles east of Alamosa and is maintained by the Colorado Historical Society. It contains military memorabilia and folk art from the San Luis Valley.

Mexican Wedding Cake

2	cups sugar
2	eggs, well beaten
1	20-ounce can crushed pineapple
2	cups flour
2	teaspoons baking soda
1	cup chopped nuts

Frosting

4	ounces butter
1	8-ounce package cream cheese
1	teaspoon vanilla
1½	cups powdered sugar

Serves 16

Preheat oven to 350°.

Place all ingredients in mixing bowl in order given. Blend together. Pour into an ungreased 9x13-inch pan. Bake for 35 minutes.

While the cake is cooling, mix together all frosting ingredients using an electric mixer. Spread evenly over cake when completely cooled. Cover with plastic wrap and store in refrigerator.

Excellent dessert for a potluck.

An officer and his family in front of the officers' quarters at Fort Garland, 1874

Across Colorado

Pike's Stockade

Pike's Stockade, a National Historic Landmark, is a reconstruction of a small breastwork built by Lieutenant Zebulon M. Pike and his men and used for a few frigid weeks in the winter of 1807 before they were intercepted and taken prisoner by the Spanish. Located six miles east of La Jara in Conejos County, the stockade was west of the Rio Grande River, at that time the recognized boundary between United States and Spanish territory. The Colorado Historical Society reconstructed and maintains the stockade.

Fiesta Cake (Pinto Bean Cake)

1	cup sugar
4	ounces butter (at room temperature)
1	egg, beaten
2	cups pinto beans, mashed
2	cups all-purpose flour
1	teaspoon baking soda
1/4	teaspoon salt
1	teaspoon cinnamon
1/2	teaspoon ground cloves
1/2	teaspoon allspice
2	cups apples, peeled and diced
2	teaspoons vanilla
1/3	cup raisins (optional)
1/2	cup nuts, chopped

Orange Sauce

1/2	cup sugar
1/2	cup orange juice
2	tablespoons cornstarch

Serves 16

Preheat oven to 375°. Grease and flour 9x13-inch cake pan.

In a large bowl, using an electric mixer, cream sugar and butter. Add beaten egg and mashed beans. Sift dry ingredients together and add to bean mixture. Add apples, vanilla, raisins, and nuts. Mix well. Pour into prepared pan and bake for 45 minutes.

To prepare orange sauce, mix ingredients and cook to thicken. Cool. When serving, top each piece of cake individually with orange sauce or sprinkle with powdered sugar.

Darlene Maes Vallejo, who contributed this recipe, is owner of the Ute Cafe on Main Street in Fort Garland.

Across Colorado

Seventeenth Street, Denver, about 1910, looking southeast from the Union Station through the Welcome Arch. The arch was demolished in 1931.

Across Colorado

The Denver Metropolitan Area

"The founders of Denver built better than they knew, for it is not likely the visions of their wildest dreams ever pictured anything approaching the reality that is before us now."

Could William H. Larimer, Jr., looking across Cherry Creek in 1858, have envisioned the traffic rushing along its banks almost a century and a half later? Could William N. Byers, setting up his printing press above a saloon in 1859, have imagined the kind of development the *Rocky Mountain News* reports today? The words of Denver's historic historian, Jerome Smiley, ring truer now than when he wrote them in 1901: "The founders of Denver built better than they knew, for it is not likely the visions of their wildest dreams ever pictured anything approaching the reality that is before us now."

Denver was born as a terminal for the stages and supply wagons coming west to the gold fields. Miners came down from the mountains for tools and grubstakes; settlers looked around and decided to stay; entrepreneurs saw opportunity. When the Union Pacific bypassed Denver, worried businessmen created the Denver Pacific Railway. But it took more than pick, shovel, and a few saloons to build a railroad. Banks appeared, investors followed. The town was no longer dependent on mining. In a few short years the railroad transformed a mining camp into the "Queen City of the Plains."

Mining mogul–turned–politician H. A. W. Tabor set the example. He built his five-story Tabor Block at Sixteenth and Larimer Streets in 1880. Seventeenth Street soon burgeoned with architectural elegance—the Denver Club, the Equitable, the Brown Palace. Department stores came—the "Denver Dry" in 1894, Daniels & Fisher, The Fair, Joslins, and the May Company. The United States Post Office, the Opera House, and the Court House rounded out downtown.

Women arrived at this new frontier. They established homes, supported schools, encouraged the arts, and brought refinement to the West. They were doctors and lawyers, teachers and nurses, bankers and businesswomen—and always homemakers. They were some of the first women in the country to vote.

Today Denver is the regional center for industrial development, communication technologies, manufacturing, health and education, agriculture and ranching, sports and tourism. It is both a mile-high cow town and a sophisticated center for culture and entertainment. You can feast southwestern or midwestern, Creole or corn-fed. The variety is endless. Enjoy the diversity. Enrich your experience. Salud!

Across Colorado

Denver's First Christmas

On December 25, 1858, far from home and feeling the absence of women and children in the holiday season, the hopeful prospectors in the Spooner camp at the Platte River gold diggings celebrated as best they could. The camp leaders, Captain Spooner and A. O. McGrew, invited fifty guests, among them several persons whose names now read like a Denver street directory: General William Larimer, Colonel S. S. Curtis, and E. P. Stout.

The bill of fare included "venison à la mode, buffalo smothered, elk, wild turkey and sage hen." Also potatoes, beans and vegetables (which the men had brought from home), dried mountain plums, and prickly pear. Biscuits and pies were baked over the campfires. The final item was "Taos Lightning"—the wagonload of whiskey that had arrived on Christmas Eve from Taos, New Mexico.

Christmas in Denver, 1928

Across Colorado

Party Chicken Breasts

3	large whole chicken breasts, boned, skinned, and halved
1	cup soy sauce
1	cup lemon juice
2	teaspoons fresh gingerroot, chopped
2	teaspoons poultry seasoning
1	teaspoon freshly ground black pepper
4	tablespoons flour
¾	cup vegetable oil
1	cup hot water
1	10-ounce package frozen white onions, thawed
2	10-ounce packages frozen artichoke hearts, thawed and quartered (or canned artichoke hearts)

Serves 6

Preheat oven to 350° when ready to bake chicken.

Mix soy sauce, lemon juice, gingerroot, and seasonings. Add chicken and marinate in refrigerator for several hours or overnight. Reserve marinade. Roll chicken in flour and brown in hot oil. Place in casserole. Add marinade and 1 cup hot water. Bake for 35 minutes. Add onions and artichoke hearts and bake 20 minutes longer. Serve with rice.

A drive into the country on a Sunday afternoon

Across Colorado

Commuting to Denver—1920

Hundreds of commuters drive from the Evergreen–Bergen Park area to Denver each day, quickly covering the distance on multi-laned Interstate 70. However, the journey was not so easy for Lucius Edwin Humphrey, who is believed to have been the first year-round commuter between Bergen Park and Denver. In the early 1920s, Humphrey, who was head of the *Rocky Mountain News* copy desk, drove a Model T he called "Mary Ann."

Humphrey's daughter, Hazel, in later years recounted his drive home each day in Mary Ann: "He would take the cement road from Denver to Golden, where he would fill up his battery with water at an old spring house. From there, he drove up Lariat Trail over Lookout Mountain to Genesee. A second stop for water took place at Ralston Ranch before he arrived in Bergen Park and then on to his ranch."

Not a Model T but a fancier car with running board rack and rumble seat

Oven Roasted Chicken

1	3½–4 pound whole fresh chicken
4	tablespoons vegetable oil
1	tablespoon chili powder
½	teaspoon salt
1	teaspoon black pepper
1	lemon, quartered
2	tablespoons roast garlic puree, or 4 cloves fresh garlic, crushed

Serves 4

Rinse and pat chicken dry. Mix oil, chili powder, salt, and pepper in a small bowl. Rub chicken inside and outside with seasoned oil. Gently rub oil under skin as much as possible. Place lemon and garlic inside chicken. Truss chicken. Using a rotisserie, roast for 1¼ hours. If using oven, place chicken in 9x13-inch pan, breast side up. Roast at 375° for 30 minutes. Lower temperature to 350° and roast 1 hour longer.

Wonderful aroma while roasting. Serve with mixed spring greens and vinaigrette. Choose a fruit tart for dessert.

Pearce-McAllister Cottage

Beautiful 1899 Colonial Revival architecture and the original interior furnishings highlight this structure located at 1880 Gaylord Street in Denver. The private Museum of Miniatures, Dolls and Toys leases the house from the Colorado Historical Society.

Across Colorado

A Block in Montclair

In 1890, Baron von Richthofen, the uncle of the Red Baron of World War I fame, built his "castle" in Montclair and subdivided his holdings. He sold the land by the block, with the proviso that the buyer would build his own home, costing at least $5,000, on a portion of the block. This was supposed to have great investment potential because the buyer could then sell the remaining lots in the block at profit.

Lawyer John H. Denison (who later became a Chief Justice of the Colorado Supreme Court) examined the title to the Baron's land and received a block in Montclair as his fee. He built his house, and in the middle of the block he built his own tennis court, one of the first in Denver. The tennis court is still there, played on regularly by his granddaughter and her friends, who are now in their eighties, as well as his great- and great-great grandchildren.

Denison's granddaughter, Mary Silverstein, says that although the block in Montclair never turned out to be a financial bonanza for her grandfather, his descendants have fared well with his tennis court.

The Richthofen Castle, shortly after it was completed

Across Colorado

Chicken à la Karl-a-Kate

2–3	pieces of chicken per person
	potatoes, sliced
	carrots, sliced
	onions, sliced
	rosemary
	salt and pepper
	chicken broth
	white wine

Preheat oven to 350°.

For each serving, cut a 16-inch square of heavy-duty aluminum foil. Place a layer of sliced vegetables on each piece of foil and top with chicken pieces. Add a bit of dried rosemary and season with salt and pepper. Sprinkle with 3–4 tablespoons of broth, wine, or a blend of both. Fold foil on the diagonal, forming a triangular packet. Seal edges well. Bake for 1 hour.

To make each individual packet a complete dinner, serve with salad and a roll.

Two pioneering families from Pueblo, the E. I. Crocketts and the Martin Walters (founder of the Walter Brewing Company), had children who married and lived at the beautiful Karl-a-Kate Ranch in Beulah, where this recipe originated.

Across Colorado

Big Tillie the Bouncer

A less than genteel establishment in the early 1920s was the Tremont Saloon, both a tavern and a house-of-ill-repute. Owners were Celesté Fatore (in white apron) and his wife, Big Tillie (at left), who was the madam and bouncer.

Pagliacci's Chicken Cacciatore

4	small, whole, boneless, skinless chicken breasts
2	tablespoons flour
$\frac{1}{4}$	cup olive oil
4	cloves garlic
1	medium onion, sliced
1	small red pepper, thinly sliced
1	small green pepper, thinly sliced
1	stalk celery, finely diced
$\frac{1}{4}$	cup white wine or chicken broth
1	1-pound can Italian chopped plum tomatoes
1	teaspoon dry sweet basil or 5–6 leaves fresh basil, chopped
2	teaspoons dry parsley or 4 sprigs fresh parsley, chopped
	pinch thyme
$\frac{1}{2}$	teaspoon red pepper flakes
	salt and pepper to taste
1	pound spaghetti or fettuccine noodles

Serves 4

Cut chicken breasts in half, pound lightly, and dust with flour. In a 10-inch skillet, heat olive oil over medium heat. Saute chicken breasts on both sides until lightly browned. Remove from skillet and set aside. Add garlic to pan, stirring quickly, until golden. Add onion, peppers, and celery, stirring to coat with oil. Add the wine or chicken broth and cook until liquid is absorbed. Add tomatoes and herbs. Bring sauce to a simmer and return chicken to skillet. Season with red pepper flakes, salt, and pepper. Cook gently over low heat for 30–45 minutes.

While chicken and sauce are simmering, prepare pasta according to package directions. Place chicken on pasta and top with sauce.

Romance and Food—Italian Style

Popular Pagliacci's Italian restaurant in northwest Denver has been in family hands for three generations. It was in 1940 that Frank Grandinetti met Thelma Balzano and began a romance that eventually blossomed into the establishment of Pagliacci's. Frank was a handsome Sicilian fruit and vegetable vendor who sold his produce in the manufacturing area of lower downtown Denver. Thelma was working on the second floor of a garment manufacturer.

When Thelma leaned out her window one day to flirt with the handsome vendor, Frank threw her an apple. For lovers of Italian food, the rest is history.

Pagliacci's famous minestrone soup remains a secret, but the Grandinetti family has shared the recipe for Thelma and Frank's Chicken Cacciatore.

Across Colorado

Morrison—the Place to Go

An event called the "Military Barbecue" was held at Red Rocks Park.

If you were a Denverite in 1910, you could have taken a 60-cent round-trip to Morrison on the Colorado and Southern Railway, walked or taken a burro to a picnic spot in Red Rocks Park, viewed the caves, paid 75 cents to take the cable railway to the top of Mount Morrison for a few hours, then returned to the dance pavilion at the Mount Morrison Casino on the banks of Bear Creek and ordered a fine dinner.

At dinner you might have been elbow-to-elbow with the casino and cable railway's owner, John Brisben Walker, and some of his friends, such as Mark Twain, John Jacob Astor, and President Theodore Roosevelt. Entertainment could have been provided by Marie Dressler or Mary Pickford, both of whom performed there.

Teriyaki Chicken

1	3-pound frying chicken, cut up, or equal amount of chicken pieces
$\frac{1}{2}$	cup low-salt soy sauce
$\frac{1}{3}$	cup sugar
$\frac{1}{4}$	cup Mirin (Japanese cooking wine)
1	teaspoon fresh gingerroot, grated
1	clove garlic, minced

Serves 4

Preheat oven to 325° when ready to bake.

Place chicken pieces in bowl. Mix remaining ingredients and pour over chicken. Marinate overnight in refrigerator. Place chicken pieces on a foil-lined, 10x15-inch shallow pan, reserving marinade. Bake for 1 hour, basting from time to time with marinade.

Serve with Japanese short-grain rice and stir-fried vegetables.

Grant-Humphreys Mansion

This mansion at 770 Pennsylvania Avenue was built in 1902 for the family of James Benton Grant, an early Colorado governor. The architecture mixes various building styles in grandiose proportions. The Colorado Historical Society now owns this property and makes it available for public and private events.

Across Colorado

Bear Creek Pot Luck

Summertime visitors to Morrison enjoy the flowing sight and bubbling sound of Bear Creek, unaware that it has moments of sudden and swift violence. More than half a dozen life-taking flash floods are recorded in Morrison's history. Always the high waters leave havoc and confusion.

In 1938, after a heavy storm and cloudburst farther up in the mountains, walls of water came down both Bear and Mount Vernon Creeks. Morrison's grocery store was hit and the canned goods floated out the doors and downstream, often settling in some family's backyard.

The unexpected bounty provided many a meal for these folks, meals of the "potluck" variety because the can labels washed off during their swim.

Sunday traffic jam on Bear Creek

Pigeons or Game Hens à l'Ardennaise

4	small pigeons (squab) or Cornish game hens
4	tablespoons butter (divided use)
8	thick slices bacon
20	pearl onions, peeled
3	carrots, scraped and cut into 1-inch sticks
8	cauliflower flowerets, about 2 inches in diameter
4	medium potatoes (or 8 very small)
1	cup chicken broth, fresh or canned
1/4	cup dry white vermouth or white wine
1	teaspoon dry thyme
1	bay leaf
	salt and pepper

Serves 4

When ready to bake, preheat oven to 325°.

In a skillet, melt 2 tablespoons butter. Brown squab or hens on all sides until golden. Place in large, oven-safe covered casserole. Cut bacon into 1/2-inch strips. Add 1 tablespoon butter to skillet and fry bacon until crisp. Remove bacon and add pearl onions to skillet. Brown in drippings until golden. Add carrots and cauliflower and cook 2–3 minutes. Put vegetables into casserole with squab. Peel potatoes, wash, dry, and cut in half if medium, or leave whole if very small. Add remaining butter to skillet. Brown potatoes on all sides, then add to casserole. Add broth, vermouth, and bacon, but do not add pan drippings if burned at all. Season with thyme, bay leaf, salt, and a generous grinding of pepper. Cover tightly, using foil on casserole edge to seal, if necessary. On high heat, bring to boil, then transfer to oven and bake for about 1 hour.

Serve immediately.

This classic Ardenne dish was contributed by Michel Reynders of the Belgium Consulate in Denver.

Across Colorado

Lodging in Early Denver

Wagon train arrives in Denver.

Three nationally known newspapermen arrived in Denver in June 1859 to check out the tales of the gold discovery. They were Horace Greeley, editor of the *New York Tribune*, Albert Richardson of the *Boston Journal*, and Henry Villard of the *Cincinnati Commercial*. The men first took lodging at the Denver House, a long, low gambling and drinking establishment with dirt floors, where the ceaseless noise discouraged their literary pursuits.

Richardson, in his book *Beyond the Mississippi*, described their next move: "So, according to the custom of the country we 'jumped a cabin'—selected the best one we could find, moved in our effects, and took possession. . . .

It was twelve feet square, of hewn pine logs new and smooth, the cracks within chinked with wood and outside plastered with mud."

Then Richardson relates what happened when the cabin's owner returned.

"A few days later, the owner of the cabin came down from the mines and looked in upon us quite unexpectedly; but observing that the nine points of the law were in our favor, he apologized humbly for his intrusion, (most obsequious and marvelous of land-lords!) begged us to make ourselves entirely at home, and then withdrew, to jump the best vacant cabin he could find, until the departure of his non-paying clients." *(From* History of Denver *by Jerome Smiley, 1901)*

Baked Rainbows

1	10-ounce package frozen chopped spinach
$1/4$	cup butter, softened
$1/4$	cup grated onion
6	10- to 12-inch fresh, whole rainbow trout (or other variety)
	salt and pepper
1	egg
$1/4$	cup milk
1	teaspoon salt
$3/4$	cup toasted bread crumbs
$3/4$	cup grated Cheddar cheese
$1^1/2$	tablespoons butter
	prepared tartar sauce

Serves 6

Preheat oven to 500°.

Cook spinach according to package directions. Press out excess moisture. Mix butter, spinach, and onion. Salt and pepper fish cavities. Stuff spinach mixture inside trout. In a pie pan or other flat dish, beat egg and milk with salt. Combine bread crumbs and grated cheese on a sheet of waxed paper or foil. Dip trout in egg mixture, then in crumb mixture. Place trout in buttered baking dish. Dot with butter and sprinkle with remaining crumb mixture. Bake for 15–20 minutes or until fish are tender and well browned. Serve with tartar sauce.

Across Colorado

A Bonnet—a Rare Sight

Albert Richardson, correspondent for the *Boston Globe*, wrote this description of Denver as he saw it in 1859: "It was a most forlorn and desolate-looking metropolis. If my memory is faithful, there were five women in the whole gold region; and the appearance of a bonnet in the street was the signal for the entire population to rush to the cabin doors and gaze upon its wearer as at any other natural curiosity. The men who gathered about our coach on its arrival were attired in slouched hats, tattered woolen shirts, buckskin pantaloons and moccasins, and had knives and revolvers suspended from their belts."
(From History of Denver *by Jerome Smiley, 1901)*

"Bonnets" like this one were high fashion in Denver in the 1890s.

Karouine Couscous

1	tablespoon butter
1	tablespoon olive oil
1/2	cup onion, finely chopped
3–4	cups boneless, cooked chicken, cubed
1/2	teaspoon salt
1/2	teaspoon pepper
1/4	teaspoon cayenne powder
1	teaspoon ground turmeric
2	teaspoons ground ginger
4	tablespoons tomato paste
1/2	cup chicken broth
1/2	cup canned garbanzo beans
1	cup diced vegetables, such as zucchini, yellow squash, or carrots
	chicken broth
1	cup couscous
	peel of 1 orange, grated
1	cup boiling water
1/2	stick cinnamon
5	whole cloves

Garnish

curls of orange peel and fresh mint leaves

In a large skillet, melt butter and olive oil. Add onions and cooked chicken and saute until onion is translucent. Add salt, pepper, cayenne, turmeric, ginger, tomato paste, and chicken broth. Simmer for 5 minutes to blend flavors. Add beans, vegetables, and enough chicken broth to cover. Simmer for 20 minutes.

Place couscous in a heavy saucepan with tight-fitting lid. Add orange peel, boiling water, cinnamon, and whole cloves. Cover quickly and let stand 5 minutes.

To serve: Mound couscous in center of large platter. Using a slotted spoon, place chicken mixture around it in a ring. Pour remaining liquid over all. Garnish with curls of orange peel and fresh mint leaves.

Serves 4–6

Across Colorado

Suburbanites from west Denver traveled across the Platte Valley to the inner city on this open-air trolley.

Flour and Pickles in Littleton

Littleton began as a farming community in the 1860s and continued to prosper in that capacity for many years. In 1867 several Littleton farmers established a mill on the banks of the South Platte River.

According to Richard Little, for whom the town was named, the mill "found a good market in Denver and mountain towns for every sack of flour we could grind."

Another early industry established in Littleton was the Merry Pickle Company. At this time the area was known for large gardens from which the Merry Pickle Company obtained the vegetables it processed. In the 1890s the company employed about fifty workers. Perhaps the company's greatest impact was to encourage the adoption of the name "Pickletown" for the area. "Pickletown" is still a familiar term to old-time Littleton residents.

Roasted Tomatoes, Asparagus, Shrimp, and Pasta

1	head garlic
12	fresh Roma tomatoes, quartered lengthwise
2	tablespoons olive oil
	freshly ground black pepper to taste
1	pound large shrimp, peeled and deveined
1	pound asparagus, very thin, cut into 2-inch lengths
12–16	ounces corkscrew, penne, or other type short pasta
2	teaspoons olive oil
2	teaspoons fresh lemon juice
1	teaspoon oregano
1	teaspoon thyme
	salt to taste
	grated Parmesan cheese

Serves 4

Preheat oven to 450°.

Slice the top $\frac{1}{2}$ inch off the garlic head and discard. Pull off any loose papery skin. Wrap garlic loosely in aluminum foil. Bake for 15 minutes.

In a large roasting pan toss together tomatoes and olive oil. Add some black pepper. Add garlic package to corner of roasting pan. Bake 20 minutes without stirring or until tomatoes are wrinkled and beginning to brown. Remove garlic package. Scatter shrimp and asparagus over tomatoes and roast 10 minutes longer.

Meanwhile, boil water for pasta and cook for 8 minutes or until tender but not soft. While pasta is boiling, squeeze soft pulp from garlic cloves into a small bowl. Mash into a paste. Add 2 teaspoons olive oil, lemon juice, oregano, and thyme. Mix well. Drain pasta and toss with garlic mixture until evenly coated. Then toss pasta mixture with roasted tomato mixture in roasting pan. Add salt to taste. Serve immediately with grated Parmesan cheese.

Across Colorado

The Tabor Opera House at Sixteenth and Curtis was grandiose in 1881. The mud streets were less pretentious. Photo by W. H. Jackson.

Good Food in LoDo

With the advent of major league baseball in Denver and the construction of Coors Field in the heart of Lower Downtown ("LoDo" as it is affectionately called), the neighborhood is brimming with new dining establishments and brew pubs. But LoDo and its surrounding area are no strangers to good eateries. They go with its history.

In the late 1940s, Stanley Kazuo Yoshimura established the SKY Coffee Shop and Home Bakery at 2151 Larimer Street, which became famous, especially for his pies and cakes. "Sky" (who was known by the name formed by his initials) had been employed in the kitchen of the Brown Palace Hotel after leaving the Gila River War Relocation Center in Arizona where he and his family were interned during World War II. After his death in 1964, his family operated the restaurant until 1971.

Shrimp Scampi

8	ounces butter
$^1/_4$	cup chopped onion
2	cloves garlic, minced
2	tablespoons chopped parsley
2	tablespoons bread crumbs
1	pound raw shrimp, peeled and deveined
2	cups sliced fresh mushrooms
2	cups chopped fresh tomatoes
	salt, pepper, and cayenne pepper to taste

Serves 4

Melt butter in a 10-inch skillet. Add onions and garlic and saute lightly. Add parsley and crumbs and stir. Add mushrooms and tomatoes and simmer until mushrooms are cooked. Stir in shrimp and cook 4–5 minutes. Season to taste. Serve over rice.

The sauce may be made ahead and reheated. Add the shrimp just before serving. This dish is very pretty served in a shallow casserole.

Unforgettable Baur's

There were white marble floors, white metal chairs, and a mouth-watering array of candies behind the glass display cases. Children growing up in Denver in the first half of the twentieth century remember Baur's at 1512 Curtis as the place for special birthday occasions.

Newcomers to Denver in the sixties remember Baur's in Cherry Creek. Both establishments have passed away, but Denver cooks still pass around their treasured Baur's recipes and mouths still water at the remembrance of English toffee and chocolate crunches melded within ice cream, pies, and cakes.

See the South Plains/Special Times section for Baur's Mija Candy recipe.

Across Colorado

The Art of Homemaking—1932

In 1932, Denver homemakers read their praises by F. G. Bonfils, publisher, in the foreword to *The Denver Post's Book on the Art of Homemaking*. The book also printed prize recipes, the first prize going to a "Savory 3-in-1 Beef," which made a beef broth, a beef sauce, and marrow dumplings from one Colorado beef shank bone. The recipe was clearly keyed to the Great Depression.

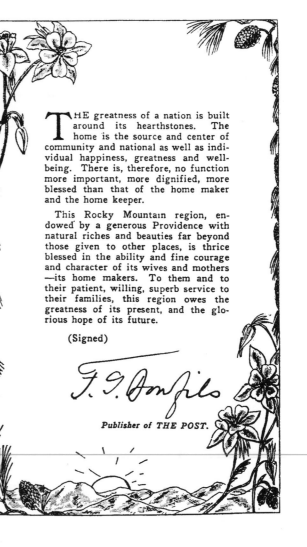

THE greatness of a nation is built around its hearthstones. The home is the source and center of community and national as well as individual happiness, greatness and well-being. There is, therefore, no function more important, more dignified, more blessed than that of the home maker and the home keeper.

This Rocky Mountain region, endowed by a generous Providence with natural riches and beauties far beyond those given to other places, is thrice blessed in the ability and fine courage and character of its wives and mothers —its home makers. To them and to their patient, willing, superb service to their families, this region owes the greatness of its present, and the glorious hope of its future.

(Signed)

F. G. Bonfils

Publisher of THE POST.

Scallops with Snow Peas and Pasta

$^3/_4$ pound fresh snow peas (pea pods) or 6 ounces frozen pea pods

2   tablespoons water

1   tablespoon oil

1   tablespoon butter

1   large red pepper, cut into $^1/_4$ x 3-inch slivers

4   tablespoons finely minced shallots

1   teaspoon finely minced garlic

1   pound fresh scallops

3   tablespoons vodka

2   tablespoons fresh lemon juice

$^1/_4$ cup half-and-half

     salt and pepper

4   tablespoons fresh cilantro, minced

10   ounces pasta, such as capellini, cooked

     dusting of Parmesan cheese

Serves 4

Place snow peas in a small saucepan. Add 2 tablespoons water. Cook over low heat, covered, for 10 minutes. Drain and set aside. In a 12-inch skillet, heat oil and butter over medium-high heat. Add cooked snow peas, red pepper, shallots, and garlic. Cook 3 minutes, stirring often. Add scallops and cook for an additional 2–3 minutes. Lower heat to medium low. Add vodka, lemon juice, and half-and-half. Season with salt and pepper. Cook gently for 5 minutes, until sauce thickens, stirring frequently. Sprinkle with minced cilantro.

Divide cooked pasta among four preheated dinner plates. Top with scallops and sauce. Dust with Parmesan cheese.

Dinner is ready in 30 minutes.

Across Colorado

Four-Mile Historic Park

Four-Mile House is located at
715 South Forest Street.

Four-Mile House is Denver's oldest home. It was built of hand-hewn logs in 1859, and named for its location four miles from what is now Confluence Park, the center of Denver at the time. An early owner was Mary Cawker, a widow with two teen-age children, who established its fame as a tavern and stage stop. Stagecoach passengers, covered with dust of the plains, stopped at Four-Mile House for food, drink and to wash up; then they proceeded to their final stop, Denver, refreshed and ready to take on the big city or the mountains beyond.

Hand Lotion Recipe:

Found on a yellowed scrap of paper:

1 wine glass glycerine
2 wine glasses Bay Rum
Yoke [sic] of one egg, well
   beaten in lotion

"I find by putting this on my hands several times in the evening I can get my hands healed so quickly I put it on 5 or 6 times in the evening before going to bed."

Tuscan Pasta Pie

8	ounces vermicelli spaghetti
2	tablespoons butter
1/3	cup grated Parmesan cheese
2	eggs, well beaten
1	pound ground beef, or half beef and half Italian sausage
1	medium onion, chopped
1/2	medium green pepper, chopped
1	8-ounce can whole tomatoes
1	6-ounce can tomato paste
1	teaspoon sugar
1	teaspoon oregano
1/2	teaspoon garlic salt
1	cup small-curd cottage cheese
1/2	cup Mozzarella cheese, shredded

Serves 6 – 8

Preheat oven to 350° when ready to bake.

Cook spaghetti according to package directions. Drain. Place hot spaghetti into a bowl; add butter, cheese, and eggs. Mix well. Spoon spaghetti into a buttered 10-inch pie plate with a 2-inch rim. With back of spoon, spread spaghetti over bottom and up sides of plate to form a crust. (Spreads best as it cools.) Set aside.

Crumble ground beef or combination of beef and sausage into a heated skillet. Cook until meat loses red color. Add onion and green pepper and cook 5 minutes longer. Drain fat. Cut tomatoes into small pieces, then add tomatoes with liquid, tomato paste, sugar, oregano, and garlic salt to meat. Cook over moderate heat until hot.

Spread cottage cheese over spaghetti crust. Spoon meat mixture over cottage cheese. Bake uncovered for 20 minutes. Sprinkle Mozzarella cheese on top in a small circle in center of pie. Bake 5 minutes longer, or until cheese melts. Let stand for about 5 minutes before cutting.

Across Colorado

"Wo ist die schule?"

Early graduation class at Evans School

Min Ray, of Denver, recounts a frightening day of her childhood in Denver: "I was born of German parents in West Denver and couldn't speak English when I started school in 1920. The first day I walked to school alone I got lost and remember crying over and over, 'Wo ist die schule?' A kind man who either understood German or realized what I was looking for took my hand and walked me to Evans School. A short time later I lost my sweater at school and nobody understood me. Never any language problem after that! When I learned English, that ended my speaking German. However, my mother insisted on speaking to us in German, saying, 'If you won't speak it, you'll have to be able to understand it.' For which I was eternally grateful when we were stationed in Germany for three and a half years."

Gourmet Pizza

Dough

1	package dry yeast
1½	cups warm water
2	teaspoons sugar
1	teaspoon salt
1	tablespoon vegetable oil
3½–4½	cups bread flour
	olive oil

Pizza Spice Blend

(or use purchased pizza spice blend)

1	tablespoon dried basil
1	tablespoon dried oregano
1	tablespoon marjoram
2	tablespoons dried parsley flakes
1	teaspoon garlic powder
1	teaspoon ground black pepper
2	teaspoons fennel seeds
1	tablespoon garlic salt
1	teaspoon onion powder
	pinch red pepper flakes

(Ingredients continued on page 213)

Preheat oven to 450° when ready to bake pizza.

In a large bowl dissolve yeast in warm water. Add sugar, salt, and vegetable oil and blend. Add 3½ to 4 cups of flour to the liquid, ½ cup at a time, to form a smooth dough that is not too sticky. Knead dough for 8 minutes. Place dough in a greased bowl and let rise for 1 hour or until doubled.

While dough is rising prepare pizza spice and select cheeses and toppings.

When dough has doubled, punch down and divide in half. (The dough can be refrigerated at this stage for later use.) Turn dough onto a lightly floured surface and roll into a 13-inch circle.

Lightly grease or spray a pizza pan. Place dough on pan, brush dough lightly with olive oil, sprinkle liberally with pizza spice, coat with Mozzarella cheese, and sprinkle with blended Parmesan and Romano cheeses. Embellish with your choice of toppings.

Enjoy. Be creative. Have fun.

This recipe was created by Executive Chef Kurt Melle for a restaurant in Silverthorne, circa 1970. Chef Melle reports: "We got into all kinds of debates as to what wine would go best with some of these combinations. If anxiety sets in, beer always worked well for us."

See the story in the Central Mountains/Salads and Vegetables section telling how these pizzas came to the rescue of skiers trapped on I-70.

Across Colorado

Pioneer Matrons Promote Historic Preservation

The Pioneer Ladies' Aid Society was formed in 1889 "to encourage the collection of such historical incidents and matters as will serve to perpetuate the acts and deeds of pioneer men and women of Colorado."

Membership was open to women who arrived in Colorado or were born here prior to 1861, the wives and widows of such pioneers, and their female descendants.

Well-known names are among the trustees.

Articles of Incorporation
and by-Laws of the
Pioneer Ladies' Aid Society of the
State of Colorado

Organized September, 1889
Incorporated March 27, 1894

Articles of Incorporation of the
Pioneer Ladies' Aid Society

Know all Men by These Presents:
That we, Caroline C. Cornforth, Augusta L. Tabor,
Lucinda M. Mosley, Caroline E. Cutler, and Miriam Mitchell,
all residents of the State of Colorado, have associated ourselves
together as a corporation under the name and style of the
Pioneer Ladies' Aid Society of the State of Colorado for the
purpose of becoming a body corporate and politic under and by
virtue of the laws of the State of Colorado and in accordance
with the provisions of the law of said state we do hereby make,
execute and acknowledge in this certificate in writing our
intention so to become a body corporate under and by the
virtue of said laws.

Gourmet Pizza (*continued*)

Cheeses

shredded whole milk and skim milk
Mozzarella, freshly grated, imported
Parmesan, freshly grated, imported
Romano, or other cheeses such as
Swiss, Cheddar, Havarti dill,
Monterey Jack, Gouda, Feta

Memorable Combinations of Toppings

cooked shrimp, broccoli, capers

tomato, artichoke hearts, broccoli

crisp bacon, lettuce, tomato,
cooked filet slices, mushrooms,
green onions

cooked salmon bits, tomatoes,
capers, Havarti dill cheese

cooked chicken, onions,
mushrooms, black olives

other combinations with peppers,
sausage, olives, sauteed leeks,
sundried tomatoes, fresh basil,
cilantro, exotic mushrooms
such as Portabello

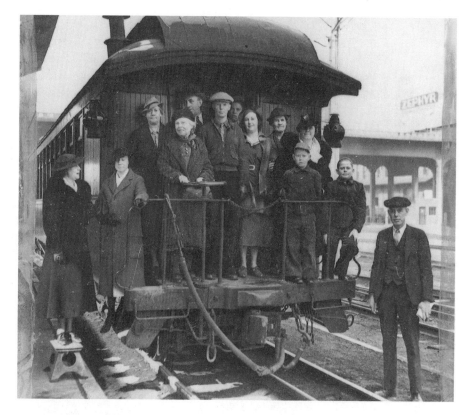

Last Train to Leadville

These passengers were aboard the Colorado and Southern as it left Denver's Union Station for the last time to travel the narrow-gauge route through South Park to Leadville. The final trip was made April 9, 1937.

Across Colorado

Josephine Roche

Josephine Roche had a graduate degree in social work from Columbia University when she became Denver's first policewoman in 1912. Later she inherited her father's place on the board of the Rocky Mountain Fuel Company and was elected its president.

Roche became the nation's first woman mine operator and the first mine operator in Colorado to recognize the newly organized United Mine Workers. Later, President Franklin Roosevelt named her an assistant secretary of the Treasury responsible for the Public Health Service, and a few years later, head of the National Youth Administration.

Roche often alienated other mine owners by siding with workers.

Marinated Grilled Lamb for Two

1	pound boneless lamb steaks, 1 inch thick
1	teaspoon curry powder
1	teaspoon five-spice powder
1	teaspoon sugar
½	teaspoon salt
2	tablespoons oyster sauce
½	medium onion, chopped
1	inch gingerroot, cut in small pieces
2	stalks lemongrass, chopped
1	small head iceberg lettuce, shredded
2	tomatoes, cut into wedges
1	cucumber, peeled and sliced

Serves 2

Place lamb in a 9x9-inch glass dish.

Mix the curry powder, five-spice powder, sugar, and salt with the oyster sauce, onion, gingerroot, and lemongrass. Spread this marinade mixture over meat and allow to marinate in refrigerator for 8 hours or overnight.

Over charcoal or gas, grill the lamb to desired doneness. Slice grilled lamb into strips. Garnish a platter with shredded lettuce, tomato, and cucumber. Place grilled lamb strips in center. Serve with hot rice.

This Vietnamese recipe is from Chef Anna at the T-WA Terrace.

Across Colorado

The Society of Colorado Pioneers

The Society of Colorado Pioneers held their first annual banquet and reunion at the Windsor Hotel in Denver, January 25, 1881. The program for the evening compared the pioneer food in 1859 to their own sumptuous fare. Names on the evening's program included Richard Sopris, presiding officer; Fred Stanton, who presented Denver's early history; George West, who represented the pioneer press; W. A. H. Loveland, who discussed transportation; and Colonel John Wanless, who gave a tribute "to those who have gone over the range."

–1859–

GRUB

Beans Bacon Hardtack
Dried Apples   Taos Lightning

–1881–

MENU

Raw Oysters

Mock Turtle Soup

Baked Filet of Trout Larded, Madeira Sauce

Parisian Potatoes

Boiled Leg of Mutton, Caper Sauce

Sweetbreads, Glazed, with French Peas

Tenderloin of Beef, Braized with Mushrooms

Roast Beef with Yorkshire Pudding

Roast Young Turkey Stuffed, Giblet Sauce

Boiled Potatoes, Green Peas, Stewed Tomatoes

Browned Mashed Potatoes   Spinach with Cream

Roast Quail Larded, with Jelly

Celery   Lettuce   Queen Olives

English Plum Pudding, Rum Sauce

Mince Pie Assorted Cake Lemon Meringue Pie

Confectionery Port Wine Jelly Orange Ice

Neapolitan Ice Cream

Fruit   Cheese   Coffee

Leg of Lamb with Lemon-Herb Stuffing

1	3½ pound boned leg of lamb
4	garlic cloves, slivered
	salt and pepper
2	teaspoons dried oregano, crumbled
1	lemon

Stuffing

4	cups dry bread cubes (may use packaged stuffing)
2	tablespoons minced onions
½	teaspoon salt
2	teaspoons sugar
¼	cup chopped fresh parsley or 1 tablespoon parsley flakes
½	cup chopped celery
¼	teaspoon each thyme, marjoram, sage
¼	cup melted butter
2	teaspoons lemon juice
½	cup water

Serves 6

Preheat oven to 350°.

In a large bowl, mix together all ingredients for stuffing. Open boned leg of lamb and place stuffing in cavity. Close cavity and tie with kitchen string. Place lamb in a 9x13-inch roasting pan. Make small cuts in surface of meat and insert garlic slivers. Rub roast with salt, pepper, and oregano. Squeeze juice from lemon over lamb. Roast uncovered for 1½ hours.

Since the 1890s, generations of Denver natives and their houseguests commingle their memories of childhood, summer, and Elitch's. Rides in the goat cart were a popular pastime when the Gardens first opened.

Across Colorado

Colorado Led the Way

In 1893, Colorado men voted to give the women of the state the right to vote. Women voted in the election of 1894 and elected three of their sex to the Colorado State Legislature. Colorado was the second state, following Wyoming, to grant women's suffrage.

A Denver polling place, possibly 1894

Across Colorado

Pork Tenderloin with Mustard Sauce

2	pork tenderloins, about 1–1$\frac{1}{2}$ pounds each

Marinade

$\frac{1}{2}$	cup vegetable oil
$\frac{1}{4}$	cup white wine vinegar
4	garlic cloves, minced
$\frac{1}{2}$	teaspoon salt
	pepper
$\frac{1}{2}$	teaspoon dried oregano
$\frac{1}{2}$	teaspoon dried rosemary
$\frac{1}{2}$	teaspoon dried thyme

Sauce

$\frac{1}{2}$	cup Chardonnay
6	tablespoons butter, sliced
2	teaspoons Dijon mustard
1–2	tablespoons country-style whole grain Dijon mustard
$\frac{1}{8}$	teaspoon dried tarragon
$\frac{1}{8}$	teaspoon dried chervil
$\frac{1}{2}$	cup cream
1	egg yolk

Preheat oven to 300°.

Place all marinade ingredients in a blender jar. Blend until emulsified. Place pork tenderloins in a glass or stainless steel bowl. Pour marinade over meat and marinate for 8 hours or overnight in refrigerator. When ready to roast, remove loins from marinade. Place meat in a 9x13-inch pan and roast for 55 minutes, turning halfway through roasting period.

In a 2-quart saucepan, over medium-high heat, reduce wine by half. Whisk in cold butter slices, whisking constantly. Reduce heat to medium low. Whisk in mustards and herbs. Add cream and egg yolk. Whisk thoroughly and keep sauce warm over low heat. Slice tenderloins and arrange on a serving platter. Pour warm sauce over slices.

S e r v e s   4

Across Colorado

Remember the Windsor

Parlor at the Windsor Hotel

A graying coed remembers:

"In 1952, the old Windsor was a derelict hotel, on a derelict street, housing impoverished people. It was long past its glory days of the 1880s. I remember this old Windsor well, because on the night of my twenty-first birthday a batch of us drove in from CU in Boulder to celebrate my maturity on its legendary floors. The Windsor was in its last throes of life.

"Upstairs in the Belle Starr room, we joined 'the locals' and danced to a small combo on that fabulous ballroom floor, constructed with birch and mahogany stripes and suspended so that you could dance all night without tiring. We shared my huge birthday sheetcake with the hotel's luckless inhabitants, who seemed amused by and welcomed the crazy kids from Boulder.

"We explored all the hotel, including the huge rosewood bar, with its assortment of bullet holes.

Two of our celebrants remember the wine cellar best—they were locked in it by mistake and weren't discovered until the next morning, just their dispositions the worse for wear."

In 1959, all of the Windsor's furnishings were auctioned away to souvenir collectors prior to the wrecker's ball.

Venus and Adonis adorned the Windsor's downstairs bar.

Pork Tenderloin with Orange Sauce

2	pork tenderloins, 1–1½ pounds each
1	tablespoon vegetable oil

Marinade

⅓	cup vegetable oil
¼	cup white wine vinegar
4	garlic cloves, minced
½	teaspoon salt
½	teaspoon black pepper
½	tablespoon dried rosemary
½	tablespoon dried oregano
½	tablespoon dried thyme

Sauce

2	tablespoons butter
2	unpeeled oranges, sliced
2	tablespoons dark brown sugar
¼	cup dark rum

Serves 4

Place all marinade ingredients in blender jar and process until emulsified. Place pork tenderloins in a glass or stainless steel bowl and cover with marinade. Allow to rest for 8–24 hours in the refrigerator. Remove meat from marinade and reserve liquid. Place 1 tablespoon oil in a 10–12-inch skillet and heat over medium-high heat. Sear pork in skillet for 5–8 minutes, turning so that all sides are browned. Add reserved marinade liquid to skillet and cover. Cook for 20 minutes over medium-low heat.

Meanwhile, make sauce. In another skillet melt butter and add orange slices. Cook over medium high-heat. Add brown sugar and rum and lower heat. Mash orange slices with a potato masher to release juice. Remove tenderloins to a cutting board. Add pan juices from the cooked pork to the sauce skillet. Simmer for 3–5 minutes. Adjust flavor for sweetness. Slice meat and arrange slices on a serving platter. Strain sauce and pour over meat slices or pass sauce in sauceboat.

Across Colorado

Buffalo Bill's Horse

Hazel Humphrey (1917–1995), a cofounder of the Jefferson County Historical Society, spent her childhood on a ranch in Bergen Park. Hazel told the story that Buffalo Bill died the same week that she was born (December 17, 1917) and that her father bought Buffalo Bill's horse at an estate sale. However, the horse refused to adjust to the quiet and serenity of Bergen Park. He loved noise and brass bands but the rustling of a bush would "spook" him. Finally the Humphreys had to stable the horse in Denver.

A city horse draws Daniels and Fisher's delivery wagon.

Grilled Pork Tenderloin

3	pounds pork tenderloin (3 loins)

Marinade

$\frac{1}{4}$	cup soy sauce
$\frac{1}{4}$	cup bourbon
2	tablespoons brown sugar

Sauce

1	tablespoon dry mustard
$1\frac{1}{2}$	teaspoons vinegar
$\frac{1}{3}$	cup sour cream
$\frac{1}{3}$	cup mayonnaise
	salt to taste
1	tablespoon chopped green onions

Serves 4 – 6

Place tenderloins in a glass or stainless steel bowl. Mix together all marinade ingredients and pour over tenderloins. Marinate for 8 hours or overnight in refrigerator.

Grill tenderloins for 10–12 minutes per side.

Mix together all sauce ingredients, folding in green onions last. Serve cold with meat.

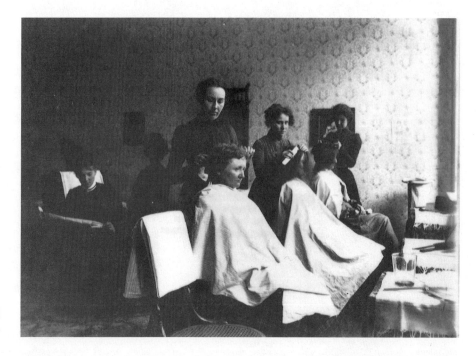

Getting beautiful at the first School
of Hairdressing in Denver

Across Colorado

Larimer Street in Denver, 1884. The telephone poles were 80 feet high.

Inner-City Danger

In the 1870s, newcomers streamed through Denver by the thousands on their way to the Colorado mining towns. Their enthusiasm for gold sometimes had to take a backseat to the realities of the new city. One early arrival who came through Denver from Maine in 1879 wrote back to his mother and sisters that he thought Denver was the prettiest city he had yet seen. Despite such praise, truth forced him to add that he had found it somewhat dangerous to be out on the street after dark on account of so many hogs running about. One was in danger of falling over them. *(From a letter written by Arthur B. Foster, as quoted in* Pioneers of the Roaring Fork *by Len Shoemaker.)*

Veal Scallopini

4	large fresh tomatoes or 2 pounds canned whole tomatoes
4	tablespoons butter (divided use)
4	tablespoons olive oil (divided use)
1	pound fresh mushrooms, sliced
$\frac{1}{2}$	green pepper, cut into $\frac{1}{4}$-inch dice
$\frac{1}{2}$	red pepper, cut into $\frac{1}{4}$-inch dice
1	onion, finely chopped
2	cloves garlic, minced
$\frac{2}{3}$	cup dry white wine or Italian white vermouth
	salt and pepper to taste
$\frac{1}{2}$	teaspoon dry tarragon leaves, crushed
2	pounds veal scallops, thinly sliced
$\frac{3}{4}$	cup freshly grated Romano cheese

Serves 4–6

Skin tomatoes and cut in half crosswise. Gently press out seeds and juice. Chop coarsely. Measure 3 cups and set aside. Over medium-high heat, heat 3 tablespoons butter and 2 tablespoons olive oil in a skillet with tight-fitting cover. Place mushrooms, peppers, onions, and minced garlic in skillet and saute until the onions are translucent. Add tomatoes, wine, salt, pepper, and tarragon. Mix well. Reduce heat to low. Cover and simmer sauce for approximately 30 minutes, stirring occasionally.

Wipe veal scallops with damp paper towels. Season with salt and pepper. In another skillet, heat 2 tablespoons olive oil and 1 tablespoon butter. Over medium heat, saute veal scallops a few slices at a time, till lightly browned on both sides. Add veal to sauce and simmer, covered, for 5 minutes. Sprinkle with grated Romano cheese. Serve with your favorite pasta.

Entertainment—1890

Across Colorado

Silver Dollar Meets Teddy

Silver Dollar and President Theodore Roosevelt

The *Denver Post* printed this picture of Silver Dollar (Echo) Tabor, daughter of Baby Doe and H.A.W., when she met Theodore Roosevelt in 1910 at a Denver Press Club picnic in Overland Park. An aspiring author, Silver Dollar had written a song, "Our President Roosevelt's Famous Colorado Bear Hunt," that brought her some local fame.

Silver Dollar never realized her artistic ambitions and was all but forgotten until she made the newspapers again in 1925 when she was found dead in a Chicago rooming house, a victim of either murder or suicide.

Veal Forestier

1½	pounds thin veal cutlets
1	clove garlic, cut in half
4	tablespoons flour
4	tablespoons butter
½	pound fresh mushrooms, thinly sliced
	juice of ½ lemon
¼	cup chicken broth
	salt and pepper
	grated lemon peel and/or chopped parsley

Serves 4–6

On cutting board, using a meat mallet, pound cutlets to ¼-inch thickness. Rub both sides of the meat with the cut side of the garlic. Cut veal into 2-inch pieces and dredge in flour. Heat an electric skillet to 325° and melt butter. Saute the veal until brown on both sides. Heap sliced mushrooms on veal. Add lemon juice, broth, salt, and pepper. Turn the skillet down to 215°, cover, and simmer 20 minutes, or until tender. To serve, sprinkle with grated lemon peel and/or parsley.

All aboard!

Across Colorado

Beef for a President

Saturday evening diners in the Ship's Tavern at the Brown Palace Hotel have President Dwight D. Eisenhower to thank for the popular special "Slices of Beef Tenderloin Sauté President." When President Eisenhower, a frequent guest of the Brown Palace during and after his presidency, returned from his golf game one day, he asked Executive Chef Ira Dole to prepare a new dish for the presidential dinner guest that evening. Despite such short notice, Chef Dole created an original beef tenderloin masterpiece. The dish became an instant success with "Ike," who ate it for three days in a row.

Prepare Slices of Beef Tenderloin Sauté President (see next page) for your most elegant dinner party.

Lieutenant Dwight D. Eisenhower and Mamie Doud Eisenhower, in Denver, about the time of their marriage in 1916

Brown Palace Slices of Beef Tenderloin Sauté President

Roux

8	ounces butter
²/₃	cup flour

Demi-Glace

4	tablespoons vegetable oil
1	pound veal bones
1	pound beef bones
1	large onion, chopped
³/₄	stalk celery, chopped
1	small carrot, chopped
1	bay leaf
	stems from ¹/₂ bunch parsley
1	cup tomato paste

Tenderloin

3	pounds beef tenderloin, cut into 12 4-ounce slices
8	tablespoons butter (divided use)
1	pound fresh mushrooms, sliced
3	shallots, finely chopped
1	clove garlic, finely chopped
1	cup red Burgundy wine
12	stalks fresh asparagus
2	tablespoons vegetable oil

Serves 6 – 8

Preheat oven to 350° when ready to prepare demi-glace.

For the roux, melt butter, add flour, and cook over medium to medium-high heat until mixture has a slightly nutty color, stirring constantly with a whisk. Set aside.

For the demi-glace, place vegetable oil in a 9x13-inch roasting pan. Add bones, onions, celery, and carrot. Place in oven and roast for 20 minutes. Add bay leaf, parsley, and tomato paste and roast approximately ¹/₂ hour longer, until golden brown. Transfer to a large stockpot. Add 4 quarts of water, season to taste with salt and pepper, and whisk in roux. Simmer for several hours until demi-glace is reduced to 1 quart. Remove bones, then strain through cheesecloth.

Place 2 tablespoons butter, mushrooms, shallots, and garlic in a saucepan and saute until tender. Add Burgundy wine and reduce by two-thirds. Add 2 cups of the demi-glace and simmer gently for 1 hour. Save remaining demi-glace for future use. Place asparagus in 10-inch pan with 2 tablespoons butter. Salt lightly. Cover with water and cook until tender. Set aside.

Melt remaining butter with 2 tablespoons vegetable oil in 12-inch pan and heat to frying point. Season slices of beef with salt and pepper and cook 3–4 minutes on each side to medium rare. Place slices of beef on serving platter. Pour sauce over beef, lay asparagus on top, and serve immediately.

This is the recipe that Executive Chef Ira Dole created on short notice and by special request of President Dwight D. Eisenhower.

Across Colorado

The Buckhorn Exchange

In 1893, Henry H. Zietz opened the Buckhorn Exchange at 1000 Osage Street in Denver. The

Henry Zietz (center) with some of the thirty Sioux tribal members who made a ceremonial visit to the Buckhorn Exchange in 1938. Zietz was presented with General Custer's sword, taken by the victors from the general's body after the Battle of the Little Big Horn. Sitting Bull had requested that after his death the sword be presented to Zietz to honor their long-term friendship. *(Photo courtesy of the Buckhorn Exchange)*

restaurant has been famous for more than 100 years for the wild game on its walls and the wild game on its menu.

At the age of thirteen, Zietz became a member of William F. Cody's band of buffalo scouts. While working for Buffalo Bill, Zietz met Chief Sitting Bull who bestowed on him the name "Shorty Scout." In 1938, the nephew of Sitting Bull, Chief Red Cloud, along with a band of Sioux Indians, visited Zietz at the Buckhorn. They set up their tepees in the north parking lot and during a solemn ceremony, presented him with Sitting Bull's Colt 45 and a sword taken from General George Custer at the Battle of the Little Big Horn. A photo of the event still hangs in the Buckhorn; the gun and sword were kept by the Zietz family when they sold the restaurant in 1973.

The walls of the Buckhorn are covered with more than 500 taxidermy pieces. These mounted heads and whole animals create a unique atmosphere where patrons may indulge in venison or buffalo in the presence of their dinner's ancestors.

See the South Mountains/Southwest Flavors section for the Buckhorn's famous recipe for Red Chili with Buffalo and Sausage.

Buckhorn Exchange Roasted Loin of Venison

venison loin

olive oil

sea salt

freshly ground black pepper

Sauce

1	cup apricot puree
2	cups water
1	tablespoon finely diced shallots
2	cups sundried cranberries
12	juniper berries
1	teaspoon black pepper
2	cups Cabernet Sauvignon
3	tablespoons cornstarch
$1/4$	cup water

Preheat oven to 350° when ready to prepare venison loin.

Combine apricot puree and water in a heavy saucepan and bring to boil. Reduce to a simmer. Add shallots, cranberries, juniper berries, pepper, and wine and return to boil. Reduce by one-fourth. Combine cornstarch with $1/4$ cup water and add to sauce. Return to boil and simmer for 5 minutes. Remove from heat.

Rub venison loin with olive oil and season with sea salt and pepper. Roast loin in oven for 30–40 minutes or until internal temperature reaches 120°. Remove roast from oven and let stand for 5–10 minutes before slicing. Serve $1/4$-inch-thick slices with warm sauce spooned over top.

Across Colorado

Aunt Clara Brown

Aunt Clara Brown was born a slave in Virginia in 1803. At the age of three, she and her mother were sold to a slave trader in Kentucky. She married in Kentucky and saw her husband and two daughters sold to different slave owners. She managed to purchase her freedom and moved to Leavenworth, Kansas, and then to Denver in 1859.

Aunt Clara had a keen business sense. She opened a laundry and boardinghouse and invested in grubstaking miners in Central City. Eventually she stockpiled enough money to fulfill a dream— returning to Kentucky twice to lead wagon trains of black pioneers back to Colorado.

In Denver, Aunt Clara started the first Sunday School and in Central City she founded the St. James Methodist Church. Shortly before she died in 1895, she realized a lifelong hope—she was reunited with one of her daughters.

In Central City, look for the bronze plaque honoring Aunt Clara in the St. James Methodist Church and for her Chair of Honor in the Opera House. At the Colorado capitol building, admire the stained-glass window designed in her honor for the Colorado Centennial-Bicentennial celebration.

Beef Goulash, German Style

2	pounds beef stew meat or chuck or round steak, cubed
3	tablespoons cooking oil
2	large yellow onions, thinly sliced
1	tablespoon Hungarian paprika
2	tablespoons red wine vinegar
1	tablespoon caraway seeds
$\frac{1}{2}$	tablespoon dried marjoram
$\frac{3}{4}$	teaspoon salt
$\frac{1}{2}$	teaspoon garlic salt
	pepper
3	tablespoons flour
2	cans beef broth or $2\frac{1}{2}$ cups homemade beef stock

Serves 4

In a 10–12-inch skillet, heat oil over medium-high heat. Add onions, lower heat, and cook until onions are translucent, about 15–20 minutes. Add paprika and cook 5 minutes longer. Add meat and cook until meat is lightly browned. Add vinegar, caraway seeds, marjoram, salt, garlic salt, and pepper. Stir in flour. Cook for 2–3 minutes. Add beef broth. Mix well, cover, and cook over very low heat for 1 hour. Serve with buttered noodles.

Mary Elitch was the spirit behind the creation of Elitch Gardens, taking over its management after the death of her husband. Here Mary is in the bear pit, directing the performance of her trained bears.

Across Colorado

A Medical Pioneer

Florence Sabin, M.D.

Florence Sabin was born in Central City in 1871 and went on to become a renowned physician and researcher at Johns Hopkins University and the Rockefeller Institute for Medical Research. After retirement, she straightened out Denver's public health services and became famous again for her public health work. Her statue represents Colorado in the U.S. Congress Statuary Hall.

A woman of many interests, Dr. Sabin died in 1953 while standing up to take a seventh-inning stretch while watching a Brooklyn Dodgers baseball game on television.

Elk or Venison with Mushrooms and Red Wine

2	pounds boneless elk or deer meat, cubed
2	tablespoons vegetable oil
2	tablespoons flour
	salt and pepper
1	cup red wine
$\frac{1}{2}$–$\frac{3}{4}$	cup beef bouillon
3	yellow onions, thinly sliced
$\frac{1}{2}$	pound fresh mushrooms, sliced
	hot cooked rice

Pour oil into a large skillet. Heat over medium-high heat. Add meat and brown. Sprinkle with flour and season with salt and pepper. Add red wine, beef bouillon, and onions. Stir gently and simmer 30–60 minutes, or until meat is tender. Add mushrooms and cook for an additional 15 minutes. Serve over rice.

Serves 4–6

Round 'Em Up Brisket

1	4–5-pound beef brisket
3	tablespoons vegetable oil

Sauce

1	package dry onion soup mix
1	onion, diced
2	stalks celery, minced
1	cup chili sauce
$\frac{1}{2}$	cup water
1	12-ounce bottle full-flavored beer

Preheat oven to 200°.

In a heavy skillet, brown brisket in vegetable oil. Place meat in a foil-lined roasting pan. Mix all sauce ingredients in a small bowl and pour over browned meat. Seal foil. Place in oven and bake for 3 hours. Open foil and bake 2 hours longer. Meat should be very tender.

Even better when made in advance and reheated. This brisket makes delicious sandwiches.

Serves 12

Across Colorado

Byers-Evans House

The Byers-Evans House reflects the character of two pioneer families that contributed to Denver's early civic community. It was built in 1883 by *Rocky Mountain News* publisher William Byers, and sold in 1889 to William Gray Evans, the son of John Evans, Colorado's second territorial governor. Evans family members occupied the house until 1981. Colorado Historical Society tour guides take visitors through the residence, which is filled with many of the original furnishings. Nestled on the northeast corner of Thirteenth and Bannock, the house is open daily except Mondays.

Beef Sukiyaki

½	cup low-salt soy sauce
3	heaping teaspoons sugar
¼	cup sweet white wine or sake
2	pounds beef sirloin or fillet, partially frozen
1	small package rice thread (saifun)
3	bunches green onions with tops, cut into 1-inch lengths
8	ounces mushrooms, quartered
2	cups bean sprouts
2	cups celery, cut into diagonal slices
1	can bamboo shoots, sliced diagonally, or 1 can water chestnuts, sliced
	fresh spinach, watercress, napa cabbage, or other vegetables in season
	radish roses
	fresh parsley
2	tablespoons vegetable oil
1	8-ounce package firm tofu, cubed

Serves 6 – 8

Combine soy sauce, sugar, and wine in a bowl and set aside. Slice partially frozen beef very thinly, using a sharp, heavy knife. Soak rice thread in boiling water for about 15 minutes. Drain in colander.

Arrange all vegetables attractively on a platter. Garnish with radish roses and parsley. Refrigerate until ready to cook. Preheat an electric skillet or wok. Add 2 tablespoons vegetable oil to hot skillet. Add meat to skillet and stir. When meat is almost cooked, cover with soy sauce mixture. Let it come to a boil without stirring. Add half of vegetables. Add greens last and cook until just tender. Add tofu.

Ingredients should not be mixed together as in stir-fry. Each should be placed separately in skillet or wok. Do not cook all the meat and vegetables at one time. Cook as much as is needed for the first serving. Keep adding more as needed.

Japanese food markets sell beef that is already sliced for sukiyaki.

Across Colorado

The long trip across the plains promised free land and a brighter future.

Across Colorado

The North Plains

The Pawnee Grasslands are archetypal of the northeast plains— just land, grass, and a wide-open sky. Then the Pawnee Buttes rise high to break up what some call the monotony of the landscape and others call the rolling ocean of golden grasses.

They came on foot and horseback. They came in covered wagons and carts. They crossed mile after mile of unbroken prairie, and after a while the wheels of their wagons cut tracks in the sod that left a record lasting for generations.

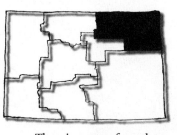

The pioneers of northeast Colorado were people who came to stay. They were not looking for the pot of gold at the end of the rainbow or nuggets of gold at the bottom of streams. They were looking for free land to homestead and for a brighter future. They cut sod and built houses and barns.

Babies were born and children grew. Soon there were teachers and preachers. Carpenters and blacksmiths came, then merchants and doctors. Before long towns dotted the prairie.

There were good times and bad. Success escaped some. The Colorado homesteaders had to adjust their dreams to Colorado reality: the scarcity of water. They were used to the heavy rainfall and humid air of the East and Midwest, but here they built canals and irrigated their crops or learned new ways of dry dirt farming. In the 1930s, the federal government bought back a total of 772,000 acres that now compose the Pawnee National Grasslands, mute testimony to the desperation of farmers during the Dust Bowl and Depression days.

The Pawnee Grasslands are archetypal of the north plains— just land, grass, and a wide-open sky. Then the Pawnee Buttes rise high to break up what some call the monotony of the landscape and others call the rolling ocean of golden grasses.

The South Platte River is the lifeline through the region. Its irrigation waters form a greenbelt that flows north to meet the North Platte. Along this greenway grows much of the food for the exploding population of Front Range cities—sugar beets, vegetables of all descriptions, corn, and beef; farther away from the river and its tributaries grow crops that require less water—wheat, milo, and three new cash crops— popcorn, sunflowers, and birdseed.

Mary Ellen's Diary

"Home is where the heart is."

without grub for a day. Say they want dinner for 18.

March 5—Baked 15 loaves of light bread. Got a letter from my loving friend Sally. She says she thinks I'm very near the jumping off place. But home is where the heart is. Love will make endurable a thing which else would overset the brain or heart. My good man got home from Crow Creek.

May 24—Commenced to teach school today in our parlor; nine scholars.

May 26—Milked the cows, got breakfast, dressed 44 pounds of butter and did the chores. Now it is time to begin school.

Many pioneer stories of the plains are written in the diaries of the women who came west as brides. Mary Ellen Bailey came in 1868 and settled with her new husband in northeastern Colorado. Excerpts from her diary:

February 8, 1869—Well, here is my good man home at last. All of them from the Junction been

Delicate Cream Wafers

Cookie Dough

1	cup sugar
8	ounces butter, softened
2	cups sifted flour
$\frac{1}{3}$	cup whipping cream

Filling

2	ounces butter, softened
$\frac{3}{4}$	cup powdered sugar
2	tablespoons whipping cream
1	teaspoon vanilla

Makes about 4 dozen

Preheat oven to 350°.

Place 1 cup sugar on a plate and set aside. Mix together butter, flour, and whipping cream to form a smooth dough. Wrap dough in plastic wrap and refrigerate until firm but not hard, 1–2 hours. Remove from refrigerator. Divide dough in half. Return half of dough to refrigerator.

Place other half of dough on a floured surface. Using a floured rolling pin, roll dough out to $\frac{1}{8}$-inch thickness. Cut dough with 1-inch round cookie cutter. Transfer each cookie to the plate of sugar and coat both sides with sugar. Place cookies on large baking sheet, prick with a fork, and bake for 7–9 minutes. Remove to a cooling rack. Repeat with remaining half of dough.

While cookies are cooling, prepare filling. Cream together butter and powdered sugar. Mix in cream and vanilla. Stick pairs of rounds together with filling.

This is an elegant holiday treat. Use red or green food coloring to give filling a festive Christmas appearance. Wafers freeze well.

Across Colorado

One Woman, Two Names

In the late 1800s, the old Overland Park racetrack in Wray was the place to go on a summer day. Few people were aware that Mrs. C. D. Thompson, whose horses consistently won ribbons at horse shows and often won at the track, was really the famous Mattie Silks of Market Street. Market Street in 1890 was Denver's most notorious sporting district and Mattie Silks was Queen of the Courtesans. Then why were her twenty-one horses stabled in Wray and why did she spend significant time there?

Mattie was born in 1847 and came from either Terre Haute, Indiana, or Buffalo, New York—she was never clear on that. She followed the railroads west, always as a madam. Somewhere in Kansas, she met Corteze D. Thompson, a dashing Texan. Over the years, a Frankie and Johnny romance developed—he was her man, but he did her wrong! His occupation seemed to be gambling and he was never noticeably successful. Mattie continually bailed him out and finally set him up on the ranch near Wray where he managed and trained her racehorses.

Mattie Silks made over a half million dollars from the world's oldest profession, but a dashing Texas gambler won and broke her heart.

Triple Threat Biscotti

2	cups flour
½	cup cocoa
1	teaspoon salt
1	teaspoon baking soda
6	tablespoons butter, softened
1	cup sugar
2	eggs
½	cup semisweet chocolate chips
1½	cups white chocolate chips (divided use)

M a k e s   2 4 – 3 0   b i s c o t t i

Preheat oven to 325°. Butter and flour one large cookie sheet.

In a large bowl, blend together flour, cocoa, salt, and baking soda. Using an electric mixer, cream together butter and sugar until light and fluffy. Add eggs and beat well. Using a wooden spoon or spatula, thoroughly blend flour mixture into butter mixture. Fold in semisweet chocolate chips and ½ cup of white chocolate chips.

With floured hands, divide the dough in half and form each half into a log approximately 12 inches long and 2 inches in diameter. Place on prepared cookie sheet and bake 30 minutes or until slightly firm to the touch. Remove from oven and cool for 10 minutes. With serrated knife, cut each log diagonally into ¾-inch slices. Place each slice flat on cookie sheet and bake for 5 minutes. Turn and bake for an additional 5 minutes. Cool on wire rack.

Place remaining white chocolate chips in a microwave-safe bowl. Heat on medium power until chips are melted. Stir to blend. Dip ends of cooled biscotti in melted chocolate; set on wire rack and allow chocolate to harden before storing in airtight container.

Biscotti will keep in a covered container for 1–2 weeks.

This recipe comes from the River Run Inn in Salida. Read about the early times at this establishment in the South Mountains/Southwest Flavors section.

Across Colorado

Lamb Day in Fort Collins

Lamb Day was a major event in turn-of-the-century Fort Collins. Its purpose was to remind the world that Fort Collins was one of the largest lamb-producing districts in America.

SPECIAL for LAMB DAY ONLY

10% BELOW COST on all Vehicles, Surreys and Delivery Wagons

P. ANDERSON MERCANTILE CO.
Dealers in Shelf and Heavy Hardware

FORT COLLINS, COLORADO   PHONE SHERWOOD 41

(above) Fort Collins' merchants celebrated Lamb Day with special sales in 1910. (right) Lambs feeding in pens southeast of Fort Collins, 1924

In 1909 all of Fort Collins participated in the event—200 lambs were roasted in a pit the full length of a city block on Oak Street. Local butchers carved and

students at Colorado Agricultural College (now CSU) served. It took more than two hours just to hand around plates to the 15,000 local and out-of-town guests who had arrived by excursion trains from

neighboring towns and as far east as Chicago.

The following year, rain and hail failed to dampen the spirits of the 20,000 participants who devoured

even more than the 200 lambs, 500 pounds of beef, 3,200 loaves of bread, two barrels of pickles, and the 100 gallons of coffee consumed in 1909. The chairman of the event scoured all the mint beds of Larimer County to find enough leaves to make the 10 gallons of mint jelly needed to complement the lamb.

Sponsors of the event—the merchants of Fort Collins and the local sheep feeders—proclaimed, "We have let America know where to come for lamb chops."

Italian Almond Biscotti

8	ounces butter, at room temperature
1½	cups sugar
4	eggs
1	teaspoon vanilla
4½	cups flour
1	teaspoon baking powder
2	cups blanched slivered almonds

Makes 4 dozen

Preheat oven to 375°.

Using an electric mixer, cream butter and sugar together until light and fluffy. Add eggs and vanilla and beat well. Using a wooden spoon or spatula, blend in flour and baking powder to form a smooth, firm dough. Fold in almonds.

Divide dough into quarters and form each quarter into a roll 1½ inches in diameter. Place rolls on a large cookie sheet and bake for 25 minutes or until golden. Remove from oven and cool for 10 minutes. Slice each log into ¾-inch slices. Place slices flat on cookie sheet and return to 250° oven. Bake for 8 minutes, then turn biscotti over, and bake for an additional 8 minutes or until biscotti are dry and crisp.

Cool and store in airtight container. These cookies keep for several weeks and are traditional with espresso drinks.

Across Colorado

Legal Lady Citizens

A Petition to the Honorable City Council of Fort Collins, 1905: "We, the undersigned, legal lady citizens of Fort Collins, Colorado, do hereby respectfully petition your honorable body as follows:

"It is generally known that the crowds which collect during the afternoons and evenings on several corners of our city, particularly the northeast corner of College and Mountain Avenues, at the northwest corner of Linden and Walnut Streets and on the First National Bank corner, are a detriment to business houses and cause a great intimidation to ladies who wish to pass said places, not caring to be remarked at or trail their dresses through tobacco spit.

"Therefore, we respectfully petition your honorable body to pass an Ordinance prohibiting such crowds to gather, or any other means which your honorable body deems necessary to prevent such gatherings."

A street corner in Fort Collins about 1905 where crowds of rowdies intimidated lady passersby

A more recent picture of the Fort Collins main thoroughfare in 1922

Tamarade Cherry Strip

2	cups flour
$^1/_4$	cup sugar
$^3/_4$	teaspoon salt
1	tablespoon baking soda
$^1/_4$	cup shortening
1	egg, well beaten
$^1/_2$	cup milk
1	21-ounce can cherry pie filling
$^1/_2$–$^3/_4$	cup sifted powdered sugar

Serves 12

Preheat oven to 350°.

Mix flour, sugar, salt, and baking soda in a large bowl. Cut shortening into flour mixture, using a pastry blender, until mixture forms large crumbs. Stir in egg and milk and mix to form a soft dough. Press two-thirds of dough into the bottom of a 10x15-inch jelly roll pan. Top with cherry pie filling.

Roll out remaining third of dough on a lightly floured surface into a long rectangle. Cut dough into strips and place them in a crisscross pattern over top of filling. Bake for 20–30 minutes. Cool slightly and sprinkle with sifted powdered sugar to form a glaze. Serve freshly baked.

Chocolate Scotcheroos

1	cup sugar
1	cup light corn syrup
1	cup peanut butter
6	cups crisp rice cereal
1	6-ounce package chocolate chips
1	6-ounce package butterscotch chips

Makes 2 dozen

Butter a 9x13-inch pan.

In a 3-quart saucepan over moderate heat, cook sugar and corn syrup until mixture boils. Remove from heat. Stir in peanut butter and cereal. Press mixture into prepared pan.

Place chocolate and butterscotch chips into a small glass bowl. Cover with plastic wrap and microwave on low power until chips are melted. Stir to blend, then spread over cookie mixture. Chill until firm, then cut into bars.

Beloved by teenagers, their parents, and grandparents.

Across Colorado

In Praise of Horsepower

Skiing on the plains with horsepower

In her recorded memories of a childhood in northeastern Colorado, Alice Wells Helzer remembered the importance of horses on ranches, farms, and homesteads: "Few people can imagine nowadays how important, useful, and downright indispensable horses were. They were our only source of power to break and cultivate the ground, to cut and stack hay, and to thresh grain. We were dependent on horses for all transportation and travel. In driving and caring for cattle, nothing takes the place of a saddle horse."

Alice called horses a source of security and safety. "In that big country, one felt like a very small, unimportant, helpless human being. On a horse with his strength, instinct and intelligence working for you, nothing could harm you. There is no companion like a good horse. People who call a dog man's best friend have never owned or made friends with a horse."

Across Colorado

Homesteaders' Coffee Cookies

1	cup raisins
1	cup boiling water
1	cup granulated sugar
1	cup light brown sugar
1	cup shortening or margarine
1	cup cold, very strong coffee
1	teaspoon vanilla
3	eggs
5	cups flour
1	teaspoon baking soda
1$\frac{1}{2}$	teaspoons baking powder
1	teaspoon cinnamon
1	teaspoon nutmeg
1	teaspoon salt
1	cup walnuts, chopped

Makes 6 dozen big, soft, friendly cookies

Preheat oven to 350°. Grease cookie sheets generously.

Place raisins in a small bowl. Cover with 1 cup boiling water and set aside for 5 minutes. Drain raisins, reserving $\frac{1}{2}$ cup of liquid. Place drained raisins and reserved liquid in a large bowl. Add sugars and shortening. Stir to melt shortening and dissolve sugars. Allow to cool for 15 minutes. Add coffee, vanilla, and eggs and mix well. Sift together dry ingredients and gradually add to the raisin-sugar mixture. Blend well and add nuts. Drop by tablespoon onto prepared cookie sheets. Flatten slightly with fork dipped in cold water or bottom of a glass dipped in sugar. Bake for 10 minutes. Remove to cooling rack.

Across Colorado

Burlington's Elitch Carousel

A seahorse, a lion, a camel, a tiger, and a giraffe with a snake encircling its neck—animals in rows of three prancing around in circles to the booming tones of a Wurlitzer military band organ. It sounds intriguing but was considered folly by the frugal citizens of Burlington, when in 1928, three county commissioners purchased the elegant, twenty-three-year-old carousel from Elitch Gardens in Denver and installed it at the Kit Carson County fairgrounds. Unfortunately, the Great Depression hit Burlington and the county had to forgo its fair. By 1937, when the fair was resumed, mice had destroyed the organ rolls and the exotic animals made their rounds to mundane recorded music.

But the carousel was destined for better times. In the mid-seventies a group of concerned citizens began the painstaking restoration of the carousel. All of the animals were meticulously repaired and repainted. The original paintings were returned to their former beauty and the organ to its original grandeur. Today the Kit County Carousel is listed in the National Register of Historic Places and a new generation is enjoying the sight, sound, and a rollicking ride on an animal that exists only in the imaginations of the young at heart.

Elitch's carousel

Across Colorado

Christmas Applesauce Cake

2	cups applesauce
1	tablespoon baking soda
1	cup sour cream
2	cups sugar
3	cups all-purpose flour
1	tablespoon ground cloves
1	tablespoon cinnamon
$^1/_4$	teaspoon salt
3	eggs, lightly beaten
1	cup chopped walnuts
1	cup raisins

Serves 12

Preheat oven to 350°. Grease and flour a 9x13-inch pan.

Place all cake ingredients into a large bowl and mix well with a wooden spoon. Pour batter into prepared pan. Bake for 45 minutes, or until a wooden toothpick inserted into center of cake comes out clean. Cool cake completely.

Serve with vanilla ice cream or frost with prepared frosting of your choice.

Delicious any day of the year.

Household Hints—1902

Was there ever a publication—newspaper, magazine, cookbook—without household hints? In 1902 you might have read:
- A linen-covered sachet filled with fragrant dried leaves from an oriental shrub induces sleep.
- A small box of lime in the pantry will help keep the air dry and pure. It should be renewed occasionally.
- A few drops of turpentine in hot starch add luster to ironed linen.
- Grass stains on children's clothing may be eradicated by rubbing moistened cream of tartar on them, or by dipping them in alcohol.

Making hay and enjoying it,
about 1911

Oatmeal Chocolate Chip Cake

1¾	cups boiling water
1	cup quick oatmeal
4	ounces margarine
1	cup granulated sugar
1	cup firmly packed brown sugar
2	eggs
1¾	cups flour
1	teaspoon baking soda
½	teaspoon salt
1	tablespoon cocoa
1	12-ounce package chocolate chips
½–¾	cup nuts, chopped

Serves 12–16

Preheat oven to 350°. Grease and flour a 9x13-inch cake pan or two 9-inch round pans.

In a large bowl, pour boiling water over oatmeal. Let stand 10 minutes. Add margarine and stir until melted. Add sugars, eggs, flour, baking soda, salt, and cocoa and mix well. Fold ½ cup chocolate chips into batter. Pour into prepared pan. Sprinkle nuts and remaining chocolate chips on top. Bake for 35–45 minutes. No frosting is necessary.

Unlikely Intellectual

Who would have expected—in 1842—to find a European-educated fur trader camped on an island in the Platte River, near what is now Fort Morgan? The camp was under the direction of a man named Chabonard, who had acquired a classic education and could converse quite fluently in German, French, and Spanish, as well as English and several Indian languages.

Chabonard was actually Jean Baptiste Charbonneau, who as an infant had been carried papoose-style on the back of his famous mother, Sacajawea, Bird Woman, as she guided Lewis and Clark. William Clark became fond of the child and arranged for him to be educated in St. Louis. Later the youth spent six years traveling throughout Europe.

However, the call of the West was strong, and he returned to America in 1829 to trap for the American Fur Company. For the next half century, he was a familiar figure throughout the western frontier.

Across Colorado

Creative Cookery

Wood ranges of grand proportions were needed to cook all the food a large and hungry family required.

In 1907 the pioneers of Larimer County held a reunion in Fort Collins. The ladies talked about their cooking experiences when necessity was the mother of invention. How Mrs. Stuart made squash pie has gone down in history. She said, "I make a good many pies. I made 35 last week."

"You did? What kind, dried apple? It must have been quite expensive," was the chorus with which the statement was received. "Well," said Mrs. Stuart, "they weren't so expensive the way I made them. They were squash pies. I did not use milk or eggs. I mashed the squash and sweetened it with molasses, then put in plenty of spice to make them tasty, and as for the crust, instead of lard, I bought suet at the market and rendered it myself and used that for shortening."

Everyone present imagined the taste of those pies. "You certainly have the gift of invention," said Mrs. D. W. Taft politely. Mrs. Stuart looked pleased. Then someone less tactful said, "Why, I shouldn't think they would be good." Mrs. Stuart straightened up and with pride and dignity replied, "Father and the boys liked them."

Across Colorado

Spud 'n Spice Cake

1³/₄	cups sugar
1	cup cold mashed potatoes
³/₄	cup shortening
¹/₂	teaspoon salt
1¹/₂	teaspoons cinnamon
1	teaspoon nutmeg
3	eggs
1	teaspoon baking soda
1	cup buttermilk
2	cups flour

Quick Caramel Frosting

1¹/₄	cups butter
³/₄	cup firmly packed brown sugar
¹/₄	cup milk
2	cups powdered sugar, sifted
1	teaspoon vanilla

Serves 12

Preheat oven to 350°. Grease and flour two 9-inch round cake pans.

Using an electric mixer, cream together sugar, potatoes, shortening, salt, and spices. Beat for 4 minutes on medium speed. Add eggs and beat until thoroughly blended. In a glass measuring cup, combine soda with buttermilk and add alternately with flour, beginning and ending with flour. Pour batter into prepared pans. Bake for 40 minutes, or until a wooden toothpick inserted into center of cake comes out clean. Cool thoroughly.

While cake cools, prepare frosting. Melt butter over low heat. Stir in brown sugar. Cook over low heat for 2 minutes. Add milk. Bring to full boil. Cool to lukewarm without stirring. Blend in powdered sugar and vanilla and beat until smooth and of spreading consistency. Spread evenly on layers and sides of cooled cake.

Across Colorado

Utopia in Colorado

Greeley is one of the few planned utopias that can be labeled a success story. Horace Greeley, publisher of the *New York Tribune,* and his agricultural editor,

Nathan Meeker, established the Union Colony at the confluence of the Cache la Poudre and South Platte Rivers in 1870. They sold memberships in their colony for

$155, but only to "temperance men of good character." With the membership fees, Greeley and Meeker purchased 12,000 acres for $60,000. In return, the members received a town lot and land for farming.

Although some scoffers laughed at Greeley's anti-drinking views and considered teetotaling a blemish on the frontier character, the colony and its town of Greeley prospered. An irrigation system was built, as was a library; there were organized concerts and lectures, a farmers' club, and a dramatic association. Intoxicating liquors were strictly forbidden, a circumstance that may have accounted for an extraordinary number of saloons in Evans, the small town next door.

Members of the Union Colony who settled Greeley in 1870

Out-of-the-Processor Chocolate Cake

$2/3$	cup cocoa
$2^1/4$	cups flour
$1^3/4$	cups sugar
$1^1/2$	teaspoons baking powder
$1^1/2$	teaspoons salt
$1^1/2$	cups orange juice or water
2	teaspoons vanilla
3	eggs
$1^1/4$	cups vegetable oil

Serves 10–12

Preheat oven to 350°. Generously grease and flour a 10-inch Bundt pan.

Fit the steel blade attachment on the food processor. Place all the dry ingredients in the processor bowl and process until blended (about 10 seconds). Pour in orange juice, vanilla, and eggs. Start processor, add oil through the feeder tube, and process 45 seconds. When batter is thoroughly mixed, pour into prepared Bundt pan. Bake for 55–60 minutes. Cool cake in pan upright for 10 minutes, then invert. When completely cool, remove from pan and glaze with your choice of icing or sprinkle with powdered sugar.

Jackie Davis, a Denver historian who co-authored Places Around the Bases *with Diane Bakke, contributed this recipe, which was given to her by a relative. She says, "Somehow, the process of passing recipes along hasn't changed much since 1876 when Colorado became a state."*

Plum Delicious

$1/2$	cup sugar
$2/3$	cup red wine
4	tablespoons melted butter
8	fresh, ripe Italian plums, halved and pitted
$1/4$	teaspoon grated nutmeg
$1/4$	teaspoon black pepper, freshly ground
1	pint vanilla ice cream or 1 small pound cake

In a 10-inch skillet, combine sugar and wine. Cook over medium heat until sugar dissolves. Add butter to skillet along with plum halves and cook over medium-low heat, covered, for 10-15 minutes or until plums are tender but not mushy. Remove plums from skillet and increase heat to medium high. Add nutmeg and pepper. Cook until sauce is reduced by half. Return plums to pan and reheat. Serve warm over ice cream or cake.

Serves 4–6

Across Colorado

Buffalo Bill on the Plains

Buffalo Bill standing third from right

As soon as he signed on as a pony express rider in 1860 in Julesburg at the age of fourteen, William Frederick Cody became a familiar figure in the West. His familiar nickname "Buffalo Bill" came later.

When the Civil War was over, the Union Pacific Railroad began construction westward from Omaha. The hearty appetites of many workers had to be satisfied, and since the line was going through buffalo country, buffalo became the food of choice. William F. Cody was one of those contracted to supply the meat. During his seventeen months on the job, he brought in 4,280 animals, earning him the name "Buffalo Bill," which followed him the rest of his life.

Across Colorado

Snowdrift Meringue Torte

4	ounces butter or margarine
1½	cups sugar (divided use)
4	egg yolks, lightly beaten
¼	cup milk
1	cup cake flour
1	teaspoon baking powder
1	teaspoon vanilla
4	egg whites
½	cup pecans or almonds, finely chopped
1	cup whipping cream
¼	cup powdered sugar
	fresh, frozen, or canned fruit

Serves 8–12

Preheat oven to 375°. Lightly grease and flour two 9-inch round cake pans.

Using an electric mixer or wooden spoon, beat together butter, ½ cup sugar, egg yolks, milk, cake flour, baking powder, and vanilla. Pour half of the batter into each cake pan.

With an electric mixer or wire whisk, beat egg whites until stiff, gradually adding 1 cup sugar. Spread meringue over the cake batter. Sprinkle with chopped nuts. Bake for 20-25 minutes or until torte is lightly browned. Cool cakes in pans for 10 minutes, then invert on rack, remove from pans, and cool completely.

An hour or less before serving, whip cream stiffly with powdered sugar. Spread bottom cake layer with whipped cream and, if desired, slices of fruit. Stack the two cake layers. To serve, slice cake and garnish with lightly sweetened strawberries, raspberries, blueberries, peaches, or other fresh, frozen, or canned fruit. Top with sweetened whipped cream.

Across Colorado

Wash Day at the Homestead

Alice Wells Helzer, born in 1898 in Fort Collins, described how laundry was managed on the homestead where she spent her early years. "Mama had a hand powered washer and hand wringer. She very wisely refused to use a washboard. I remember this machine because it was run by child power which oftener than not meant me. She would say, 'Run this machine full fifteen minutes.' How I watched the clock. Those were the longest fifteen minutes that ever elapsed. I was always sure the clock had stopped."

Women took their work to the porch during a hot summer's day on the plains.

Amaretto Cheesecake

Crust

1½ cups chocolate cookie crumbs

2 tablespoons butter, melted

Filling

12 ounces cream cheese, at room temperature

⅔ cup sugar

2 eggs

⅓ cup Amaretto or other almond-flavored liqueur

Topping

4 ounces milk chocolate candy, melted

½ cup sour cream

Serves 8–10

Preheat oven to 325°.

In a small bowl, mix cookie crumbs and butter until well blended. Press crumbs firmly into a deep 9-inch glass pie pan.

With an electric mixer, beat cream cheese and sugar. Add eggs and mix until well blended. Carefully stir in liqueur. Pour into prepared crust and bake for 50–60 minutes. Remove from oven and cool for 1 hour.

For topping, melt chocolate candy, add sour cream, and blend until smooth. Pour over cooled cheesecake and refrigerate for 4–8 hours before serving.

"I Vant to Go Back!"

Elizabeth Aagaard Larsen came to Brush, Colorado, with her family in 1918, when she was three years old. Her parents had emigrated from Denmark and first lived in Iowa several years, where Elizabeth was born.

In later years, the family recalled that in the fall in Brush, their father butchered their ducks and hung them to freeze up under the eaves of their house. Each evening at twilight the coyotes appeared on the sandhills horizon and began their evening serenade. After dark, the coyotes would creep down to the house, jump up on the siding, and try to snatch a duck that was so temptingly swinging by its neck.

Little Elizabeth, who spoke a mixture of Danish and English, would cry to her mother, "I vant to go back to Iova ven the coyotes they hyle at the door!"

Elizabeth Aagaard's mother and Aunt Mary are in the house-cleaning mode at their home near Brush. Note dust caps that protected hair.

Chocolate Velvet Cheesecake

Crust

2	8½-ounce packages chocolate wafers, finely ground
6	ounces butter, melted and cooled
½	teaspoon cinnamon

Filling

12	ounces high-quality semisweet chocolate or chocolate chips
2	tablespoons butter
3	8-ounce packages cream cheese, at room temperature
1½	cups heavy cream or half-and-half
1	teaspoon vanilla
1	cup sugar
3	eggs, at room temperature
3	tablespoons cocoa

Serves 12–16

Preheat oven to 350°. Place oven rack in center of oven.

Mix cookie crumbs, butter, and cinnamon. Press crumbs firmly and evenly onto bottom and up the sides of a 10-inch springform pan.

Refrigerate for 30 minutes or longer.

Using low power, microwave chocolate and butter in a small glass bowl covered with plastic wrap until chocolate is melted. Stir to blend and set aside.

Using an electric mixer, beat cream cheese for 5 minutes. Stir in cooled chocolate mixture. Slowly add cream and vanilla. Beat well. Add sugar, eggs, and cocoa. Beat at low speed, scraping sides of bowl, until batter is well blended. Pour batter into chilled crust. Place springform pan on a cookie sheet and bake for 30 minutes. Reduce heat to 325° and bake for 30 minutes longer. Turn off oven, and with door slightly ajar, leave cake in oven for an additional 30 minutes. Remove to cooling rack. Cool for 2 hours. Cover and refrigerate for at least 8 hours. Cake will keep for 3–5 days and is an absolute treat.

Across Colorado

Butter on the Go

A type of butter churn

"Aunty" Elizabeth Stone was the first white woman resident of Fort Collins, where she lived from 1864 until her death in 1895. In the meanwhile, she ran a boarding-house for the officers of Camp Collins, managed a hotel, set up Fort Collins's first school in her house, built and managed both the first flour mill and the first brickyard, and cared for her eight children. Aunty had come from New York via Minnesota, then to Denver in 1862.

On the trip west, the Stones' wagon team was composed of two cows yoked together like oxen, which they drove to Denver, milking the cows regularly and making butter on the way. In making the butter, Aunty reported that no churn was employed. It was produced by the motion of the wagon, "and it was good butter, too."

Across Colorado

Mount Garfield Peach Cheesecake

Crust

3	cups finely crushed vanilla wafers
½	cup ground pecans (use coffee grinder or food processor)
8	ounces butter or margarine, melted

Filling

1	8-ounce package light cream cheese, at room temperature
2	8-ounce packages regular cream cheese, at room temperature
1	can sweetened condensed milk
1	teaspoon vanilla
3	eggs, beaten
6	fresh peaches, peeled and chunked
1½	teaspoons cinnamon
	light whipped topping
	fresh peach slices for garnish
1	tablespoon powdered sugar
2	tablespoons lemon juice

Serves 12–16

Preheat oven to 350°.

Blend vanilla wafers, ground pecans, and butter or margarine. Press firmly onto the bottom and up the sides of a 10-inch springform pan.

Using an electric mixer, blend together the cream cheeses, sweetened condensed milk, and vanilla. Add the beaten eggs and mix well. Gently stir in the peaches and cinnamon. Pour filling into the crust and bake for 1 hour. Remove cake from oven. Cool for 15 minutes in pan, then loosen sides, and cool 30 minutes longer. Remove pan sides and chill for at least 4 hours, preferably overnight. Top with light whipped topping and garnish with fresh peach slices mixed with powdered sugar and lemon juice.

The Mount Garfield Bed and Breakfast in Clifton serves this cheesecake during peach season.

Across Colorado

Pioneer Ingenuity

It is impossible to exaggerate the ingenuity of the pioneer homemakers. Hard times encouraged inventiveness and making do became a way of life, all of which was seasoned with a dash of native creativity. Among the recipes not found in many cookbooks is this:

Nettle Soup

Collect a quantity of nettles. Wash and boil the nettle shoots, then rub the parts through a sieve. Melt a little butter, sprinkle in an ounce of flour, and add the nettles and enough milk (a little at a time) to make a soup of the desired thickness. Bring to a boil, simmer for a few minutes, and season. All kinds of nettles are worth a cautious trial.

Nettles—in soup the sting may change to zing.

Heavenly Chocolate Pie

Crust

1/2	cup sugar
1/8	teaspoon cream of tartar
2	egg whites
1/2	cup chopped pecans

Filling

1 1/2	cups semisweet chocolate chips
6	tablespoons hot water
2	teaspoons vanilla
2	cups heavy cream, whipped and slightly sweetened

Serves 6 – 8

Preheat oven to 275°. Generously butter a 9-inch pan.

Mix sugar and cream of tartar together. Using an electric mixer, beat egg whites until stiff but not dry. Add sugar mixture gradually, beating continuously until sugar is incorporated. Line buttered pan with mixture, bringing mixture up sides of pan, but not covering rim. Sprinkle pecans over "crust." Bake for 1 hour, or until a delicate brown. Cool thoroughly before filling.

Melt chocolate over hot water in a double boiler. Stir in water. Cook until thick. Cool. Add vanilla. Fold in cream. Fill meringue shell and refrigerate for 3–4 hours. Garnish with additional whipped cream if desired.

"Heavenly" is the right word for this dessert.

Cranberry Pie

1	9-inch pie shell, baked
2	cups fresh cranberries
1/4–1/2	cup sugar (or to taste)
3	tablespoons cornstarch
	whipped cream

Serves 6 – 8

Place cranberries in a 2-quart saucepan and add just enough water to cover. Bring to a boil and cook until cranberry skins pop. Remove from heat, put mixture through a sieve or mash until soft, and then strain. Add enough water to the strained pulp to make 3 cups of liquid. Stir in sugar. Place cornstarch in a small bowl. Blend in 1–2 tablespoons of water to dissolve cornstarch. Add to pulp. Place pulp in a saucepan and cook until thickened. Cool. Pour into baked pie shell. Refrigerate for 4–6 hours and serve with sweetened whipped cream. Recipe can be doubled.

Sophie Berglin brought this recipe from Sweden to Berthoud in 1898.

Across Colorado

Greeley Grasshopper Cake

Did you ever eat grasshopper cake? (No relative of Grasshopper Pie.) If you are a newcomer to Greeley, you will shrug your shoulders, turn up your nose, and shudder, but if you belong to a pioneer family there, you will smile and say, "Yes, my grandmother made it!"

Grasshoppers compounded the difficulties that the intrepid band of Greeley colonists had to overcome. Between 1872 and 1874, grasshoppers stripped the countryside of everything they could devour. The pests left nothing that was worth taking. Feed for chickens was scarce, eggs were a prohibitive price, and cake became an unknown luxury.

Mrs. Ralph Hilton, a plucky, capable woman, concocted a cake made without eggs and took it to a social. The eggless cake was christened "Grasshopper Cake" and the recipe was welcomed in all homes when the price of eggs went up. Grasshopper cake is still made by Greeley pioneer families.

Early street scene in Greeley

Lemon Cloud Pie

Pastry

1	cup all-purpose flour
$\frac{1}{2}$	teaspoon salt
$\frac{1}{3}$	cup vegetable shortening
1	egg, slightly beaten
1	tablespoon grated lemon rind
1	tablespoon fresh lemon juice

Filling

1	cup sugar (divided use)
$\frac{1}{4}$	cup cornstarch
1	cup water
$\frac{1}{3}$	cup fresh lemon juice
2	egg yolks
4	ounces cream cheese, at room temperature
$\frac{1}{2}$	cup whipping cream

Garnish

	fresh raspberries and fresh mint leaves

Serves 6–8

Preheat oven to 400°.

Sift flour and salt into a mixing bowl. Cut in shortening, using a pastry blender. Combine egg, lemon rind, and juice and sprinkle over flour mixture, stirring with fork until dough is moist enough to hold together. Form dough into a ball. Roll out on a floured surface into a $10\frac{1}{2}$-inch circle. Fit pastry into pan and trim. Put trimmings into small baking pan. Bake shell and trimmings for 12–15 minutes. Cool.

In saucepan, mix $\frac{3}{4}$ cup sugar and cornstarch. Add water, lemon juice, slightly beaten egg yolks and blend. Cook over medium heat until very thick, stirring constantly. Remove from heat, add cream cheese, and blend well. Cool. Whip cream and add remaining $\frac{1}{4}$ cup sugar. Fold into cooled lemon mixture and spoon into pie shell. Crumble baked pastry trimmings around edge of pie. Chill at least 2 hours. Garnish with a sprinkling of red raspberries and mint leaves.

An excellent, refreshing dessert.

Dried Apple Pies

Pioneers moving west soon became bored with the monotony of eating the same old food day after day. This prompted some unknown diner to write a poetic tribute to the ever-present dried apple.

Dried Apple Pies

I loathe, abhor, detest, despise
Abominate dried-apple pies.
I like good bread, I like good meat,
Or anything that's fit to eat;
But of all poor grub beneath the
*   skies,*
The poorest is dried-apple pies.
Give me the toothache, or sore eyes,
But don't give me dried-apple pies.

The farmer takes his gnarliest fruit,
'Tis wormy, bitter, and hard, to
*   boot;*
He leaves the hulls to make us
*   cough,*
And don't take half the peeling off.
Then on a dirty cord 'tis strung
And in a garret window hung,
And there it serves as roost for flies,
Until its made up into pies.
Tread on my corns, or tell me lies,
But don't pass me dried-apple pies.

A social gathering at a sod house on the northeastern plains

Across Colorado

Tangy Lemon Pudding

1	cup sugar
1	tablespoon butter
2	tablespoons flour
2	egg yolks, well beaten
1	cup milk
1	large lemon, juice and grated rind
2	egg whites, stiffly beaten

Serves 6

Preheat oven to 325°.

Using an electric mixer or wooden spoon, cream together sugar, butter, and flour. Gradually add egg yolks, milk, lemon juice, and rind. Gently fold in beaten egg whites. Pour into an ungreased 8x8-inch pan. Set pan in larger pan of hot water. Bake for 1 hour. Serve immediately.

This light, lemony dessert is as delicious today as it was 100 years ago when Mary Anderson brought it from Ohio to the ranch near the Chalk Cliffs west of Grover. Grover's annual celebration, the Earl Anderson Memorial Rodeo, is named in honor of Mary's husband.

Overnight Chocolate Bread Pudding

9	slices day-old high-quality white bread
5	ounces imported dark chocolate
2	cups whipping cream
4	tablespoons dark rum
3/4	cup powdered sugar
3	ounces butter
1/4	teaspoon cinnamon
2	teaspoons grated orange rind
3	eggs

Serves 6-8

When ready to bake, preheat oven to 350°.

Trim crusts from bread, then cut each bread square into 4 triangles. Set aside. Over hot water in top of double boiler, mix chocolate, cream, rum, powdered sugar, butter, cinnamon, and orange rind. Stir until chocolate and butter are melted. Remove from heat and cool. In a separate bowl, whisk eggs and add to cooled chocolate mixture, blending well. Spoon about one-third of chocolate mixture into a 7x9x2-inch glass baking dish. Arrange half the bread triangles over chocolate. Pour another third of remaining chocolate over bread. Add remaining bread triangles and remaining chocolate. Press down with a fork so bread is completely covered. Cover with plastic wrap and let stand for 2 hours at room temperature. Refrigerate for 24–48 hours. Bake for 30–35 minutes or until crusty. Allow to stand 10 minutes. Serve with whipped cream.

Across Colorado

Colorado pioneer life became less austere when fashions of the Gay Nineties reached Colorado. These women who lived in Ault must have prided themselves on keeping up with the times.

Flat Apple Pie

Crust

3	cups all-purpose flour
$1/2$	teaspoon salt
$1^1/4$	cups shortening (half butter)
1	egg yolk and milk to make 1 cup
$3/4$	cup crushed corn flakes or bread crumbs

Filling

9	cups apples (Jonathan or Granny Smith), thinly sliced
2	tablespoons butter
1	cup sugar
$1^1/2$	teaspoons cinnamon
$3/4$	teaspoon nutmeg
$1/8$	teaspoon mace
1	egg white, stiffly beaten

Glaze

1	cup powdered sugar
2	tablespoons lemon juice

Serves 16–24

Preheat oven to 375°.

Blend flour, salt, and shortening using a pastry blender. Place egg yolk in a 1-cup glass measuring cup. Add enough milk to equal 1 cup. Stir to mix. Pour milk mixture over flour mixture and toss with a fork to blend. Form dough into a ball and divide in half. On a well-floured surface, roll out half of dough into a 12x17-inch rectangle. Fit dough into a 10x15-inch jelly roll pan. Top the dough with the crushed corn flakes or bread crumbs.

Spread sliced apples over the crust. Dot with 2 tablespoons butter and sprinkle with the sugar and spices.

Roll out remaining dough into another 12x17-inch rectangle. Place on top of the apples. Seal edges. Brush top crust with stiffly beaten egg white. Bake for 1 hour.

Combine powdered sugar with lemon juice. Spread glaze over pie while pie is warm. Can be made in advance and reheated.

Across Colorado

Fort Vasquez

Fort Vasquez, the most active rival of Bent's Fort, was built in 1836 by Louis Vasquez. Military forts assumed the protective functions for the area; Fort Vasquez was a trading post and served as a thriving trading center for Indians, hunters, and trappers. Fort Vasquez was abandoned in 1842, but was used again in the 1860s by military troops as a base during Indian conflicts. A replica of the original fort has been reconstructed by the Colorado Historical Society. Fort Vasquez is located about 40 miles north of Denver, 1 mile south of Platteville.

Sugarless Apple Pie

2	prepared 9-inch pie crusts
4	Delicious apples, red or yellow, peeled
1	6-ounce can frozen, unsweetened, concentrated apple juice
2	tablespoons flour
1	teaspoon cinnamon
1/4	teaspoon nutmeg
4	tablespoons margarine, cut into bits

Preheat oven to 400°.

Slice apples into unbaked pie crust. Bring apple juice to a boil. Mix flour and spices in a small bowl and whisk in apple juice to form a paste. Spread over apples. Dot with margarine. Cover with top crust. Crimp edges and cut several small vents. Brush a small amount of water over top crust with a pastry brush and sprinkle with nutmeg. Bake for 40 minutes, then reduce oven temperature to 375° and bake for an additional 10 minutes.

This is a very good, low-calorie dessert.

Serves 8

Springtime Strawberry Pie

1	9-inch pie crust, baked
1	8-ounce package light cream cheese, at room temperature
1/2	cup powdered sugar
2	pints fresh ripe strawberries
1	cup granulated sugar
3	tablespoons cornstarch
1	cup water
2	tablespoons dry strawberry gelatin
	whipped cream (optional)

Blend cream cheese and powdered sugar. Spread in bottom of prebaked shell. Wash and stem strawberries, slicing large berries. Place strawberries in a large bowl. In a small saucepan, mix sugar and cornstarch, then add water, stirring until smooth. Over medium heat, cook until thick and clear. Stir in dry gelatin. Mix well, cool, then pour over berries, tossing gently. Spoon berry mixture into baked crust. Chill for 4–6 hours before serving. Top with whipped cream if desired.

Serves 8

Across Colorado

This remnant of a cafe is a lonely reminder of Dearfield, an African-American colony that thrived briefly between Greeley and Fort Morgan before World War I. The colony was established by seven black families and their leader, O. T. Jackson, with encouragement from the Colorado governor, John T. Shaforth. By 1921 the colony was home to 700 people. However, financial problems and a farm depression undermined Dearfield, and its colonists slowly moved away.

Candy Bar Pie

9	ounces plain or almond milk chocolate bars
$^3/_4$	cup milk
30	marshmallows, regular size
2	cups refrigerated non-dairy whipped topping (divided use)
1	9-inch prepared graham cracker pie shell

Break chocolate bars into small pieces. In medium-size saucepan, combine milk, chocolate pieces, and marshmallows. Cook over low heat, stirring, until chocolate and marshmallows are melted. Pour into a shallow pan and place in freezer 5–10 minutes to cool. Fold 1–1$^1/_2$ cups whipped topping into chocolate mixture and mix thoroughly. Pour into pie shell. Return to freezer for 10 minutes to chill. Remove from freezer and spread remaining whipped topping over pie. Refrigerate 4–6 hours before serving.

Serves 8

Old Plantation Peaches and Cream Pie

1	9-inch pie shell, unbaked
8	fresh Colorado peach halves, peeled
2	egg yolks
1	cup heavy whipping cream
$^2/_3$	cup sugar
$^1/_4$	teaspoon salt
$^1/_2$	teaspoon nutmeg
1	tablespoon cornstarch

Preheat oven to 350°.

Arrange peach halves, cut side down, in prepared pie shell. Beat egg yolks lightly, add cream, and mix until smooth. Mix sugar, salt, nutmeg, and cornstarch. Add to cream mixture and stir until smooth. Pour over peaches. Bake for 40–50 minutes, or until filling is firm. Serve warm. Refrigerate leftovers.

Serves 6–8

Across Colorado

Young ladies take instruction in an industrial arts class at what is now the University of Northern Colorado, known in 1912 as Greeley Normal School or Greeley Teachers' College.

Jack O'Lantern Pumpkin Pie

1	9-inch deep-dish pie shell, unbaked
1	15-ounce can pumpkin
1/2	cup evaporated milk, warmed
1/2	cup milk, warmed
2	tablespoons butter, melted
1/2	cup dark brown sugar
2	eggs
1/4	cup honey
2 1/4	teaspoons cinnamon
1/8	teaspoon cloves
1/2	teaspoon ginger
1/2	teaspoon nutmeg

Preheat oven to 375°.

Place all filling ingredients in a 2-quart bowl. Whisk together until well blended. Pour into prepared pie shell. Bake for 1 hour, or until a knife inserted into the center comes out clean. Cool for 1 hour before serving.

Serves 6–8

Across Colorado

A new steam threshing machine lightened the work of men, boys, horses, and oxen during harvest, about 1912.

The South Plains

*"It's God's country
all right—only God
and I know it's
there."*

—Mary Ann Mincic

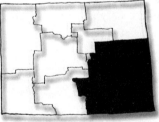

Before the settlers found their way into the Arkansas Valley, before the trappers and traders made their way along the Santa Fe Trail, even before the Spaniards came seeking the wealth and wonders of Cibola, this wide prairie grassland was the domain of the ancestors of the Comanche, the Apache, and the Kiowa. They left their records in petroglyphs along the creek canyon walls. They grew crops along the streams and rivers. They hunted the bison and deer.

For many years, this vast region knew no master, then it was claimed first by Spain, then by France, and back again to Spain. At the end of the Mexican War in 1848, it finally became a permanent part of the United States. Little trace of the French occupancy remains, but there is still much influence from the early Spanish settlers. Although its name has been shortened, there is still El Rio de las Animas Perdidas en Purgatorio—the River of the Souls Lost in Purgatory.

Then civilization began to encroach. Lieutenant Zebulon Montgomery Pike and his exploration party, bent on finding the sources of the Arkansas and Red Rivers, tried and failed to reach the summit of "Pikes Peak" in 1806. In 1820, another army officer, Major Stephen H. Long, led a "scientific exploration" into Colorado and labeled the north and south high plains "the Great American Desert." But travel continued. Traders carried guns, knives, tools, sugar, coffee, flour, cloth, and other useful goods from St. Louis to Taos and Santa Fe. They returned with buffalo robes, beaver pelts, silver, and turquoise. Midway they stopped at Bent's Fort—a fortified trading post built in the early 1830s on the Arkansas River. Bent's Fort was a haven for all who arrived—Indians, traders, trappers, and settlers. Their footprints and wagon wheels etched the Santa Fe Trail across Colorado's "desert."

The Arkansas River waters this region as it flows eastward into Kansas. South of the Arkansas, the Comanche National Grasslands form a complex blend of canyons and buttes—a 410,000-acre habitat for three bighorn sheep herds, snakes, coyotes, elk, mountain lions, birds, badgers, bears, and cattle.

In the 1870s, the Arkansas Valley became the inspiration for an agricultural experiment when a settler planted seeds of cantaloupe, watermelon, and vegetables and gave them Arkansas River water to drink. Look for and relish the flavor of Arkansas Valley melons, fruits, and vegetables when you visit the south plains. At harvest time, bask in a golden glow from rippling acres of ripened wheat.

Across Colorado

Not Gone—Just Forgotten

"It's God's country all right. Only God and I know it's there," said Mary Ann Mincic as she was being interviewed in 1988 about early times in Las Animas County. Mrs. Mincic was a lifelong resident of the Piñon Canyon area in the far southeast corner of Colorado.

A new bicycle was an unusual possession and worthy of a family photograph about 1910 on the southeastern plains.

Another southeast plains family lines up for a picture.

Across Colorado

Spring Brunch for a Bunch

Powderhorn Gin Fizz*
or
Chilled Assorted Juices
Fresh Fruit Bowl with
Orange-Yogurt Dressing*
Too-Good-to-Believe French Toast*
or
Trinidad Waffles*
Crab Casserole*
Castle Marne Royal Scones
(see Breads)
with
Lemon Curd
(see Jams and Sauces)
Shortbread Cookies Dipped
in Chocolate*
Flavored Coffees

A Brunch for Eight

Recipe Follows

Powderhorn Gin Fizz

4	ounces gin
4	ounces Triple Sec
6	ounces heavy cream
4	egg whites
3	tablespoons plus 1 teaspoon fresh lime juice
2	tablespoons powdered sugar
	dash mace
2	cups crushed ice

Combine all ingredients in blender jar. Process until frothy. Serve in prechilled, 9-ounce glasses. Make another batch in exactly the same manner for 8 servings.

Start your brunch with a delicious gin fizz and some "cool" jazz on the sound system.

M a k e s   4   g e n e r o u s   s e r v i n g s

Crab Casserole

6	slices white bread (divided use)
2	6-ounce cans crabmeat
½	cup chopped onion
½	cup chopped green pepper
½	cup mayonnaise
3	large eggs
1½	cups milk
	salt and pepper to taste
1	10-ounce can cream of mushroom soup, undiluted
½	cup shredded Cheddar cheese

Preheat oven to 350°. Grease a 3-quart casserole.

Cut two slices of bread into small cubes and place in bottom of casserole. Mix crabmeat, onion, green pepper, and mayonnaise in a bowl. Top bread cubes with crabmeat mixture. Cut remaining 4 slices of bread into quarters diagonally and place on top of mixture. In a separate bowl, beat eggs well; add milk, salt, and pepper. Pour over casserole. Spread soup over all. Bake 1 hour. During last 10 minutes of baking time, sprinkle top with cheese.

Serve piping hot.

S e r v e s   8

Across Colorado

On the South Plains with Augusta and H.A.W.

Augusta Tabor

In the 1930s an anonymous benefactor mailed two yellowed pages of a faded penciled diary to the Colorado Historical Society. These fragments are the only known surviving entries in a journal Augusta Tabor kept as she and her husband, called H.A.W., crossed Colorado's southeastern plains, probably in 1859 or 1860. They traveled in an oxen-drawn covered wagon and may have been in the vicinity of present-day Monument, on their way to the mining camps of Oro and Buckskin Joe, when these entries were recorded.

Traveling with the Tabors was Nathaniel Maxey, a good friend of the Tabors. However, the Tabors' toddler son and only child, named Nathaniel Maxey after the friend, was also with them. This makes the references to Nat and Nattie confusing. The Historical Society has searched in vain for more of Augusta's diary and for the mysterious donor.

The entries begin midsentence and end midsentence. **(undated)**—pitched tents, made a fire. Some had a hot dish of coffee for supper. Nat is highly delighted with camp life once more. Retired for the night at six. The boys made themselves merry a singing songs.

March 1—The sun rose bright and beautiful, not a cloud to be seen. Nat prepared us breakfast of venison ham and sasaphras [sic] tea. This I call a poor appology [sic] for coffee. We camped fore noon at the mill. The wind blew very high. I had a walk after dinner. At night we camped on plum creek. The wind blew all night.

March 2—The morning is very windy. Nattie has a bad cold and is very cross; breakfast of venison ham and coffee. We stopped under a hill to break the wind up and to have dinner. Glover is tiard [sic] and has stretched himself on the grass to sleep. Kellogg, Mc. and Marcy are indulging in a smoke. 4 o'clock we camped for the night beside a log cabin in which lived a woman and five raged [sic] dirty children. There the prairie caught afire and the men worked an hour or so in trying to keep the fire from a small haystack but in vain. We retired early as usual and slept sound until the sun was up.

March 3—Windy and cold. I kept the bed all the morning. At noon we stopped at a ranch and built a fire in the cabin but the smoke was so bad we were obliged to move it outside. The wind is still blowing high. Have kept the bed all the afternoon. The weather was to [sic] disagreeable to do anything but sleep. The sun half an hour high and we are in camp on monument creek.

March 4—Sunday—The wind is still blowing. We come near to the mountains and passed some natural monuments some nearly white as marble and standing nearly thirty or forty feet high. We drove into a beautiful valley and halted for noon. There was a man overtook us with some cows and kindly offered us some milk for coffee which was thankfully received as we had had no milk for coffee since we left civilization. After dinner I proposed to Horace that we walk along ahead. So off we started and Mr. Kellogg with us. We passed a beautiful place for a farm but the soil was very poor. We walked until we were weary and stopped to repose under a large pine tree. Here Kellogg gathered . . .

Fresh Fruit Bowl with Orange-Yogurt Dressing

6	cups of the ripest, freshest fruits of the season: halved strawberries, sliced fresh peaches, watermelon and cantaloupe balls, fresh pear pieces, red and green seedless grapes, grapefruit sections, sliced bananas; also mandarin orange slices and canned pineapple tidbits (drained)
1	cup nuts, chopped (optional)
1	cup shredded coconut (optional)
4	kiwis, sliced, for garnish

Dressing

1	cup vanilla yogurt
2	tablespoons frozen orange juice concentrate

Serves 8

Mix together your favorite combination of fresh fruits. Fold in nuts and coconut (if desired). Stir yogurt and orange concentrate until well blended. Pour yogurt mixture over fruit and blend carefully. Chill. Serve on Bibb lettuce leaves on individual plates garnished with kiwi slices, or in a large bowl lined with lettuce leaves.

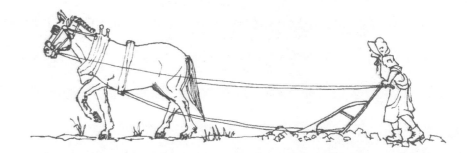

Across Colorado

Bent's Fort

Bent's Fort
(reconstructed)

The Bent brothers, Charles and William, came west from St. Louis and in the early 1830s established a trading post on the north bank of the Arkansas River, between present-day La Junta and Las Animas, in the midst of Arapaho and Cheyenne Indian country.

Bent's Fort dominated the beaver trade, then the buffalo robe trade, for twenty years. Fur trappers traded their animal pelts for knives, guns, coffee, salt, and other supplies; Indians traded their buffalo robes. The veteran mountain men—Jim Bridger, Kit Carson, Dick Wootton, Jim Beckwourth, Jim Baker, and Tom Fitzpatrick—made Bent's Fort their home base.

Interesting note: William Bent was married to Owl Woman, daughter of Grey Thunder, a Southern Cheyenne medicine man. Charles Bent's mate was Ignacia Jaramillo, mother of his five children and older sister of Kit Carson's wife.

Too-Good-to-Believe French Toast

1	16-ounce loaf French bread
3	cups whole or 2% milk
6	large eggs
1	teaspoon vanilla
1	teaspoon cinnamon
$\frac{1}{2}$	teaspoon nutmeg

Topping

4	ounces margarine, at room temperature
1	cup brown sugar
1	cup chopped pecans
1	teaspoon dark corn syrup

Serves 8

When ready to bake, preheat oven to 350°. Spray 9x13-inch pan with nonstick cooking spray.

Slice French bread into 8 slices, 1½–2 inches thick, and place flat in pan. Mix milk, eggs, vanilla, cinnamon, and nutmeg with hand beater or whisk. Pour mixture over the bread. Cover and refrigerate overnight. In the morning, place margarine and brown sugar in a small bowl. Using a pastry blender, cut sugar into margarine to form crumbs. Add pecans and corn syrup and stir well. Sprinkle crumb topping over milk-soaked bread slices. Bake uncovered for 40 minutes. Serve immediately, or allow to cool for 1 hour and reheat before serving.

This is a favorite do-ahead breakfast for the Back-In-Time Bed and Breakfast in Glenwood Springs. The Back-In-Time is a restored home, built in 1903. Over the years, it has served as doctors' offices, lawyers' offices, and an antique store.

Across Colorado

The DAR at Bent's Fort

In 1912, Colorado members of the Daughters of the American Revolution (DAR) erected and dedicated a marker at Bent's Fort, commemorating its historic significance.

Reverend Rice

The Reverend Rice, president of Baker University in Kansas, knew his destiny was to form a church in the West. He headed out on the Santa Fe Trail in 1869 and stopped in Trinidad. There he started the First Methodist Church of Trinidad. His wife started the first school. The United Methodist Men of Trinidad have sponsored the community waffle dinner for many years, using the waffle recipe on the next page.

Trinidad Waffles

4	cups flour
1/4	cup sugar
2	tablespoons baking powder
1	teaspoon salt
3	cups milk
3/4	cup melted butter, cooled
4	beaten eggs

Serves 8

In a large bowl, sift flour, sugar, baking powder, and salt together. Stir in milk and melted butter. In another bowl, using an electric mixer, beat eggs at medium-high speed until light and frothy. Fold beaten eggs into batter. Pour batter into heated waffle iron and bake until crisp. Topping suggestions: maple syrup or serviceberry, raspberry, strawberry, or chokecherry syrup.

This is a reliable recipe for high altitudes and can be multiplied to serve dozens or "the multitudes."

Shortbread Cookies

1/2	cup butter
1/2	cup margarine
1/2	cup powdered sugar
1	teaspoon vanilla extract
1	teaspoon almond extract
2	cups flour
4–6	ounces bittersweet chocolate

Makes about 3 dozen cookies

When ready to bake, preheat oven to 350°.

Cream butter, margarine, and sugar until light and fluffy. Stir in extracts. Add flour and mix well. Shape dough into two rolls. Wrap separately in plastic wrap and chill overnight. When ready to bake, cut into 1/4-inch-thick slices. Bake on cookie sheet 15–20 minutes, or until lightly browned. Cool cookies on a wire rack.

An optional touch: Place bittersweet chocolate in a small glass bowl and microwave on low power until chocolate is melted. Dip half of each cookie in chocolate and cool on a wire rack until chocolate has hardened.

This is a recipe of Ruth McEntire Warshauer's, who lived in Antonito and later in Denver. See the stories about the Warshauers in the South Mountains/Southwest Flavors section.

Across Colorado

Maria Josephina (or Josefa) Carson

Josefa Jaramillo married Kit Carson in Taos in 1843 when she was fifteen years old. In the spring of 1868, Josefa, nine months pregnant, went from Taos to Fort Lyon, Colorado, on the Arkansas River to be with Kit who was returning from Washington, D.C., gravely ill. She died there April 23, giving birth to their seventh child. Kit died in the same place, exactly one month later.

See the South Mountains/Southwest Flavors section for Josefa's recipe for Capirotada from the Volunteers of the Colorado Historical Society's 1963 cookbook and her recipe for the Bowl of the Wife of Kit Carson, given to us by Sam Arnold of The Fort restaurant in Morrison. Both recipes originally came from Leona Wood, Josefa and Kit's granddaughter.

Labor Day Barbecue

Berry Rum Pitcher Punch* or
Cold Beer and Fruit Drinks
California Hummus* with Pita Chips
Yuma County Cattlewomen's Dip
(see Appetizers)
Fresh Veggie Relish Tray
Cherry Creek Dip
(see Appetizers)
Charlie Brown's Pit Barbecued Beef* or
Mom's Beef Barbecue*
German Potato Salad* or
Doc's Deer Camp Taters*
Picnic Baked Beans*
Redlands Mesa Peach Ice Cream*
or
Poncha Springs Peach Cobbler*

A Barbecue for 12 (or 200)
Recipe Follows

Berry Rum Pitcher Punch

2	quarts chilled cranberry juice
2	6-ounce cans frozen, undiluted pineapple juice, thawed
1/2	cup fresh lime juice
1 1/2	cups dark rum
	crushed ice

Pour cranberry, pineapple, and lime juices and rum into a large bowl. Stir well. Cover and refrigerate for several hours, until punch is very cold. At serving time, pour into a pitcher or punch bowl and add crushed ice.

This punch has a beautiful color with a bright sparkle served from a clear glass punch bowl.

Serves 10–12

California Hummus

10	sundried tomatoes (not oil packed)
1	cup boiling water
1	19-ounce can garbanzo beans, drained
1	clove garlic, minced
1/2	cup light mayonnaise
1	tablespoon extra virgin olive oil
1/4	cup grated Parmesan cheese
2	tablespoons fresh lemon juice
1	teaspoon salt
1/4	teaspoon freshly ground black pepper
1/2	teaspoon fresh basil and/or
2	tablespoons parsley, finely minced

Pour boiling water over dried tomatoes. Allow to sit for 2 hours or longer. Drain. Place tomatoes and remaining ingredients in bowl of food processor or blender. Process until smooth. Serve with pita chips.

This can also be used as a spread for vegetarian sandwiches with lettuce, tomato, avocado, or sprouts.

Makes 2 cups

Across Colorado

Charlie Brown's Pit Barbecued Beef

3–4	12- to 18-pound beef shoulder roasts, mesh covered
6–8	large onions
	salt and pepper
	other seasonings as desired

Equipment

1	tractor with blade (or shovels and 3 or 4 helpers)
1	cord scrub oak, dry and green kindling
1–2	rolls extra-heavy aluminum foil
	burlap
	baling wire
1	tub or wheelbarrow
1	hose
	water source
	rebar
	piece of tin (slightly larger than small pit)
	insulated coolers (optional)

Serves 150–200

(The Way They Do It in Maybell Every Labor Day)

In Mr. Brown's Own Words

First, dig a hole about 4x8 feet and at least 1 foot deep out in the pasture. Inside this hole, make a deeper hole a foot or so deep, leaving about 8–10 inches all the way around. You now need a pickup load of scrub oak—a mixture of both dry and green. The bigger-sized oak works well.
Put paper, cardboard, and scrap wood on the bottom of the smaller pit and get the fire going, then put on the oak. Burn the oak down until you have a good bed of coals—approximately 3–4 hours. While the fire is burning down (and when you can safely leave it) get the meat ready. Use 12–18-pound rolled beef shoulder roasts with string-mesh covering. How you flavor them is up to you. We use salt, black pepper, and a couple of onions on each roast.

Next, wrap each roast with extra-heavy-duty aluminum foil. Roll off 3 feet of foil—two pieces for each roast. Lay one piece of foil on top of the other, folding the edges of the pieces together a couple of times to make one big piece about 3 feet square. Put a roast with the seasoning and onions on each square, bringing the foil up around the roast and making it as airtight as possible.

Now wrap the foil-covered roasts with burlap or put them into small burlap bags. Fasten with baling wire or wrap chicken wire around the burlap. Place your roasts in a tub or wheelbarrow and spray water on them, making the burlap good and wet. The roasts are now ready.

Across Colorado

Maybell Pit Barbecue (continued)

Have ready at the pit some rebar to lay across the top of the smaller pit and an old piece of tin a little smaller than the larger pit so that it will fit inside.

Next comes the fast work. Have three or four people ready with shovels. (We use a tractor with a blade if we are shorthanded.) Give your helpers instructions so everybody knows what to do. It should work like this:

(1) Toss the roasts into the firepit, spreading them out on the coals.

(2) Put the bars across the firepit on the ledge and put the tin on top of the bars.

(3) Shovel dirt into the large pit. Work fast because until you shut off the oxygen from the meat, the burlap and meat can burn up. Once the dirt is in, make sure there is no sign of smoke coming out of the dirt. If there is, pack on more dirt.

Leave the meat in the pit for at least 12 hours. (You can leave it for as long as 16 hours.) Remember, no matter how long it is in the pit, the meat cannot burn without oxygen. The meat will be very moist, tender, and juicy (sometimes a little pink), but it will be very well done and tender.

Take out one roast at a time, leaving the others in the open pit while you slice and serve one, or put them in insulated coolers where they will stay hot until served.

WARNINGS! You MUST use OAK. No other wood in the area will work. Make sure the pit is DRY. A pit dug in a swampy or wet area will not work. You MUST have a GOOD BED OF COALS. Burn at least a pickup load or a full cord of oak.

DO NOT ALLOW ANYONE TO WORK AROUND THE BURNING PIT ALONE.

KEEP A WATER HOSE HANDY. Wind can spread fire very rapidly.

Across Colorado

The Harvey Girls

More than 100,000 "Harvey Girls" answered advertisements in eastern newspapers and magazines between 1880 and 1950 and "came west" to work in Fred Harvey restaurants and hotels along the Santa Fe Railway. About half of these women returned home after their Harvey contracts were completed, but the other half remained in the West, married, and often became the founding "mothers" of small cattle, mining, and railroading towns in Kansas, Colorado, New Mexico, and Arizona.

A Harvey House in La Junta opened in 1883 and in Trinidad in 1895. Here the Harvey Girls were told where to live, what time to go to bed, whom they could date, and what to wear. Such close supervision and attention to detail was necessary in a day when single, working women were viewed with suspicion by the "respectable" matrons of the town. For most of the Harvey Girls, their choice to "go west" as waitresses was prompted by adventurous spirits, economic necessity to support themselves, and the knowledge that the West had an oversupply of single men.

Many Fred Harvey establishments continued to serve travelers on the Atchison, Topeka and Santa Fe Railway until the traveling public turned to airports in the 1950s and 1960s.

The Harvey House at Trinidad

Across Colorado

Mom's Beef Barbecue

3	tablespoons vegetable oil
1	onion, chopped
5	pounds sirloin steak, cut in strips
$\frac{1}{2}$	cup flour for dusting steak
1	cup red wine
	salt and pepper

Sauce

1	cup ketchup
1	teaspoon dry mustard
2	tablespoons sweet pickle juice
2	tablespoons brown sugar
3	tablespoons vinegar
1	teaspoon celery seed

Serves 12

Place oil and onion in 4-quart pressure cooker. Heat over medium-high heat. Lightly dust strips of sirloin in flour, add to cooker, and cook until meat is browned. Pour in wine, add salt and pepper, seal pressure cooker with lid, and lower heat to medium. After pressure has come up, cook for 20 minutes. Remove cooker from heat and allow steam to exhaust gradually. (This recipe can also be made without a pressure cooker. Gently simmer meat for 2–2½ hours in a large stockpot until meat falls into shreds.)

Place all sauce ingredients into a small saucepan and cook until slightly thickened. When pressure in cooker is exhausted, open lid and mash meat with a potato masher. Meat should fall apart into shreds. Add warm sauce and mix well. If mixture is too thick, thin with red wine. Serve on hamburger buns or crusty rolls.

Great made in advance.

Across Colorado

Wait for the Rocky Fords

Rocky Ford cantaloupes
waiting to go to points east

In 1874, George Washington Swink with his neighbors built the first cooperative irrigation canal in the Arkansas River Valley, at a place called Rocky Ford. Swink planted an experimental, irrigated garden of vegetables on his homestead acres. The cantaloupe did exceptionally well. He experimented until he found a melon with just the right flavor. By the turn of the century, Rocky Ford melon growers were shipping millions of melons to New York City alone. One hundred years later we still wait for the Rocky Fords—they set the standard for cantaloupe flavor.

German Potato Salad

5	pounds red potatoes

Dressing

8	ounces bacon, diced
3	tablespoons flour
1	cup sugar
$^3/_4$	cup white vinegar
$^3/_4$	cup water
1	small onion, finely minced
	salt and pepper to taste

Scrub potatoes well but do not peel. Dice potatoes into 1-inch cubes. Steam or boil until tender. Drain and keep warm.

While potatoes cook, make dressing. In a large skillet, fry bacon until crisp. Drain off half of the fat. Add flour to skillet and blend. Add sugar, vinegar, water, and onion. Blend well and cook over low heat for about 4 minutes. Season with salt and pepper. Pour dressing over warm potatoes. Salad can be served warm or refrigerated for later use.

Serves 12

Picnic Baked Beans

1	16-ounce can each of cut green beans, cut wax beans, lima beans, kidney beans, chili beans, pinto beans with jalapenos
1	can tomato soup
1	6-ounce can tomato paste
1	cup brown sugar
1	12-ounce bottle barbecue sauce
$1^1/_2$	cups chopped onion
2	pounds bulk Italian sausage

Preheat oven to 300°.

Drain green beans, wax beans, lima beans, and kidney beans. Place in a very large mixing bowl along with all other ingredients except sausage. Mix well. Brown the sausage in a large skillet, crumbling sausage as it cooks. Drain sausage well and stir into beans. Spoon mixture into two 9x13-inch baking dishes. Bake for 60–90 minutes, or until bubbly.

Serves 12-20

Across Colorado

Mr. Prospective Colorado Farmer

In the early 1900s, "booster" civic groups and promoters of many small towns and "colonies" in Colorado flooded eastern newspapers with glowing advertisements of their attractions.

The Commercial Club of Manzanola, in Otero County southeast of Pueblo, published a brochure with this enticing invitation:

Manzanola (Meaning "Apples All Over")

Would not a section producing the medal winning Cherries at the St. Louis World's Exposition appeal to YOU, Mr. Prospective Colorado Farmer?

Would not that section appeal further to YOU when YOU know that it is located in the county that produced the Prize Apples of the same World's Exposition?

Would it not interest YOU further to know that this county is located in the valley that produced the winning Sugar Beets of the country? And that in this county are located three of the seven beet sugar factories in the valley?

And further that this county leads the State of Colorado in value of agricultural products for the year 1909?

The section referred to, Mr. Prospective Colorado Farmer is Manzanola; the county Otero, in the Arkansas Valley of Colorado.

The Manzanola Commerce Club feels that you will be interested, and presents the following information for you to read and think about.

Doc's Deer Camp Taters

6	potatoes
1–2	onions, sliced
	vegetable oil
	chili powder to taste
	salt and pepper to taste
	rum to taste or lite beer

Serves 6

Peel potatoes and slice into wafers $\frac{1}{8}$ inch thick. Heat oil about $\frac{1}{2}$–1 inch deep in Dutch oven over a hot open fire or camp stove. Add potatoes and onions to pot. Fill the palm of your hand with chili powder and toss it in the pot. If you like, fill the other palm and toss in some more. Cook for a bit over high heat, then add salt, a good dose of black pepper, and a shot or two of rum or $\frac{1}{4}$ can of your favorite lite beer. Cook until potatoes are just slightly crisp. Cooking time varies, depending on altitude and attitude.

Recipe can be repeated for a multitude of campers or "deck diners" where the gas-fired BBQ grill can take the place of the campfire. Camp Taters are better made in small batches.

You can't go wrong with this one, according to Ed Connolly, formerly of the historic Jackson Hotel in Poncha Springs. A little of this, a little of that. Cook it till you're tired of cooking and if you are not satisfied with the taste, add another shot of rum. By the time it's gone, everyone will think it's great. Serve with steak or barbecued beef and beans at camp or for a backyard picnic.

Joys of the Stagecoach Traveler

When the gold rush to Colorado began, the staging company, Russell, Majors, and Waddell, of St. Joseph, Missouri, created the Leavenworth and Pike's Peak Express Company to provide daily coach service between Kansas and Cherry Creek. They had forty stagecoaches, each capable of carrying eight passengers. The fare was $100 to $125 for a one-way trip, including meals. The coaches traveled continuously, day and night, making short stops at stage stations. At the start, the trip took twelve days, but later they shortened the route to about a week.

Horace Greeley, editor of the *New York Tribune*, was on one of these coaches in June 1859, bound for Denver, when it had a mishap crossing the plains. Albert Richardson, another newspaperman and Greeley's traveling companion, described the accident:

"Descending an abrupt hill, our mules, terrified by meeting three savages, broke a line, run down a precipitous bank, upsetting the coach which was hurled upon the ground with a tremendous crash and galloped away with the fore-wheels. I sprang out in time to escape being overturned. From a mass of cushions, carpet-sacks and blankets soon emerged my companion [Greeley], his head rising above the side of the vehicle like that of an advertising boy from his frame of pasteboard. Blood was flowing profusely from cuts in his cheek, arm and leg; but his face was serene and benignant as a May morning."

Across Colorado

Redlands Mesa Peach Ice Cream

3   cups fresh Colorado peaches (6–8),
peeled and coarsely mashed
(if it's winter and you are desperate,
use frozen peaches)

3   cups sugar

$^1/_4$ cup fresh orange juice
juice of $2^1/_2$ lemons

1   quart whole milk

1   pint whipping cream

1   can sweetened condensed milk

Serves 12

In a large bowl, mix peaches, sugar, orange juice, and lemon juice. Let stand for 3 hours. Stir in milk, cream, and sweetened condensed milk and blend well. Pour mixture into ice cream freezer. Freeze according to manufacturer's directions.

Across Colorado

Election Night *at the Broadmoor, November 2, 1920*

Menu

In Cup, Madrilaine, 35   *Essence of Celery, 35*

Caviar Sandwich, 1.00   *Club Sandwich, 65*

Crab Meat Patty, 90

Minced Chicken à la King, 1.50

Lamb Chop with Beechnut Bacon, 80

Mignonette Potatoes, 30

Broadmoor Salad, 30

Peach Melba, 70   *Parfait Moka, 50*

Petit Noir, 20

* * *

Election Night

November 2, 1920

Did you Put in the Box one for Harding, or Cox?

Over Whom did you Rave and Enthuse?

Who'll soon Dominate our Affairs of State?

Who'll Step in the President's Shoes?

Did you Think that the League would Prevent Fatigue,

And Give every Nation its Dues;

That 't would Banish all Spites, Give Ireland her Rights,

. . . [And Accommodate Everyone's Views.]

Did you Ponder and Dwell, Study each Subject Well,

Meditate and Most Earnestly Muse,

What Effect this yere Vote will have on your Goat,

And how Much you're Out if you Lose?

Did you Think you'd Select the Man We Elect?

Well, Wait till you get All the News!

But, Whatever you Did, you'll Find you're not Rid

Of an Appetite! Eat as you Choose!

Across Colorado

Poncha Springs Peach Cobbler

4	cups fresh, ripe peaches, peeled and sliced
1/2–2/3	cup sugar
	(depending on sweetness of peaches)
1	teaspoon grated lemon zest
1	tablespoon lemon juice
1/2	teaspoon almond extract

Topping

1 1/2	cups all-purpose flour
1	tablespoon baking powder
1/2	teaspoon salt
1/2	cup sugar
1/3	cup vegetable shortening
1	egg, lightly beaten
1/4	cup milk
2	tablespoons sugar
1	tablespoon cinnamon
	whipped cream or ice cream

Serves 12

Preheat oven to 400°. Butter a 2-quart baking dish.

Peel peaches by dropping them into boiling water for 1 minute, then drain and plunge into cold water. Skins will slip off easily, and both time and fruit will be saved by using this method instead of a paring knife. Put peaches in a large bowl and stir in sugar, zest, lemon juice, and almond extract. Place peaches in baking dish and bake for 20 minutes.

While peaches bake, mix flour, baking powder, salt, and sugar. Using a pastry blender, cut in shortening until mixture resembles coarse crumbs. Combine egg and milk and mix with dry ingredients until just combined. Remove peaches from oven and spoon dough over them, covering completely. Mix sugar and cinnamon and sprinkle over dough. Bake 15–20 minutes, or until top is golden brown.

Serve with fresh cream, ice cream, or whipped cream flavored with almond extract or peach brandy.

After Colorado Governor Roy Romer was served dinner in Poncha Springs while on a sweep through the state, he wrote the Poncha Springs mayor a special thanks for this peach cobbler.

Across Colorado

Shattering News over the Wire

Mable Shoemaker Smith traveled with her parents in a wagon train from Illinois to western Kansas when she was three weeks old. Four years later her parents joined another wagon train and took her and her three-month-old brother to Trinidad, Colorado Territory, where they settled.

In later years Mable's grandchildren asked her to tell and retell the story of how, as a little girl, she was sent on an errand to the Atchison, Topeka, and Santa Fe depot in west Las Animas where she watched the telegraph operator take down a message from the clicking instrument. Then he read it to all the men present and consternation ensued. The message was the disastrous news of the Battle of the Little Big Horn.

Santa Fe Depot at La Junta

Across Colorado

An Elegant
Autumn Night's Dinner

Palisade Peach Aperitif* or
Fireside Hot Cider*
Zucchini Appetizer
(see Appetizers)
Mushroom Barley Soup
(see Soups)
Mango Salad
(see Salads and Vegetables)
Roast Leg of Lamb
with Turmeric Pickle Sauce* or
Alpenaire Venison Chops*
Wild Rice with Green Grapes*
Ice Box Yeast Rolls
(see Breads)
Irish Cream Cheesecake*
Coffees

A Dinner for Six

*Recipe Follows

Palisade Peach Aperitif

4	large fresh peaches, very ripe
2	tablespoons sugar
1	tablespoon fresh lemon juice
1/4	cup (or more) French Cognac or California brandy
2	24-ounce bottles of fruity white wine, such as Riesling or off-dry Sauvignon Blanc, chilled

Makes 12 6-ounce servings

Peel, pit, and chunk peaches. Place peaches and remaining ingredients EXCEPT wine in blender jar. Blend until smooth. Taste and adjust sweetness. Pour puree into 1-quart glass jar. Place in refrigerator to chill. Puree should be made several hours in advance of serving time. Mixture will keep in refrigerator for up to one week.

At serving time, place 2–3 tablespoons of peach puree in each wine glass. Pour in 4 ounces of wine and stir gently. Drop in 2–3 ice cubes. Serve. Sparkling wine also may be used, but must be added slowly to prevent foaming. TOAST: "A votre santé."

Fireside Hot Cider

1	16-ounce can frozen, unsweetened apple juice concentrate, thawed
2	16-ounce cans water
1	12-ounce can lemon-lime soda, diet or regular
1/4	cup small cinnamon candies, or to taste
6–7	cinnamon sticks, broken in half
12	whole cloves

Serves 8–10

Mix apple juice concentrate with water. Stir in soda. Pour into 12-cup electric coffee percolator. Place cinnamon candies, cinnamon sticks, and cloves in basket of coffeemaker. Perk as for coffee. Recipe can be doubled or tripled for a larger group, using a 30-cup percolator. Also wonderful for a holiday open house.

Across Colorado

Early Trail Mix

"Son of a Gun Stew" was a favorite of cowboys on the trail in the days of the great cattle drives. It was a stew made of the chopped tongue, liver, heart, kidney, sweetbreads, and brains of a freshly killed calf. Mexican drivers and vaqueros brought this delicacy with them to Texas, then on to the plains of Colorado.

Chuckwagon in Las Animas County

Roast Leg of Lamb with Turmeric Pickle Sauce

1	4-pound leg of lamb

Marinade

1	16-ounce jar sweet pickle relish
10	peppercorns
3	large cloves garlic, crushed
3	bay leaves
3	whole cloves
¹⁄₂	teaspoon dried thyme

Turmeric Pickle Sauce

	reserved marinade from lamb
3	tablespoons flour
3	tablespoons dry onion soup mix
¹⁄₄	teaspoon turmeric
¹⁄₂	cup regular or low-fat sour cream

Serves 6

When ready to bake meat, preheat oven to 325°.

Place lamb and marinade ingredients into a large glass or stainless steel bowl. Cover and allow to marinate overnight in refrigerator. Strain and reserve marinade and pickles separately. Place lamb on rack in shallow roasting pan. Bake for 2 hours or until meat thermometer registers 175° for medium doneness.

While lamb bakes, prepare pickle sauce. Pour reserved marinade into a large measuring cup and add enough water to measure 3 cups. Place flour in a saucepan and gradually stir in about ¹⁄₂ cup marinade to form a smooth paste. Add remaining marinade, stirring constantly. Add onion soup mix, turmeric, and reserved pickles. Simmer for 30 minutes over very low heat. Just before serving, add sour cream and heat. Serve sauce with roast lamb.

Extraordinary ingredients combine for a wonderful, sophisticated flavor.

Across Colorado

Morning at the Boice Ranch on the Cimarron River in the far southeast corner of Colorado

Venison Chops from the Alpenaire Inn

2	8-bone French racks of venison
	flour
	salt and pepper
½	cup dried juniper berries
½	cup green peppercorns
4	tablespoons butter
4	tablespoons extra virgin olive oil
1½	cups Madeira wine

Serves 6

Rinse the meat in cold water. Pat dry. Cut into 16 chops. Very lightly dredge the meat with flour; season lightly with salt and pepper. Place the juniper berries in a brown paper sack and pound with a mallet. Add peppercorns and crush again lightly. Heat the butter and oil in a large, heavy skillet. When butter foams, add the meat a few pieces at a time, browning quickly, and then remove to a warm plate.

With the skillet very hot, CAUTIOUSLY pour in the wine. It should bubble furiously. TAKE CARE. When the alcohol burns off, add the crushed berries and peppercorns. Simmer sauce a few minutes, then add the venison pieces and juices off the plate. Cook on high heat about 3 minutes for rare or up to 5 minutes for medium, depending on thickness of the meat. Serve with the sauce and spices on top. Excellent accompanied by an apple raisin chutney. This recipe could also be made with lamb.

The Alpenaire Inn, built in Estes Park in 1909, is said to be inhabited by a beneficent ghost, the daughter of the original owner. After caring for her father until his death, she lost the house to her brothers and had to move out. After her own death, she moved back in.

Across Colorado

"Mother Jones" in Trinidad

A picturesque woman of history and an ardent Socialist, Mary Harris, better known as "Mother Jones," came to Trinidad in 1913 at the age of eighty-two to bolster the spirits and efforts of coal miners, who were engaged in a bitter strike against mine operators over wages and living conditions. Here Mother Jones leads a demonstration on the streets of Trinidad. Her sign says, "Has the governor [Governor Ammons] any respect for the state?"

Across Colorado

Wild Rice with Green Grapes

2	ounces butter
1	cup chopped onions
1	cup chopped green pepper
1	cup wild rice
3	cups chicken broth
	salt and pepper to taste
3/4	cup green grapes, cut in half

Melt butter in a large, heavy saucepan. Add onions, green pepper, and rice. Toss well. Saute until onions are translucent. Add chicken broth, salt and pepper. Cover and simmer slowly over low heat until wild rice is tender and cracks open and curls (1½–2 hours). Add more broth if rice seems dry. Just before serving, stir in green grapes and quickly reheat.

Serves 6

Irish Cream Cheesecake

Crust

6	whole graham crackers
2	ounces butter, melted

Filling

3	8-ounce packages cream cheese, at room temperature
7	tablespoons sugar
1	tablespoon flour
2	large eggs, lightly beaten
1/4	cup plus 2 tablespoons sour cream
1/4	cup plus 2 tablespoons Irish Cream liqueur
1	teaspoon vanilla extract
	chocolate syrup for garnish

Preheat oven to 350°.

Finely grind graham crackers. Mix with melted butter. Press onto bottom (not sides) of 9-inch springform pan. Bake 8 minutes. Remove from oven and let cool for 10 minutes.

Using an electric mixer, beat cream cheese and sugar until smooth. Add remaining ingredients and beat well. Pour filling into crust and bake 10 minutes at 350°, then reduce oven temperature to 250°, and continue baking until cheesecake is set, approximately 40 minutes longer. Remove cheesecake from oven and cool in pan for about 10 minutes. Cover loosely with waxed paper and refrigerate overnight.

Before serving, drizzle a little chocolate syrup over the cake.

Serves 8–12

Across Colorado

Colorado City/Denver Express

The ladies are riding side-saddle in this W. H. Jackson photograph, taken near Colorado City. Pikes Peak, in the background, has faded from this century-old picture.

An advertisement in the *Colorado City Journal*, November 28, 1861, read: "Coaches run every week between the above points [Colorado City and Denver] carrying the U.S. mail. Express matter and passengers, leaving Colorado [City] every Sunday morning arriving in Denver Monday afternoon and departing Denver Thursday morning arriving in Colorado [City] Friday afternoon." Apparently this stagecoach traveled the approximately 140 miles in 28–30 hours, averaging about 5 miles per hour.

Across Colorado

Applesauce Fruitcake

$\frac{1}{2}$	cup vegetable shortening
1	cup sugar
2	eggs, well beaten
$2\frac{1}{4}$	cups all-purpose flour (divided use)
1	teaspoon baking powder
1	teaspoon baking soda
$\frac{1}{4}$	teaspoon salt
1	teaspoon cinnamon
1	teaspoon ground nutmeg
$\frac{1}{4}$	teaspoon ground cloves
$\frac{1}{4}$	teaspoon allspice
$1\frac{1}{2}$	cups unsweetened applesauce
1	cup raisins
1	cup dates or figs, chopped
1	cup walnuts or pecans, chopped
$1\frac{1}{2}$	cups candied fruit mix
	candied red and green cherries (optional)
	candied pineapple rings (optional)

Makes 1 large or 2 small cakes

Preheat oven to 350°. Spray a 10-inch angel food pan or two 4x8-inch loaf pans with cooking spray.

Cream shortening and sugar thoroughly. Add eggs and mix. Sift together 2 cups flour, baking powder, soda, salt, and spices. Add to creamed mixture, alternating with applesauce. Lightly flour the raisins, dates or figs, nuts, and fruit mix with remaining $\frac{1}{4}$ cup flour. Add to batter and mix. Turn batter into prepared pan/pans. Decorate top of cake with candied cherries and/or pineapple if desired. Bake 60 minutes or until toothpick inserted into center of cake comes out clean. Do not overbake. You may need to lower oven temperature to 325° if cake seems to be baking too quickly.

Make this cake around Thanksgiving and store in refrigerator or cool place until Christmas.

Across Colorado

Colorado Springs Pioneers' Museum

Pioneers' Museum in the original El Paso County Courthouse (Photo courtesy of Pioneers' Museum)

The outstanding antiquities collection of the Colorado Springs Pioneers' Museum was begun in 1896 and housed in the corridors of the El Paso County Courthouse when it was built. However, by 1937 the collection had grown so large it was crowding the lawyers out of the building, and it had to go.

After a new courthouse was constructed in 1977, the museum moved back into the elegant, old, restored courthouse. Marshall Sprague, a well-known Colorado historian, described the old courthouse thus: "You will remember that the remarkable Neo-Renaissance structure, the El Paso County Courthouse, opened in 1903. It was—and still is—a monument to the eclectic skill of the architect A. J. Smith, who gave it touches of every architectural style through the ages, from Egyptian to Graeco-Roman, to Edwardian."

Baur's Mija Candy

8	ounces butter, melted (do not use margarine)
1	cup sugar
1	tablespoon white corn syrup
2	tablespoons water
$1/2$	pound milk chocolate bar, shaved or grated
$1/3$	cup nuts, finely chopped

Butter an 8x8-inch pan.

Place melted butter, sugar, corn syrup, and water in a heavy skillet and cook over medium to medium-high heat until a shade darker than brown sugar. Pour in an 8x8-inch pan and top immediately with the chocolate. Sprinkle top with nuts. Cool completely. Break into pieces, using a kitchen mallet.

Read in the Denver Metro/Main Dishes section about Baur's renowned restaurants.

Microwave Peanut Brittle

1	cup sugar
$1/2$	cup white corn syrup
$2^{1/2}$	cups raw peanuts
$1^{1/2}$	teaspoons baking soda
$1/4$	teaspoon salt
1	tablespoon butter or margarine
1	teaspoon vanilla extract

Cover two 9x12-inch cookie sheets with heavy-duty aluminum foil and spray with cooking spray.

Combine sugar, corn syrup, and peanuts in $1^{1/2}$-quart glass, microwave-safe bowl and microwave on high for 10 minutes, stirring every 2 or 3 minutes. Stir in baking soda, salt, butter, and vanilla. Pour onto cookie sheets. When cool, break into serving-size pieces.

Don't tell anyone how quick and easy this candy is. It tastes like you worked very hard.

Wild Turkey for New Year's

In Trinidad, Colorado Territory, the Oddfellows Lodge held its installation ceremonies on New Year's night, 1875. However, instead of the expected 100, 300 men showed up for the banquet of wild turkey, shot in the Raton Mountains. The *Colorado Chronicle*, January 7, reported that the ladies [presumably the cooks] were not upset but stretched the turkey supply to serve everyone present.

Celebrating the Fourth of July in early Trinidad

Grandma Short's Mincemeat—Circa 1890

1	bowl suet or margarine
3	bowls lean cooked ground meat (elk, deer, or beef)
1	bowl brown sugar
1	bowl apple cider or apple juice
3	bowls apples, chopped
1	bowl raisins
1	bowl currants
4	bowls sugar
1	bowl molasses
2	spoonsful ground cloves
2	spoonsful ground cinnamon
2	spoonsful nutmeg
1	spoonful salt
	juice of 4 lemons
1	orange peel, ground (optional)

A 1-quart "bowl" makes about 3 gallons of mincemeat

Melt suet or margarine and mix with all ingredients in a large pot. Stir well and bring to boiling. Pack in hot, sterilized, 1-quart Mason jars with lids. Store in refrigerator until gift-giving time.

The size of the "bowl" can vary as long as the same bowl is used for measuring all ingredients. Use teaspoon or tablespoon for "spoonful" measurements according to size of bowl used. For smaller amounts, substitute "cup" for "bowl."

A real taste of the past. This is a surprisingly superior mincemeat recipe.

Read about pioneer Grandma Short in the Southwest Slope/Soups section. Mincemeat was the white settlers' version of pemmican, the Plains Indians' staple, made with buffalo meat.

Across Colorado

Old-Time Words to the Wise

Beautiful maidens—aye, Nature's fair queens!
Some in your twenties, some in your teens,
Seeking accomplishments worthy your aim;
Striving for learning, thirsting for fame;
Taking such pains with the style of your hair;
Keeping your lily complexions so fair;
Miss not this item in all your gay lives,
Learn to keep house—you may some day be wives.

Beautiful maiden, pause ere you wed—
Learn to boil coffee, learn to bake bread;
Learn, oh, sweet girl, that one road to man's heart
Lies through his stomach—they are not far apart.
He loves your sweet face, he praises your eyes,
Has a tooth for your puddings, dotes on your pies.
Then beautiful maidens, be sure ere you wed
That you learn to make coffee, learn to bake bread.

—from Golden Gate Compressed Yeast Company's
Handy Book for Handy People,
"The Young Wife's Friend" (published about 1900)

Kahlua Bars

Crust

8	tablespoons butter or margarine, at room temperature
$\frac{1}{2}$	cup firmly packed light brown sugar
1	cup flour

Filling

2	large eggs
$\frac{1}{4}$	cup Kahlua or other coffee liqueur
1	cup firmly packed light brown sugar
$\frac{1}{4}$	cup flour
1	teaspoon baking powder
1	cup flaked coconut
1	cup pecans, coarsely chopped

Frosting

$1\frac{1}{2}$	cups sifted powdered sugar
4	tablespoons butter, at room temperature
1	tablespoon Kahlua or other coffee liqueur
$\frac{2}{3}$	cup semisweet chocolate chips, melted

Preheat oven to 350°. Grease and flour a 9x13x2-inch pan.

Cream together butter and brown sugar. Stir in flour and mix well. Spread crust mixture over bottom of prepared pan and press mixture firmly into pan. Bake for 10–12 minutes. While crust is baking, make filling.

Beat eggs in a medium-sized bowl. Add coffee liqueur and sugar and beat until fluffy. Stir in flour and baking powder. Fold in coconut and pecans. Pour filling over partially baked crust, return to oven, and bake 20 minutes longer. Cool.

Place powdered sugar, butter, and coffee liqueur in a mixing bowl. Beat to form a smooth frosting. Spread frosting over cooled bars. Drizzle melted chocolate on top of frosting and swirl with a table knife. Place in refrigerator for 1 hour before cutting into bars.

Makes 48 bars, $\frac{3}{4}$ x $1\frac{1}{2}$ inches

Across Colorado

Purgatoire or Picketwire

The Purgatoire River, which flows through southeastern Colorado, was named by Spanish settlers. Its full name was El Rio de las Animas Perdidas en Purgatorio. English translation: the River of the Souls Lost in Purgatory. When American settlers came from the East, they had trouble saying the Spanish words and called it the "Picketwire River."

Admiring his crop on the southeastern plains

Slovac Christmas Sausage (Kolbasky)

(According to Dr. John Moyer)

2	cloves garlic, minced
5	tablespoons salt
2½	teaspoons caraway seed
2	cups water
10	pounds pork shoulder, ground twice

M a k e s   1 0   p o u n d s   s a u s a g e

Mix garlic, salt, and caraway seed in water. Blend into ground pork and mix well. Sausage may be left in bulk and made into patties when ready to cook, or it can be cased into links if you have a sausage-casing machine. Frozen casing can be found in most meat markets. This sausage is great cooked on a grill and then eaten on Kaiser rolls.

Dr. Moyer has a large smokehouse and enjoys experimenting with all types of smoked food. To make smoked sausage from this recipe, add 1 tablespoon of Morton's Insta-Cure. Smoke sausages for 6–7 hours at about 165°. Check meat periodically—color will determine how the meat is smoking.

Makes an unusual and wonderful gift.

Contemplating Canning—1884

"There is genuine satisfaction in contemplating the rows of cans filled with the different kinds of fruit, showing clear and distinct through the glass, and we are conservative enough to hope that the time will not come when the business of canning fruit shall be relegated entirely into the hands of the mercenary factory owner with his tin can with its overdrawn label.

—*from* The Successful Housekeeper,
published by M.W. Ellsworth Company, 1884

Trinidad History Museum

This Colorado Historical Society complex features four attractions: the Santa Fe Trail Museum (it celebrated the 175th anniversary of the trail in 1996), the Baca House, the Bloom Mansion, and the Historic Gardens. The Baca House is an adobe home featuring Hispanic folk art and Victorian furniture; the Bloom Mansion next door is a Victorian home. Brick pathways lead to the Historic Gardens, filled with herbs and vegetables common to the Hispanic Southwest. The museum is located at 300 East Main Street in Trinidad and is open daily from May 1 through September.

Bloom mansion in Trinidad, built in 1882

Topping It Off with Jams and Sauces

Lemon Curd*

Lost Blend Jam*

Colorado Marmalade*

Old-Fashioned Rhubarb Conserve*

Tangy Rhubarb Sauce for Meat*

Mrs. Webster's Tomato Relish*

*Recipe Follows

Lemon Curd

2 cups sugar

4 ounces butter

2 lemons (grated peel and juice)

3 eggs, well beaten

Makes 2 cups

Melt sugar and butter in a double boiler, blending well. Add grated lemon peel and juice. Slowly stir in eggs. Cook over hot water until thick and glossy, about 15 minutes, stirring constantly to keep mixture from scorching. Let cool and spread on bread, scones, or cake. Will keep for 1 week when refrigerated.

This recipe comes from Devonshire, England, by way of a Fort Collins pioneer family.

Lost Blend Jam

5 pounds fresh apricots, pitted

1 quart fresh red raspberries

1 20-ounce can crushed pineapple with juice

sugar (amount determined by number of cups of fruit)

1 package dry pectin

Makes 10–12 glasses of jelly

Grind apricots or process in blender or food processor.

Measure apricots, berries, and pineapple into a large kettle, counting the cups of fruit. Add one cup of sugar for each cup of fruit. Cook fruit slowly, bringing to a full rolling boil. Add pectin. Bring to boil again and cook for 1 minute. Pour into hot, sterilized jars. Seal with new lids and rings. Process in boiling water bath for 15 minutes or according to glass manufacturer's instructions. Store unprocessed jam in refrigerator.

Harriet Kelly Davis, a San Francisco debutante who had a degree in Home Demonstration Arts from Columbia University, created this recipe using apricots and raspberries from her yard in Aspen. Harriet lived in Aspen while her husband served as lawyer for the Smuggler Mine.

Across Colorado

El Pueblo Museum

This regional museum of the Colorado Historical Society, located in Pueblo, portrays the history of southern Colorado and Pueblo and examines the many cultural groups whose paths crossed at this point on the Arkansas River. The permanent exhibit, "Crossroads on the Arkansas," displays artifacts of the native peoples, trappers, traders, soldiers, Hispanic and American settlers, ranchers and cowboys, miners, and industrialists who left their marks on this region. Located at 324 West First Street in downtown Pueblo, the museum is open Monday through Saturday, 10 a.m. to 4:30 p.m.; Sundays noon to 3 p.m.

Colorado Marmalade

2	cups thinly sliced, unpeeled oranges
1	9-ounce can crushed pineapple, drained (reserve juice)
	water to make 2 cups with reserved pineapple juice
5	cups sliced, ripe peaches
6	cups sugar
5	ounces maraschino cherries
2	peach kernels (cracked seeds, unpeeled)

Boil orange slices 1 hour in water and pineapple juice, uncovered. While orange slices are cooking, mix peaches with sugar and let stand 1 hour. Add peaches to orange mixture. Cook ½ hour. Add cherries, peach kernels, and pineapple and cook ½ hour or longer until thick and of marmalade consistency. Remove peach kernels. Pour into hot, sterilized half-pint jars and seal with new lids and rings. Process in boiling water bath for 15 minutes or according to glass manufacturer's instructions; or store unprocessed marmalade in refrigerator.

Makes eight 8-ounce jars

Tangy Rhubarb Sauce for Meat

2	tablespoons honey
1¾	cups rhubarb, very finely diced
1	teaspoon prepared horseradish
2	teaspoons lemon juice
1	teaspoon prepared mustard
¾	cup mayonnaise

Mix together honey and rhubarb and refrigerate overnight, stirring occasionally. The next day, quickly bring mixture to a simmer for 1 minute. Remove from heat and cover tightly. Let set for 3–5 minutes until rhubarb is tender. Add remaining ingredients.

Excellent on baked fish and also good with sandwiches, chicken, and roast beef.

This recipe comes from the pioneer Haefeli family in Monte Vista, whose honey has been famous for many years.

Makes 2 cups

Across Colorado

Bumper Crop

Sugar beet growers use the latest technology for loading their crops and getting them to market.

Old-Fashioned Rhubarb Conserve

2	pounds fresh rhubarb, cut into 1-inch pieces
3	cups sugar
½	cup raisins
1	whole lemon, sliced
1	whole orange, sliced
1	cup walnuts, coarsely chopped

Put rhubarb in a stockpot and cover with sugar. Add remaining ingredients except nuts. Let stand until juice accumulates. Stir well. Bring to boil, then reduce heat, and gently simmer until thick, stirring often to prevent sticking. Add nuts and boil 2 minutes longer. Pour into hot, sterilized jelly glasses and seal with new lids and rings. Process in boiling water bath for 15 minutes or according to glass manufacturer's instructions. Store unprocessed conserve in refrigerator.

Makes about 4 cups

Mrs. Webster's Tomato Relish

12	medium to large ripe tomatoes, unpeeled
3	medium green peppers, chopped medium fine
1	large onion, chopped medium fine
½–1½	cups sugar, to taste
½–1	teaspoon each ground cloves, cinnamon, allspice (to taste)
½–1½	teaspoons cayenne (to taste)
1	tablespoon salt (or less to taste)
1	cup vinegar

Place tomatoes in large kettle and boil until soft. Put through a sieve to remove skin and seeds. Return pulp to kettle add peppers, onions, sugar, spices, salt, and vinegar. Simmer mixture 3 hours over low heat or until cooked down to preferred consistency. Stir frequently to keep from sticking. Pour into pint or smaller sterilized jars and seal with lids and rings. Process in boiling water bath 15 minutes or according to glass manufacturer's instructions. Store unprocessed relish in refrigerator.

Your grilled cheese sandwiches and hamburgers will have new personality topped with Mrs. Webster's relish!

Makes 8 pints

This recipe has traveled throughout Colorado from one good cook to another, making its way from a Mrs. Webster in Ridgway (about 1930) to Aurora, Erie, and Boulder.

Across Colorado

Recipe Testers

Testing Co-Chairmen
Kathleen Cook
Anne Taylor

Gwen Arnold
Judy Atwater
Beth Brown
Jill Browning
Linda Bryan
Becky Buckbee
Nancy Buter
Betty Cartlidge
Aileen Christenson
Sandra David
Donna Delmonico
Jane DeMerritt
Martha Ewald
Mary Flowers
Charlene Gail
JoAn Goodman
Arlene Hansen
Barbara Hemenway
Eleanor Hixon

Lorraine Kahler
Jean Larrick
Paula Lucas
Vina McLeod
Ann Mulford
Nancy Nelson
Janet Notary
Pat Rauchenstein
Sharon Riker
Mary-Nelle Ryan
Phyllis Shotkoski
Laura Snapp
Phyllis Sumners
Delphine Tramutt
Susan Turman
Teresa Vanfeldt
Martha Von Hagen
Betty Wallace
Elaine Walsh

Contributors

Peggy Adams
Arlene Ahlbrandt
Marty Alexandroff
Jean Allard
Alliance-Francaise
Vivian Wright Allison
Betsy Andrews
Ramona S. Antonelli
Barbara Anuta
Arapahoe Cafe
Kay Armstrong
Opal I. Armstrong
Gwen Arnold
Sam Arnold
J. Atwater
Virgina Auge
Aurora Historical Society
Avery House Guild

Jerry Baier
Anne Bailey
M. Barbee
Pauline Barkley
Vivienne N. Barrack
Esther Barrett
Peggy Barr
Alice Bauer
Eileen Beamer
Catharine Bearden
Doreen Beenck
Ruth Beethe

Ray Beighle
Joan Bell
John A. Berglin
Donna Bielenberg
Darlene A. Blair
Boulder Museum of
   History
Cherie Braun
Beth Brown
Charlie Brown
Brown Palace Hotel
Jill Browning
Edwina Bruder
Janey Buchanan
Becky Buckbee
Buckhorn Exchange
Laurene Buehler
Barbara Buettner
Winnie Burdan
Leslie Burger
Robert E. Burgess
Nancy Buter
Alline Buttrill
Byers-Evans House

George E. Carlberg
Bonnie Carter
Betty Cartlidge
Castle Marne B & B
Jan Catlow
Christine Chandler

Ruth Chenoweth
Aileen Christenson
Jeanne G. Clark
RoseMary Clisdal
Elizabeth M. Cohu
Joanne Colin
Colorado Springs Pioneer
   Museum
Ed Connolly
Norma L. Connors
Roberta Cordova
Pauline Corlett
Velma Corlett
Nelle Cornelius
Peggy Bietz Cox
Gertraud R. Crawford
Creede Historical Society
Creede Repertory Theatre
Joan Crocker
Katie Cymbala

Dante Alighieri Society
Col. R. F. Darden, Jr.
Sandra David
Joan Day
Lowella Day
Jeanne Dodson
Fay Dorman
Lucile Downer
Hazel B. Draper
Luetta Dressel

Contributors

Margaret Duckett
Dutch Community

Dorothy Eastin
Irene Eastin
Bonnie Eklund
Peg Ekstrand
Susan Ellis
Jeanette Emrick
Sandy Engelbrecht
English-Speaking Union
Virginia Erickson
Jane B. Eubank
Tana Rae Evenson
Martha Ewald

Janis Falkenberg
Betty Jo Fassett
Clella Fassett
Joan Fedel
Leland Feitz
Mary Ferrier
Louise Ficco
Rebecca Finch
Asta Finney
Beverly Firth
Dave Fishell
Susan Fitzgerald
Mary McInnes Flowers
Peggy A. Ford
Fort Collins High School

Friends in Silver Cliff
Friends in West Cliff

Ramona Garcia
Kittie Gates
John & Lila Gigikos
Barbara Gigone
Ghost Town Club of
    Colorado
Marion Goldsmith
Helen L. Gonzales
Mabel Googins
Mary Eleanor Gordon
Carol Gossard
Greek Community
Dr. Doris Gregory
City of Greeley Museums
Sophie Griffith
Grover Depot Museum

Marj Haagenson
Lucille Hadad
Pat Haefeli
Kathy Hall
Rosa Halls
Joan Hancock
Peg Hayden
Edna Heeren
Barbara Hemenway
Elaine Henderson
Angie Henn

Roger Henn
Virginia Hilander
Eleanor Hixon
Kay Hoch
Betty L. Hodge
Reva Jane Hopkins
Marjorie Hornbein
Hotel Colorado
Jonney Howe
Bobbe Hultin
Hungry Gulch Books
Corinne Hunt
Sue Hutchinson
Elizabeth Hutchison

Irish Society
Kent & Betsy Irwin
Marge Israel

Mary Hale Jackson
Jan Jacobs
Robyn Jacobs
Verena Jacobson
Rev. Kim James
Jefferson High School
Lois Jensen
Jean Johannes
Johnstown High School
Louise Ann Jones
Gail Jossi
Betty Juhl

Alice Jurjovec

Lorraine Kahler
Jerre Kappel
Guido Karrer
Helena Kelling
Lynn Kelly
Jennifer Kemp
Bonnie Kibble

Lafayette High School
Lafayette Miners Museum
Margaret Lamb
Lois Lange
Rose Ann Langston
Jean Larrick
Gloria Lee
Jim Lee
Patty Lindley
Annabeth Lockhart
Joyce Loeffel
Linda Loftis
Jean Lowe
Edith Lowery
Paul Lucas
Marjorie Lutz

R. and C. Mancinelli
Phyllis Marcantonio
Eva Mate
Irene Mattivi

Bee McClure
Sue McCulloch
Patti McFerran
Todd & Carey McKay
Maxine McKee
Fr. Jerry B. McKenzie
Vina McLeod
Barbara McMurry
Beverly Meier
Lois Meining
Doris Mekelburg
Violet Mekelburg
Kurt Melle
Margareth Merrill
Rachel Merritt
Barbara Meyer
Judith Meyers
Cheryl Miller
Laura Miller
Monte Vista High School
Gwanda Moody
Agnes T. Mooney
Judy Morley
Mount Garfield B & B
Mount Hayden Rebekah
    Lodge
Ann Mulford
Elaine Munzing
Marjie Murphy

Contributors

Eva Nelson
Shirley Nelson
Virginia Nemmers
Thelma Neuschwanger
Sharon Newman
Allen Nossaman
Janet Notary

Joan Ogren
Old Town Museum
Michelle Olin
Gladys Olsen
Susan O'Hanlon
Dorothy O'Ryan

Pagliacci's Italian
    Restaurant
Penny Pappas
Kathleen Paradise
Anne Parker
Linda Parker
Marlene Parrish
Pawnee High School
Marge Pearsall
Diane Peiker
Della Perlenfein
Norah Perotin
Annabelle Petranovich
Henry Tuoc V. Pham
Burldeen Phillips
Phyllis Plehaty

Delores Plested
Poncha Springs Visitor
    Center
Poudre Landmarks
    Foundation
Prairie View School
    District
Dean Prentice
Marie Prentice
Pat Quade

Ramona M. Radcliff
Rilla Rader
Min Ray
Chris Reece
Virginia Reed
Dr. Michel Reynders
Florence Richmond
Sharon Riker
River Run Inn
Emilie Robbins
June Robinson
Rocky Mountain Jewish
    High School
Mary A. Rogers
Wren Roob
Gloria Rosener
Jean Rusk
Jayne Russell
John Russell
Judy Rutledge

Mary N. Ryan
Charlene Sachter
Rae Sanders
Nancy Sandoval
Karen Saxton
Sue Schulze
Dorothy Schutz
Gary Schwanke
Darlene Scott
Alice Seedorf
Jane & Steve Short
Phyllis Shotkoski
Mary Silverstein
Addie A. Sim
Whitney Simmons
Mike & Lois Smith
Helen Snyder
Societa Nativi di Polenza
    Lodge
Lena Spicola
Starck Family
Donald R. Starnes
Shirley Starnes
Doris Stewart
Kathryn Strainer
Strater Hotel
LaVern Stumpenhorst
Betty Summers
Phyllis Sumners
Surface Creek Valley High
    School

Kirsten Swenson
Gwen Tague
Janette Taylor
Willi Tebow
Louanne Timm
Tirolesi-Trentini of CO
    Club
Delphine Tramutt
Tread of Pioneers
    Museum
Jesse Troutman
Susan Turman
Esther Tweden

Helen Ulrich
Unitarian-Universalist
    Church
Pat Upton

Darlene Maes Vallejo
Joyce Vogel
Anne Vondracek
Teresa Vonfeldt
Martha Von Hagen

Ann Waldbaum
Ann Wall
Betty L. Wallace
Ann Walsh
Elaine Walsh

Marcella & Kurt
    Warshauer
Jeanette L. Watkins
Rene Weder
G. Weinel
Grace Weinel
Joyce Weng
Kathryn Wenger
Marie Wetterich
Dorothy Whitaker
Cynthia Whiteside
Menke Anne Whiteside
Shirley Wiggin
Ann Willard
Joyce Williams
Mary Wilson-Nichols
Frances Wither
Earlene Wolfers
Louise Worley
Kay Wyley
Nell Wyley

Youko Yamasaki
Marty Yochum
Frances Young
Yuma Museum

Shirley Zabel
Judy Zimmerman
Ruth Zollinger

Index

Index

Index

Index